SCHOOL LIBRARY MEDIA SERIES

Edited by Diane de Cordova Biesel

1. *Chalk Talk Stories*, written and illustrated by Arden Druce, 1993.
2. *Toddler Storytime Programs*, by Diane Briggs, 1993.
3. *Alphabet: A Handbook of ABC Books and Book Extensions for the Elementary Classroom, second edition*, by Patricia L. Roberts, 1994.
4. *Cultural Cobblestones: Teaching Cultural Diversity*, by Lynda Miller, Theresa Steinlage, and Mike Printz, 1994.
5. *ABC Books and Activities: From Preschool to High School*, by Cathie Hilterbran Cooper, 1996.
6. *ZOOLUTIONS: A Mathematical Expedition with Topics for Grades 4 through 8*, by Anne Burgunder and Vaunda Nelson, 1996.
7. *Library Lessons for Grades 7–9*, by Arden Druce, 1997.
8. *Counting Your Way through 1-2-3 Books and Activities*, by Cathie Hilterbran Cooper, 1997.
9. *Art and Children: Using Literature to Expand Creativity*, by Robin W. Davis, 1996.
10. *Story Programs: A Source Book of Materials, second edition*, by Carolyn Sue Peterson and Ann Fenton, 1997.
11. *Taking Humor Seriously in Children's Literature: Literature-Based Mini-Units and Humorous Books for Children Ages 5–12*, by Patricia L. Roberts, 1997.
12. *Multicultural Friendship Stories and Activities for Children Ages 5–14*, by Patricia L. Roberts, 1997.
13. *Side by Side: Twelve Multicultural Puppet Plays*, by Jean M. Pollock, 1997.
14. *Reading Fun: Quick and Easy Activities for the School Library Media Center*, by Mona Kerby, 1998.

Multicultural Friendship Stories and Activities for Children Ages 5–14

Patricia L. Roberts

School Library Media Series, No. 12

The Scarecrow Press, Inc.
Lanham, Md., & London
1998

SCARECROW PRESS, INC.

Published in the United States of America
by Scarecrow Press, Inc.
4720 Boston Way
Lanham, Maryland 20706

British Library of Cataloguing in Publication Information Available

Library of Congress Cataloging-in-Publication Data

Roberts, Patricia, 1936–
    Multicultural friendship stories and activities for children ages
5–14 / Patricia L. Roberts
        p.   cm. — (School library media series ; no. 12)
    Includes bibliographical references and index.
    ISBN 0-8108-3359-X (pbk. : alk. paper)
    1. Multicultural education—United States—Activity programs.
2. Friendship in children—Study and teaching—United States.
3. Storytelling.   4. Children's stories.   I. Title.   II. Series.
    LC1099.R623   1998
    370.117—DC21   97-15975
CIP
ISBN 0-8108-3359-X (pbk. : alk. paper)

Dedicated to J. E. and J. M.

Acknowledgment
Special thanks to Gail Zimmerman
from McClatchey High School, Sacramento, California,
for the extra reading suggestions on friendship and love.

Contents

Series Editor's Foreword ix
Introduction 1

 I. Stories and Activities for Children Ages 5–8 7
  1. Family Friendships 9
  2. Community, Neighborhood, and School Friendships 41
  3. Friendships around the World 71

 II. Stories and Activities for Children Ages 9–14 95
  4. Family Friendships 97
  5. Community, Neighborhood, and School Friendships 121
  6. Friendships around the World 149

 III. Bibliography 175
  7. Ages 5–8 177
   Family Friendships 177
   Community, Neighborhood, and School Friendships 189
   Friendships around the World 202
  8. Ages 9–14 209
   Family Friendships 209
   Community, Neighborhood, and School Friendships 215
   Friendships around the World 226

Title, Author, and Illustrator Index 235

About the Author 243

Editor's Foreword

The School Library Media Series is intended for the school library media specialist, particularly the building level librarian. The multifaceted role of the librarian as educator, collection developer, curriculum developer, and information specialist is examined. The series includes concise, practical books on topical subjects related to programs and services.

Dr. Roberts has compiled a manual of primarily contemporary works for the librarian or teacher who wishes to foster compassionate multicultural relationships between and among children.

Engaging and creative activities are provided for the stories suggested, including role-playing, journal writing, and making greeting cards. One could call this book a "skill builder" for friendship.

Diane de Cordova Biesel
Series Editor

Introduction

Violence on television, in homes, at the movies, and in the neighborhood daily affects some children's lives and demonstrates a need for children of all ethnic groups and cultural heritages to develop ongoing friendship skills. Some children exhibit few friendships due to personal, family, or environmental misfortunes or ongoing life stress. All children—those with few friends or many—can benefit from building new friendships and rebuilding old ones.

How do the characters in children's books develop their friendships? Hearing and reading stories about how children from different cultural heritages build friendships can be a valuable experience for children. This resource book aims to help teachers, librarians, parents, and others find those stories. It provides an annotated bibliography of children's books and accompanying activities that will help children build associations with others, understand the value of support groups (e.g., dyads, buzz groups, informal small groups), and recognize the value of friendly relations with people. Sample lessons related to selected books show educators and parents how such literature might be used to help children develop friendships by living vicariously through these characters and understanding their thoughts and actions.

HOW TO USE THIS BOOK

The literature in this book was selected carefully to reflect aspects of building friendships that have been associated with children who are friendly and are able to develop friendships despite obstacles in their path. Activities are suggested that extend the lessons of the selected stories.

Part I contains a broad sampling of quality picture books and related activities for children ages 5–8. Part II features books without pictures and activities for children ages 9–14. Each part is divided into chapters on family friendships; community, neighborhood, and school friendships; and friendships around the world. Selected books in both parts are annotated and highlight the heritage of the book's main characters as well as the age levels for which they are intended. For each selected book, there are detailed plans, materials to use, objectives, activities, and discussion questions to demonstrate ways the books can be used to foster friendship skills. Not every activity listed is appropriate for the entire age range given. Educators are encouraged to select from all options the activities for their particular class. Note that some activities call for Venn diagrams, or character diagrams, or webs. Here are some examples:

- A Venn diagram is suggested as one of the activities related to *A Day's Work* (Clarion, 1994, ages 6–8) written by Eve Bunting and illustrated by Ronald Himler. This story is Francisco's testimonial to his grandfather who has newly arrived from Mexico to live with his daughter and her family. Related to the story, the children are asked to compare their individual characteristics as a good friend with Francisco's characteristics as a friend. In the intersection of two circles drawn on the board, the children are asked to dictate or to write the characteristics that are similar.

- A character diagram is suggested as an activity to examine how John Chapman (Johnny Appleseed) was viewed differently by poets writing at different times. After reading aloud a poem about this friendly man, the children are asked to share descriptive words about him—words that describe his clothing, his travels, and so on. Have the children dictate or write their suggestions on the diagram. The diagram can be similar to the following:

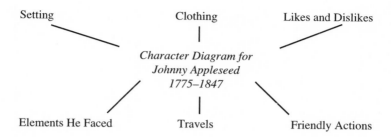

Setting   Clothing   Likes and Dislikes

Character Diagram for Johnny Appleseed 1775–1847

Elements He Faced   Travels   Friendly Actions

- After reading aloud information from another poem about Appleseed, ask the children to prepare another character diagram with the same headings and add more facts. Have the students discuss their lists to see if they can discern some major facts about Johnny Appleseed, his actions, his life, identified by the poets.

Finally, Part III is a bibliography of additional friendship stories for children that includes the books entered by the author's last name. The entries are numbered and annotated and provide appropriate information such as title, illustrator, place of publication, publisher, and publishing date. *In the index, the numbers refer to entry numbers in the bibliography and not page numbers.*

The quotes by public figures on the division pages are in the public domain. They are available, however, on posters in a set titled *Inspirational Quotations II* (Knowledge Unlimited, 1994) and suitable for a room display.

READINGS A\ND RESOURCES FOR ADULTS

Aaserg, N. (1987). *The Peace Seekers: Nobel Peace Prize.* Minneapolis, MN: Lerner Publications.

Allen, J. (1992). *Cultural Awareness for Young Children.* New York: Addison-Wesley.

Andrews, S. V. (1994). *Teaching Kids to Care: Exploring Values Through Literature and Inquiry.* Terre Haute, IN: Indiana State University; Bloomington, IN: ERIC/REC and EDINFO Press.

Applebee, A. N., and J. A. Langer, consultants (1993). *Multicultural Perspectives.* Evanston, IL: McDougal, Littell.

Baltuck, N. (1995). *Apples from Heaven: Multicultural Folk Tales About Stories and Storytellers.* New Haven, CT: Linnet Professional Publications/Shoe String Press.

Banks, J. A. (1988). *Multiethnic Education: Theory and Practice, 2nd Ed.* Needham Heights, MA: Allyn and Bacon.

Banks, J. A. (1987). *Teaching Strategies for Ethnic Studies, 4th Ed.* Needham Heights, MA: Allyn & Bacon.

Banks, J. A., and C. A. McGee Banks (1989). *Multicultural Education: Issues and Perspectives.* Needham Heights, MA: Allyn & Bacon.

Bruchac, J., ed. (1983). *Breaking Silence: An Anthology of Contemporary Asian American Poets.* New York: Greenfield Review Press.

Carlson, L. M., ed. (1994). *Cool Salsa: Bilingual Poems on Growing Up Latino in the United States.* New York: Henry Holt.

Chipasula, S., and F. Chipasula, eds. (1995). *The Heinemann Book of African Women's Poetry.* Portsmouth, NH: Heinemann.

Condon, C., and J. McGinnis (1988). *Helping Kids Care.* St. Louis, MO: Institute for Peace and Justice.

Curriculum and Instruction/Charles County Public Schools (1984). *Education That Is Multicultural: A Curriculum Infusion Model.* College Park, MD: University of Maryland.

Day, F. A. (1994). *Multicultural Voices in Contemporary Literature: A Resource for Teachers.* Portsmouth, NH: Heinemann.

Derman-Sparks, L. (1989). *Anti-Bias Curriculum—Tools for Empowering Young Children.* Washington, DC: National Association for Young Children.

Garcia, R. (1981). *Education for Pluralism: Global Roots Stew.* Phi Delta Kappa Educational Foundation. ED 192 380.

Gillan, M. M., and J. Gillan, eds. (1994). *Unsettling America: An Anthology of Contemporary Multicultural Poetry.* New York: Penguin Books.

Gollnick, D. M., and P. C. Chinn (1994). *Multicultural Education in a Pluralistic Society, 4th Ed.* New York: Macmillan.

Glover, D. M. (1994). *Voices of the Spirit: Sources for Interpreting the African-American Experience.* New York: American Library Association.

Grammar, R. (1980). *Teaching Peace Audio Cassette.* Peerskill, NY: Smiling Atcha Music.

Gray, S., ed. (1989). *The Penguin Book of Southern African Verse.* New York: Penguin Books.

Haverluck, B. (1992). *Perspectives on Peace and Conflict.* Winnipeg, Manitoba: Pequis Publishers.

Heath, R. B., ed. (1989). *Trade Winds: Poetry in English from Different Cultures.* London: Longman.

Heltshe, M. A., and A. B. Kirchner (1991). *Multicultural Explorations: Joyous Journeys with Books.* Littleton, CO: Teacher Ideas Press.

Hirschfelder, A. B., and B. R. Singer, eds. (1992). *Rising Voices: Writings of Young Native Americans.* New York: Ballantine Books.

Hongo, G. (1993). *The Open Boat: Poems for Asian Americans.* New York: Anchor/Doubleday.

Hopkins, S. (1990). *Discovering the World, Empowering Children to Value Themselves and Others*. Philadelphia, PA: New Society Publishers.

Hornbeck, D. W. (1984). *Guidelines for Multicultural Education*. Baltimore: Maryland State Board of Education.

Irving, J., and R. Currie (1991). *From the Heart: Books and Activities about Friends*. Littleton, CO: Teacher Ideas Press.

Izuki, S. (1994). *Poems about Americans of Asian and Pacific Islander Descent*. Chicago: Children's Press.

Johnson, D. W., and R. T. Johnson (1955). *Reducing School Violence Through Conflict Resolution*. Alexandria, VA: Association for Supervision and Curriculum Development.

Kemple, K. M. (1991). "Preschool Children's Peer Acceptance and Social Interaction." *Young Children* 45 (3): 70–75.

Kovacs, E. (1993). *Writing Across Cultures*. Blue Heron, LA: Blue Heron Inc.

Kreidler, W. J. (1994). "Welcome to the Peaceable Classroom." *Instructor* 104, (2): 33–34.

Ladd, G. W. (1990). "Having Friends, Keeping Friends, Making Friends and Being Liked by Peers in the Classroom: Predictors of Children's Early School Adjustment." *Child Development* 61: 1081–1100.

Lambert, W., and O. Klineberg (1967). *Children's Views of Foreign People: A Cross-Cultural Study*. New York: Appleton-Century-Croft.

Livingston, M. C., selector (1992). *A Time to Talk: Poems of Friendship*. New York: Margaret K. McElderry Books.

MacDonald, M. R. (1992). *Peace Tales: World Folktales to Talk About*. New Haven, CT: Linnet Professional Publications.

Marantz, S., and K. Marantz (1994). *Multicultural Picture Books: Art for Understanding Others*. Columbus, OH: Linworth Publishing.

Norton, D. E. (1990). "Teaching Multicultural Literature in the Reading Program." *The Reading Teacher* 44: 28–40.

Nye, N. S., selector (1992). *This Same Sky: A Collection of Poems from Around the World*. New York: Four Winds Press.

Nye, N. S., selector (1995). *The Tree Is Older than You Are: A Bilingual Gathering of Poems and Stories from Mexico with Paintings by Mexican Artists*. New York: Simon & Schuster.

Purves, A. C., ed. (1993). *Tapestry: A Multicultural Anthology*. Englewood Cliffs, NJ: Globe.

Roberts, P. L., and N. L. Cecil (1993). *Developing Multicultural Awareness through Children's Literature: A Guide for Teachers and Librarians, Grades K–8*. Jefferson, NC: McFarland.

Slapin, B., and D. Seal, eds. (1992). *Through Indian Eyes: The Native Experience in Books for Children*. Philadelphia: New Society Publishers.

Stott, J. C. (1995). *Native Americans in Children's Literature*. Phoenix: Oryx.

Tiedt, P. L., and I. M. Tiedt (1995). *Multicultural Teaching: A Handbook of*

Activities, Information, and Resources, 4th Ed. Needham Heights, MA: Allyn & Bacon.

Totten, H. L., and R. W. Brown (1995). *Culturally Diverse Library Collections for Children.* New York: Neal-Schuman.

Ward, H. H. (1988). *My Friends' Beliefs: A Young Reader's Guide to World Religions.* New York: Walker & Co.

Yolen, J., ed. (1994). *Sleep Rhymes Around the World.* New York: Boyds Mills Press.

Yolen, J., ed. (1992). *Street Rhymes Around the World.* New York: Boyds Mills Press.

Zepeda, O., ed. (1982). *When It Rains: Papago and Pima Poetry.* Phoenix: University of Arizona Press.

I Stories and Activities for Children Ages 5–8

The truth is that there is nothing noble in being superior to somebody else. The only real nobility is in being superior to your former self.

—Whitney Young, civil rights leader

The strong man is the man who can stand up for his rights and not hit back.

—Martin Luther King, Jr., civil rights leader

1 Family Friendships

Book 1.1 *Aunt Flossie's Hats and Crab Cakes* (14)

Ages: 5–8

Heritage: African American

Goals: To relate friendship to an intergenerational relationship

To relate friendship to an elderly family member

To appreciate a family's oral traditions

To retell a story related to a family's collection of objects

To interpret a friendly intergenerational relationship through a sketch or drawing from the student's point of view

To develop an original story and share it aloud with others

Materials: Copy of *Aunt Flossie's Hats and Crab Cakes* (14), board, chalk, hat, and trimmings

BOOK NOTES

Aunt Flossie's Hats and Crab Cakes (Houghton Mifflin, 1991) is written by Elizabeth Fitzgerald Howard and illustrated by James Ransome. Every Sunday, great-great Aunt Flossie entertains her two nieces, Susan and Sarah, by letting them look through her boxes of wondrous hats.

9

After cookies and tea, she tells them a story about each hat, with each tale (some humorous) placed in a different setting—the big Baltimore fire, a parade after the Great War, and a pond near the family home on a Sunday walk. The intergenerational relationships (enjoying eating crab cakes together) and oral traditions are central in this African American family.

ACTIVITIES

Sound Effects

Ask children to help tell the story again and to add some sound effects to the words as you reread the story aloud. Invite them to sing the words "Hats, hats, hats, hats" to four musical notes of their choice (perhaps in a marching cadence) when you stop at an appropriate place in the story.

Hat Song

Demonstrate ways to compose new words about the hats in Aunt Flossie's collection to the tune "Here We Go Round the Mulberry Bush" and ask the children to describe some of Aunt Flossie's hats—especially the bright colors of green, blue, pink, and purple. Write their descriptions on the board and make decisions about what to sing. For example, a description could be written like this:

> And here's Aunt Flossie wearing a hat,
> Wearing a hat,
> Wearing a hat.
> And here's Aunt Flossie wearing a hat,
> The black one with red ribbons (the brown one with some buttons, the blue
>   one with a feather)

After the children suggest their descriptions, read the words back to the group, say the words aloud as a group, and then have the children sit in a friendship circle (or stand), hold hands, and sing their new words. If appropriate, ask the children to sing the song into a tape recorder. Place the recorder at a listening area so children can hear it again at a later time.

Sing the Story

With the tune of "Over the River and Through the Woods," ask the children to suggest new words to retell this story from the nieces' point of view. Sing the song together as a group to recall the melody and then elicit suggestions for different words from the children. Write the words on the board so the children can chant or sing them together. A beginning could start like this:

> Through the traffic and down the streets
> to Aunt Flossie's house we go.
> We both know the way we're happy to say
> We love Aunt Flossie—Aunt Flo-Oohh . . .
> Through the traffic and down the streets . . .

Hat Story

Bring in a hat to class that has an interesting shape or decoration as a stimulus for original storytelling. The hat could show some of the features on Aunt Flossie's hats—a red ribbon, silver buttons, faux fur, or feathers. Ask the children to meet with partners to think of their own original story about a friendly family member and interject the hat into their story in some way. Ask volunteers to share their hat story aloud with the group.

Friends Report

Invite the children to work together as friends and consider what they think would be found in Aunt Flossie's wastebasket that would reflect some of the events in her life. For instance, focusing on Aunt Flossie's interest in hats and the stories she told about them, the partners might say that they would look for trimmings for her hats, confetti and small flags from a parade (one of the settings for a Flossie hat story), and burned material from the Baltimore fire. Have them give a "friends report" and tell what they "found" in Aunt Flossie's wastebasket to the whole group.

Hats and Stories

Hats can be related to an individual's entertaining times with friends just as Aunt Flossie mentioned in this story. Have the children design their own hats to reflect events in their lives and paint the hats on paper. The hat pictures can generate new and original friendship stories, so invite the children to write their own hat stories on index cards to display with their paintings.

Intergenerational Collections

Invite children to describe a collection of one of their elderly relatives or friends: salt and pepper shakers, figurines of angels, cats, cows. Have them ask the person to tell the story behind one of the collectibles (perhaps where they got it, what memory it brings, who it reminds them of when they see it, and so on). Ask volunteers to retell the story in small groups.

Book 1.2   *Black Is Brown Is Tan* (1)

Ages:	6–9
Heritage:	Multicultural
Goals:	To recognize family friendship traits
	To portray family friendships in artwork
	To develop and expand vocabulary
	To recognize family friendships in the art of others
Materials:	Copy of *Black Is Brown Is Tan* (1)

BOOK NOTES

Black Is Brown Is Tan (HarperCollins, 1973) is by Arnold Adoff. Poetically told, it is a story of a happy integrated interracial family—two children, their black mother and white father, and their loving grandmothers from both sides of the family.

ACTIVITIES

Point-of-View Eyeglasses

Invite the children to see the story from the point of view of one of the children in the story by making paper eyeglasses that represent the children in some way (by the color of their clothing, hair, a fabric pattern, etc.). Engage the children in drawing the shape of eyeglasses and cutting them out. Have children cut small circles or ovals in the center so they can see. Attach cord, ribbon, or pipe cleaners to hold the glasses in place. Invite the children to wear their glasses when they tell their favorite part of the story from a point of view that represents one of the children and emphasizes the friendship between the members of this extended family.

Words about Family

After reading the story, ask the children to select their favorite displays of family friendship in the story and suggest action words to contribute to a word map that represents information about family friendships. Invite the children to use their word maps to write original sentences, paragraphs, or brief stories about family friendships.

Illustrations

Engage the children in looking at the illustrations in the book. Ask what actions they see and how many action words can they think of to describe the family friendships in the story. Observe the pictures to look for scenes of family friendships and doing things for one another. Relate what is seen to the children's experiences and ask the children if they do any of the things they see in the book family's actions. Record the children's suggested action words on a writing board, chart, or overhead transparency and make the words available for the children's original writing about family friendships.

Family Feelings

Invite the children to look at the illustrations again and talk about how the family members in the illustrations feel. Which family members are happy? Sad? If appropriate, relate the feelings in the story to the children's experiences. Are there feelings of joy, friendship, warmth (perhaps dislike) in the story? In the children's lives? Ask the children about ways we could build happier family friendships.

Loving Family

Ask the children what demonstrations of love and support they have received from members of their family (or from someone they know), similar to the family support the two children received in this biracial family. Write their ideas on the board. Ask children to look again at the illustrations in the book to identify family members doing things with the children that demonstrate family love and support. What events and activities in the story are similar to those experienced by the children in their own lives?

Trait

Ask the children to write or sketch five or more of their own characteristics that make them a good friend in their family. They can list almost anything they do or say in a friendly way. Have the children move into small groups and exchange their lists with other group members. Have each child introduce the child whose list has been received and tell which family friendship trait on the list impressed him/her the most.

Mural

With children in a discussion group, write the phrase "family friendships" on mural paper affixed to the writing board and ask the children what they know about family friendships or what comes to mind when they see or hear the words. Write down the children's contributions (or have student volunteers record them on the paper). Invite the children to describe one or more of their family friendships and make stick drawings on art paper to illustrate the friendships. Have children cut out around the drawings and paste them to the mural. Keep the mural on display in the room so the children can sketch and add additional images that come to mind.

Family Book

Invite the children to fold paper in half and put the pages together to make family friendship stories. Invite them to begin 5 or 10 sentences and then to trade stories. The children who receive the stories may complete the five or ten sentences. If appropriate, invite the children to read aloud their finished sentences. Encourage the children to write additional sentences about any ideas they think they can use to develop positive family friendships wherever they go.

Collage

Encourage the children to locate magazine or newspaper pictures of family members and make a collage of family friendships to display on a wall in the classroom. If the children could ask the family members a question, what would they ask them?

Invite the children to participate in a "Family Friendships News Program"—a class panel of student-speakers to talk about contributions of family members (some are poets, artists, architects, others are engineers, doctors, dentists, and still others are government and health care workers).

Graffiti

Affix light-colored, brick-patterned paper on a bulletin board to make the background for a graffiti wall. Invite children to make their own comments about family friendships on the wall. Each child can write about a family friend that he or she selects. Have them read and react to one another's comments.

Book 1.3   *A Day's Work* (3)

Ages:	6–8
Heritage:	Mexican/Mexican American
Goals:	To relate friendship to an intergenerational relationship
	To relate literature to an elderly family member
	To develop and expand vocabulary through dictation and a chart story
	To retell a story, reread, think about what was read, and reflect on the characters, intergenerational friendship, and similar situations in one's own life
	To recognize feelings in friendship relationships among family members
Materials:	Copy of *A Day's Work* (3), class chart, art materials

BOOK NOTES

A Day's Work (Clarion, 1994) is written by Eve Bunting and illustrated by Ronald Himler. This is a grandson's testimonial to his grandfather, newly arrived from Mexico to live with his daughter and her son. The grandson, Francisco, believes his grandfather, Abuelo, is a fine man and convinces someone to hire him, even though Abuelo doesn't speak English yet. Working in the man's yard, the two work hard but pull up yard plants instead of all the weeds. With honesty and integrity, the two go back to the yard the next day to correct the mistake for no extra pay. The illustrations portray an intergenerational feeling of friendship and love between the two.

ACTIVITIES

I Now Know

Have children dictate or write three things that they now know about this Mexican American family and the family's relationships that they did not know before they heard this story. Record the children's ideas on the board. Engage them in illustrating their ideas. Display.

Francisco & Me

On the board, draw a Venn diagram of two intersecting circles and ask the children to compare their individual characteristics as a good friend with Francisco's characteristics as a friend. In the intersection of the circles, have children dictate or write the characteristics that are similar. Emphasize the idea that people are more alike than different. Repeat this activity with another selected book character and ask the children to compare and contrast again for the traits of friendship.

Feelings

Look again at the illustrations in the story with the children and ask them how the people in the scenes might be feeling. After eliciting feelings the family members had for one another, elicit what feelings the man who hired Abuelo and Francisco might have felt when he discovered all the yard plants were pulled up instead of the weeds, then discuss how he might have felt when Abuelo and Francisco demonstrated their honesty and integrity and corrected their mistake. Continue and discuss:

- How could this action start a friendship?
- In what ways did the children see (or not see) feelings of friendship, love, dislike or prejudice in this story?
- At what times have the children had any of these same friendship feelings with their grandfather or other members of their family?

Family friendship feelings can be reinforced through doll or puppet play, and talking about feelings through such play can aid in resolving conflicts over items and objects.

Chart Story

Invite children to retell the story in their own words. Write their words on a class chart. Ask them to reread the chart story together, think about what they read, and respond to any or all of the following:

- Francisco and his friendship with his grandfather reminds me of myself and a friendship I had because . . .
- Abuelo, the grandfather, reminds me of someone I know because . . .
- I think the friendship between the grandfather and his grandson is a good one because . . .

- The boy's friendship with his grandfather reminds me of a similar time in my own life; it happened when . . .
- What I liked best about the family friendship in this story was . . .

Friendship Drawing

Engage the children in turning their words about a similar friendship into artwork and ask them to create a drawing that reflects an intergenerational friendship (or elderly acquaintance) they have had in their lives. Display the drawings and invite volunteers to describe an intergenerational friendship to the whole group. Invite them to consider what they could do this year to form a family friendship that they could not do last year.

Correcting Mistakes

Ask the children to think of a time when they (or someone they know) had to correct mistakes, as Francisco and his grandfather did. Invite them to tell how this was done. Emphasize the friendly and polite ways that are discussed. If a negative, hostile, or ugly situation is described, ask the children to think of and talk about alternative and friendly ways the mistake could have been corrected.

Family Friendship Language

Ask the children if they know how to say the words "family," "love," and "friendship" in a language other than English. Use the responses to create artwork about language that reflects family friendships. Children can draw, paint, sketch, make a chart, or create a collage to show the use of words that portray loving family friendships. If appropriate, invite one or two older students into the class who are bilingual and ask them to teach the children family friendship words in languages other than English.

Friendship Word Search

Ask the children to write the words, "family," "love," and "friendship," on a sheet of paper and during the school recess or lunch period, ask speakers of languages other than English to tell them how the words sound in those languages. Let the children write the word phonetically on the paper. At the end of the school day, conduct a survey to find out how many languages in which the children can write/say words such as family, love, and friendship.

Book 1.4   *Hiawatha* (16)

Ages:	5–8
Heritage:	Native American
Goals:	To relate friendship to an intergenerational relationship
	To reflect upon friendly family relationships
	To portray family friendship in artwork
	To find examples of personification in nature to emphasize the relationship Native Americans have with their environment
	To identify words and actions of friendship that are the most meaningful to the children
	To portray friendly family relations through artwork
	To develop and expand vocabulary through imaginary conversations
Materials:	Copy of *Hiawatha* (16), notebooks, paper and markers, crayons, paints to make a quilt design depicting friendship

BOOK NOTES

Hiawatha (Dial, 1983), retold by Susan Jeffers, is a story of intergenerational love and friendship. Hiawatha is raised by his loving grandmother, Nokomis. This version is based on Longfellow's poem, composed in 1855, "The Song of Hiawatha." The character of Hiawatha was based on the stories of an actual Onondaga chief as well as Indian folklore.

ACTIVITIES

Family Images

Read the poem "Hiawatha" aloud and invite students to think of some scenes for the poetic words in their "mind's eye." Encourage them to think of friendly family relationships in the boy's life as they reflect on the poem. Invite volunteers to describe their reflections aloud to the whole group and write their suggestions on the board. If appropriate, also read aloud excerpts from Longfellow's *Hiawatha's Childhood* (Farrar, Strauss, & Groiux, 1984), illustrated by Errol LeCain, to find other examples of friendship in the text and illustrations. Have the children look for similarities between examples from the book and the entries on the list on the board. Invite them to relate any of the similarities to their own life experience.

Personification in Nature

Ask the children ages 7–8 to find examples in the poem of personification in nature to emphasize the caring relationship Native Americans have with their environment. Have the children select quotes about personification and meet in small conversational groups to tell their findings. Have them write the quotes for their group. Ask the children to discuss which quote would make a good sound byte (TV byte)—for instance, a quote that is memorable and should be passed on to others. Back in the large group, have the children read aloud the quotes from each small group and record the quotes on a chart for display in the room.

Connections

Reinforce the friendship aspects of the story of Hiawatha by asking the children to work together to illustrate selected sequential events in it. Assign to each child an event and distribute art paper. Explain to the group that each child will need to make a special effort as a friend to coordinate his or her artwork with the artwork of another child. To do this, the children should make the edges of their drawings connect with the other drawings. Display the pictures as a mural in the room to show the events of the story in sequence and invite children to retell the actions of friendship from the drawings they made and *to add the acts of friendships they encountered* with other children in the room while creating their drawings.

Imaginary Conversations

Have the children work with partners to write an imaginary conversation of friendship between themselves and Hiawatha. As a group, have children describe what they would like to talk about with Hiawatha and how they would begin and end their friendly conversations. In some instances, the children might want to listen to the story again to consider what replies Hiawatha might give in a conversation. Have them also think about how Hiawatha might speak and what facial expressions and body language he might use. After the conversations are written, ask the children to read the conversations to one another and imitate Hiawatha's pronunciation, his facial expressions, and his body language.

Changes

After listening to the story of Hiawatha, have children recall some of the events of friendship in the story and list the events on the board. Invite the children to choose one of the events and suggest alternative outcomes of the event.

Events in *Hiawatha*	Suggested Changes
—He learned the language of birds and talked with them	—Could not learn the language of owls
—He learned the secrets of the beasts	—Was afraid of the animals
—He sang a song of friendship to little fire-fly	—Was disinterested in the insects —Did not like to sing

Have the children describe how the story of Hiawatha might change as a result of these alternatives—for example, Hiawatha might never have referred to the animals as his "brothers" due to his fear. Have them meet in small groups to discuss which version they prefer and why.

Interjections

With children, reread the story of Hiawatha aloud to the group. As you read the poetic words, encourage the children to interject with additional friendship words and actions. As an example, a child might suggest that a new friend walks into the action of a particular scene, or that Hiawatha has a special friendship with a younger or older sibling who helps him, or that a caring acquaintance arrives in the middle of a scene to assist a friend who is in trouble, etc. Encourage conversations about friendships and actions that might occur.

Friendship Theater

Have children divide into groups of four or five, then select one event of the story to turn it into an untitled short skit that reflects friendship. After each skit, invite members of the group to identify the event in Hiawatha's story upon which the skit was based. If appropriate, have the class identify a main idea related to the event played in the skit.

Meaningful Words

Ask the children to write down the title of the book and then to copy one quote from the story that was the most meaningful to them. Emphasize quotes related to friendship—the citing of friendly words and actions. Have the children cut around the words in a free-form shape and collect the cutouts. Paste the cutouts on a chart or mural paper and select a quote to read aloud. Have the children recall which event in the story inspired the quote. Invite the child who selected the quote to tell why the words were meaningful to him or her.

Book 1.5   *Jojo's Flying Side Kick* (37)

Ages:	5–7
Heritage:	Asian American
Goals:	To relate friendship to an intergenerational relationship
	To portray family friendship through personal stories
	To work together as friends and partners in activities
	To celebrate and recognize women of achievement who represent different ethnic and cultural groups
	To prepare a prose or poetic passage related to friendship
Materials:	Copy of *JoJo's Flying Side Kick* (37), notebooks, paper and markers, crayons, paints to make a quilt design depicting friendship

BOOK NOTES

JoJo's Flying Side Kick (Simon & Schuster, 1995), written and illustrated by Brian Pinkney, is a story of intergenerational love, family love, and friendship. JoJo wants to advance from a white to a yellow belt in her Tae Kwon Do class; to do this, she must break a board with a flying side kick. Family members offer their support. Her grandfather, a former boxer, suggests that she do fancy footwork similar to what he did before his boxing matches. Her mother suggests visualizing the action, and a friend suggests JoJo gain power by yelling "KIAH" from deep within herself. JoJo does all three in her class and earns the yellow belt she wants.

ACTIVITIES

Family Support

Ask the children to describe family support they have received from members of their family (or someone they know) similar to the family support JoJo received. List their ideas on the board. Ask the children to look again at the illustrations in the book to identify family members expressing love and support for JoJo. Ask if the children found activities in the story similar to their own. Ask the children to describe in their own words what family members are doing, such as demonstrating fancy footwork, yelling "KIAH" from deep within, and visualizing an anticipated activity.

Invite the children to review/reread the list about family support on the board, and then to dictate or write brief stories telling more about these family friendship activities.

Fancy Footwork

Ask the children to consider the advice given to JoJo by her grandfather that she do a little fancy footwork to chase away any jitters before the big test of her ability in her class. JoJo followed his advice and danced a bit before trying her flying side kick to break the board. From the children's point of view, what would JoJo's fancy footwork look like? Ask for volunteers to demonstrate the fancy footwork JoJo might have done. What advice have the children received from their parents, guardians, grandparents or friends that helped them in certain situations? What friendly advice would the class audience offer to the fancy footwork performers to improve their footwork?

Visualizing

Invite the children to meet in small buzz groups to consider the advice that JoJo's mother gave her about a visualization technique to help her succeed. They can informally respond to questions such as:

- Did you like the idea given to JoJo by her mother? Why? Why not?
- Why do you think the visualization idea was helpful/not helpful?
- Have you ever felt like JoJo when she visualized reacting to the motions of a creepy tree in her yard that had always frightened her?

Friend's Advice

A friend advised JoJo to yell "KIAH" from deep within herself to gain greater power when she tried to break a board with a flying side kick. Have children volunteer to take turns and yell aloud their own version of

"KIAH" to experience JoJo's feelings vicariously. Invite them to tell how they felt when they yelled "KIAH" and in what ways the friend's advice helped JoJo gain greater power for her class performance. If appropriate, ask volunteers to tell anecdotes about helpful advice received from a close family friend.

Tae Kwon Do

Have children research Tae Kwon Do by interviewing someone they know who has taken lessons and report back what they have learned to the whole group. Invite them to discuss how such skills might benefit a friendship. If appropriate, invite someone from a Tae Kwon Do class to visit the children to tell about the history of Tae Kwon Do, its benefits, and the significance of the belts and to demonstrate a flying side kick or other motions.

Audiotape Reading

Audiotape this story and invite the children to listen to the story on a cassette as they follow along in the book. After listening to the story, have students pair up as friends to draw-and-guess words from the story. Have one child draw a word from the following list from JoJo's story and have the other child guess what the picture is showing.

Words from JoJo's Story:

white belt	yellow belt
a board	a kick
grandfather	a boxer
mother	yelling "KIAH"
friend	scary tree

Friendship Choral Speaking

Ask students to pair up as friends and prepare a saying (e.g., "friendship makes life easier") related to friendship to present to the class. Distribute photocopies of all the sayings or display them on the board, a class chart, or overhead transparency. Different parts of the saying can be spoken by each student or they can recite it in unison. Some children, particularly those learning English as a second language (ESL), will benefit, particularly in intonation and pronunciation, by participating in this oral language activity.

International Women's Day

Each year on March 8, the history of women and their achievements are recognized through International Women's Day. Invite children to celebrate and recognize women and girls, such as JoJo, who represent different ethnic and other groups, women who have fought stereotyping, women of all races and creeds who have made contributions to others, and women's achievements by writing letters to the editors of local newspapers identifying the women they admire and explaining why.

Book 1.6   *Luka's Quilt* (13)

Ages:	5–7
Heritage:	Hawaiian American
Goals:	To relate friendship to an intergenerational relationship
	To portray family friendship in artwork, minibooks, stories
	To become aware of special events, holidays, celebrations recognized by different families
	To record what has been learned about being part of a family friendship through a story
	To explore feelings of disappointment when an expected desire is not realized
	To become aware of different types of family friendships and concerns in different locales and time periods
Materials:	Copy of *Luka's Quilt* (13), notebooks, paper and markers, crayons, paints to make a quilt design depicting friendship

BOOK NOTES

Luka's Quilt (Greenwillow, 1994), by Georgia Guback, is a story of intergenerational love and friendship. Luka and her grandmother have quarreled because the traditional plain Hawaiian quilt that her grandmother was making for Luka did not have the large beautiful flowers that Luka wanted. On Lei Day, Luka's grandmother asks that they declare a truce so they can celebrate the festival together. Luka agrees and participates in making flower leis. In return, Luka's grandmother makes a colorful fabric lei to accent the plain quilt, and this heals Luka's hurt feelings. Includes words such as tatami mat, lei, and shave ice that might be unfamiliar to some children.

ACTIVITIES

Family Friends

Reminding them that Luka and her grandmother worked together to make flower leis on Lei Day, ask the children what friendship activities they like to do with family members (or someone they know). List their suggestions on the board. Show the pictures in *Luka's Quilt* on an opaque projector and ask the children to find pictures in the book of family members doing things that portray friendship. Which friendship activities are similar to those experienced by the students in their own lives? Elicit from the children words that describe what the characters are doing in the friendship activities, such as hugging, waving hello or good-bye, working together, and so on.

Invite the children to keep a log of the friendship activities their family members engage in for a selected period of time (one day, two days, one week). Have them include their own demonstrations of friendship during times with family or important others. Invite them to report their findings back to the group.

One Who Bounces Back

Demonstrate resilience with a marshmallow as you talk about family members who bounce back to preserve friendships in the family, as Grandmother did with Luka. Press the marshmallow down in the center and let the children watch it bounce back. Distribute cupcake papers and marshmallows to the children and ask them to write a greeting on the paper, such as "To _____ with love" to give to a family member in honor of their resilience.

Friendship Calendar

Invite children to interview family members and research Lei Day and other events to include on a multicultural friendship calendar for the classroom. Discuss in the large group some special events, holidays and celebrations recognized by different groups, the names of significant people related to the events, and contributions made by various groups.

Quilt Stories and Family Friendships

Guide children who are particularly interested in feelings among family members to one or more of the following quilt stories, set in various locales and time periods. Read aloud or have children read some of the books about different types of family friendships and children's concerns. Then ask them to plan and write a day's activities as if they were a friend of the main character in the story they read. Have them explain what they learned about being part of family friendships through the stories:

- Coerr, Eleanor. *The Josefina Story Quilt.* Harper & Row, 1986. A young girl, Faith, creates a quilt that illustrates the story of Josefina, her pet hen.
- Johnson, Tony. *The Quilt Story.* Putnam, 1985. This story tells about Abigail, a small pioneer girl, who received a quilt made for her by her mother. Throughout her life, this quilt traveled with her.
- Polacco, Patricia. *The Keeping Quilt.* Simon & Schuster, 1988. This is a true story about a quilt kept by the author's family.
- Kinsey-Warnock, Natalie. *The Canada Geese Quilt.* Cobblehill/Dutton, 1989. Ages 6–8. In this story, a granddaughter's artistic sketches become a part of the family's history.
- Kurtz, Shirley. *The Boy and the Quilt.* Good Bks., 1991. Ages 5–6. A young boy sees that his sister and mother are going to make a quilt and his mother tells him that he can work on it, too.
- Flournoy, Valeria. *The Patchwork Quilt.* Dial, 1985. Ages 6–8. This story shows making a quilt in a contemporary setting, an activity that brings a family together as they recall events related to the fabric remnants.

Minibooks

Read one or two books from the previous list of quilt stories and ask the children to make their own eight-page minibooks by copying a quote about friendship from the stories on each of the minibook pages. Show children how a sheet of paper can be folded into fourths to make eight minipages (including the front and back of the sheet). For each quote on a page, ask them to write or sketch ideas for implementing the quote's suggestion for becoming a better friend.

Family Troubles

Invite the children to listen to or read one of the stories listed in the bibliography of this book and talk about feelings shared by the children and the characters in regards to family friendships. After the story, ask the children for suggestions for making family friendships stronger and list them on the board. Ask the children to illustrate some of the suggestions listed on the board. Invite them to tell how they can strengthen family friendships.

Paper Friendship Quilt

Distribute paper squares to the children and ask them to color scenes that show family friendships on them. For example, the children can use scenes from a family's history as inspiration for their artwork. Their scenes/patterns can represent activities tied to a family all through the year. Have the children sign their names on their artwork. Arrange the squares in a quilt pattern or shape on a bulletin board to display in the room. On subsequent days, ask for volunteers to tell about the family friendships they drew.

Book 1.7 *My Rotten Red-Headed Older Brother* (39)

Ages:	5–8
Heritage:	European American
Goals:	To offer friendship to a sibling
	To recognize changed behavior in a sibling
	To portray sibling friendship in artwork, want ads, stories
	To gain insight into conflict resolution and turning a teasing situation into a friendly one
Materials:	Copy of *My Rotten Red-Headed Older Brother* (39), magazines, newspapers, brochures, and catalogs; art paper, mural paper, crayons, paints

BOOK NOTES

My Rotten Red-Headed Older Brother (Simon & Schuster, 1994), by Patricia Polacco, is the story of an older brother who always outdoes his younger sister, Patricia, and brags about his achievements while grinning his greeny-toothed grin. Patricia makes a special wish on a star and the following day discovers that her brother really cares about her. He rescues her when she becomes dizzy from riding the carousel at the carnival and takes a spill.

ACTIVITIES

Want Ad

Read the story aloud and discuss its portrayal of sibling friendship. Ask the children to list the kinds of things they like to have their brothers and sisters do for them and why. Then have the children write or dictate a want ad for a perfect brother or sister. Read several aloud and invite children to pair up in groups of two and take the roles of ad writer and newspaper editor. Ask each child to initiate a friendly conversation and read his/her want ad to the newspaper editor over an imagined telephone. Later, display the ads on a display board in the room.

Family Friendship Is . . .

Provide the children with discarded magazines, newspapers, brochures, and catalogs and ask them to find illustrations that show family friendships. Have them cut out and paste the illustrations on art paper for their own mural of friendship or arrange the collages on butcher paper to make a large classroom mural. Have children dictate or write captions—such as "Family friendship is . . . "—to accompany their work and sign their names to the mural.

Sibling Sketches

Have the children draw a sketch showing a friendship with a brother or sister they have or would like to have. To accompany their sketches, ask the children to write about their friendships with someone in their family (or a caring person they know). Encourage them to write about what they have learned about their own friendships with a brother or sister through this story.

Rub It In

Ask children in small informal conversation groups to tell of a time when someone they know tried to "rub in" their achievements in a teasing way, just as Patricia's brother did. Elicit suggestions from all the children about ways to respond to such teasing and to turn this kind of situation into a friendly one.

Valued Sibling

Have the children work with partners in the group and write ten things they value about a sibling. Back in the whole group, ask some children to volunteer to read their lists aloud. As the lists are read, compare and tally the students' comments to see the extent to which the children value similar qualities.

Friendship Poster

Ask the children to look at the illustrations in the book again and respond to the following questions:

- What do the siblings in the illustrations look like?
- What are they wearing?
- What kind of house do they live in?
- What do they eat?

Have the children find other pictures of sibling friendships in discarded magazines, newspapers, catalogues, and brochures. Let them use the pictures to make posters reflecting family friendships. Suggest that the children take their artwork home and present it to someone in the family.

Sibling Feelings

Invite the children to consider the feelings of the brother and sister and answer the following questions:

- Did you like the brother? Why? Why not?
- Why do you think the brother was important in the story?
- Do you know anyone like the sister?
- In what way did the brother change?
- What things did the brother do that you thought were friendly/unfriendly?

- What things did the sister do that you thought were unfriendly/ friendly?
- What did the brother do that you thought would bring peace to the family?
- What do you think was the "friendliest" part of the story? Why?
- In what ways have you felt like the brother? The sister?
- In what other way could the story have ended?
- What have you learned about being friendly with a family member?

Help the children deal with their feelings openly and to understand that all people have feelings. This story allows children to discuss feelings of disappointment when their desires are not met and to realize that sometimes a quarrel takes place. The teacher can express personal feelings, too, such as, "I was feeling unhappy when that happened and I got angry" or "That made me feel sad and unhappy inside." Help children talk openly to others when they share their experiences related to disappointments and quarrels.

Book 1.8 *Saturday Sancocho* (47)

Ages:	5–8
Heritage:	Latino/Hispanic
Goals:	To see a family friendship that is fostered by assisting a family member
	To identify a family friendship through helpful actions
	To incorporate information and problem-solving into role-playing
	To transform thoughts and feelings into sketches and written work
	To discuss polite and friendly ways to interact with others
	To role-play a family member introduced to a new food
Materials:	Copy of *Saturday Sancocho* (47), paper lists, pencils, writing board, chalk, reference materials

BOOK NOTES

Saturday Sancocho (Farrar, Straus and Giroux, 1995), by Leyla Torres, is the story of an intergenerational friendship between Maria Lili and her grandmother, Mama Ana. Every Saturday, Maria goes to visit her grandparents, and they make *sancocho,* a chicken stew that Maria thinks is wonderful. One Saturday, Maria discovers that the only food in the kitchen is eggs and that they lack all of the ingredients to make the favorite stew. Mama Ana and Maria put the eggs in a basket and go to the open-air market, where they barter their eggs from stall to stall.

ACTIVITIES

Friends at the Market

In groups of three, have the children role-play family friendships using the scenario where Mama Ana and her grandchild are at the market bartering with a friendly person at the stalls for ingredients for the stew. Elicit children's responses to questions prior to role play so they can consider some information and problem-solving techniques for use in role playing the event:

- Who are you (Mama Ana or her grandchild or the seller)?
- Where are you?
- What might happen? Why?
- How are you feeling? What are you thinking?
- Why are you at this place?
- How do you act toward the family member in this family friendship? Toward the seller?
- How can you make this family relationship more friendly?

Have the children change roles until each child has played all three.

Thinking and Feeling

Stop the role-playing and ask the children to write/sketch what they are thinking and feeling about Mama Ana and her grandchild at this time. As part of the family friendship theme, ask the children to write an entry in their friendship journals about a family friendship they have experienced or to write what they learned about family friendships from the role-playing. Invite them to include any friendly words and actions they performed or saw performed during the role-play. After writing, ask the children to resume role-playing again in different groups of three.

Bartering

Ask the groups of three to meet with another triad and role-play a scene for one another that depicts family members bartering in a friendly manner at the market.

Curiosity

Back in the whole group, ask children in what ways the role-playing stimulated their curiosity about family friendships. Ask them how we can learn more about family friendships and list their responses on the writing board. Elicit from student volunteers something each could do to be a better friend in their families.

Sancocho

Ask the children to recall the ingredients that Mama Ana and Maria needed to make the chicken stew, *sancocho*. Write the names of the ingredients on the board. Ask them to suggest reasons why each ingredient was added to the stew. Have the children turn to a partner-friend in the group and informally share their ideas about this situation: Could the same stew be made *without* one of the ingredients? Have the partner-friends suggest ways to change ingredients and role-play the manner in which they could say something about changing ingredients in a polite and pleasant way to a family member who was cooking the stew. Ask the partners to role-play good manners, making suggestions to the cook about the stew in a polite way that would not hurt the cook's feelings.

American Foods

Discuss with the children the idea that several "American" foods came to America from other countries. Invite the children to suggest their favorite foods and their family members' favorite foods and list them on the board. Invite the children to guess which of the foods are native to America and put a check by the food names. Ask them to meet in buzz groups of five or six and imagine sharing one of the foods they like (or do not like) with a younger brother or sister. In the buzz groups, have the children suggest friendly comments and pleasant remarks they might make in their conversations with a sibling.

Two Friends

Ask for student-volunteers to work together in a friendly way to research the country of origin of some of the foods in the previous or subsequent list and report their findings back to the class. In their reports, ask the children to imagine what two friends would say (liked the food, did not like the food) when first tasting a food from a country other than America and to share their remarks with the group.

cornflakes (America)	chop suey (America)	doughnuts (Netherlands)
French fries (France)	hamburgers (Germany)	hot dogs (Germany)
ice cream (France)	popcorn (America)	potato chips (America)

Have the children pretend they are meeting a family relative from France, Germany, or the Netherlands and are introduced to one of the foods from the relative's country for the *first time*. Thus, the children would be imagining what it would be like to eat French fries, ice cream, hamburgers, doughnuts, or hot dogs for the first time with a family relative from another country. What would they think? See? Feel? Taste? Say to the new family relative? Have children volunteer to play the part of the family relative who introduced the "new" food.

Visitor

Invite a parent or community member into the classroom to introduce a food that is unfamiliar to many of the children. Before the visit, hold a class meeting to talk about some of the polite and friendly ways the children can invite the visitor (perhaps with an invitational letter or phone call), ask questions about the food, talk about the tasting experience with the visitor, make comments about trying the unfamiliar food, and thank the visitor upon his or her departure.

Book 1.9   *The Second Princess* (35)

Ages:	6–7
Heritage:	European American/folk literature
Goals:	To discuss feelings among siblings
	To relate friendship to a sibling
	To develop and expand vocabulary through friendship sayings

To recognize peacekeeping (conflict resolution) in a
family
To recognize friendly traits in family members
To portray family peacekeeping in expressive art, i.e., a
mobile or poem
Materials: Copy of *The Second Princess* (35), paper for friendship
mini-almanacs, clothes hanger, yarn, and art paper to
make mobile

BOOK NOTES

The Second Princess (Artists & Writers, 1994), by Hiawyn Oram, is a
story of a second princess who thinks the first princess gets better treatment than she does at the palace and wants to be rid of her. Her schemes
are discovered by her mother, the queen, who helps the two princesses
become friends and declares that the princesses will alternate days of being "first" through the royal week, and on Sundays, the entire royal family will be "first" together.

ACTIVITIES

Princess' Feelings

Invite students to meet in pairs to discuss the feelings of the second
princess and informally tell one another their responses to each of the following as you read the questions aloud:

• Did you like the second princess? Why? Why not?
• Why do you think the second princess was important in the story?
• Do you know anyone like the second princess? Tell about her.
• In what way did the second princess change?
• What things did the second princess do that you thought were friendly?
  Unfriendly?
• What did the queen do that you thought would bring peace to the sec-
  ond princess and to the family?
• What do you think was the "friendliest"/"unfriendliest" part of the
  story? Why?
• In what ways have you felt like the second princess?
• In what other way could the story have ended?
• What did you learn about family friendships from the story?

Better Treatment

Ask the children to think of a time when they thought someone else received better treatment and how that made them feel. Ask student volunteers to share their experience aloud to the whole group. Elicit responses on what they could have said to change the situation. Ask them to watch for opportunities to change situations in the future and to report back to the group if one arises.

Friendship Mini-Almanacs

Ask the children to make individual family friendship mini-almanacs with pages that record sayings of friendship. First, have the children write the words of the queen in *The Second Princess* on a page in the mini-almanac: "The first and second princesses will alternate days of being 'first' through the royal week and on Sundays, the entire royal family will be 'first' together." Ask the children to recall additional family oriented sayings, proverbs, or quotes they have heard to write in the almanacs. Here are some friendship sayings to read aloud to the children that they can include if they wish:

- A friend in need is a friend indeed. (Benjamin Franklin)
- A friend is one before whom I can think aloud. (Ralph Waldo Emerson)
- A friend is a present you give yourself. (Robert Lewis Stevenson)
- My best friend is the one who brings out the best in me. (Henry Ford)
- Make new friends and keep the old; one is silver, the other gold. (Mother Goose)

Further, the children can make up friendship sayings of their own to write on the pages. If appropriate, ask the children to include in their almanacs any times or important days in their lives when someone in their family demonstrated friendship to another person. Have the children remember to include some friendly family events that they attended, some favorite jokes that family members tell in a friendly setting, and anything else that matters to them in family friendships.

Family Friendship Qualities

Reread aloud some of the quotations about friendship from the previous list and discuss the qualities of friendship found in the quotations. Ask each child to make a list (or sketch stick figures) to record the qualities they think a sister (brother, cousin, or other family member) must possess to be a good family friend. As a comparison, have them list (or sketch) their own friendship qualities. Ask the children to compare the two lists and then reflect/write or draw the ways they could become a better friend to their brothers, sisters, or other family members.

Family Friendship Mobile

After discussing family friendships in the whole group, ask children what they think is needed to build stronger family friendships. Have the children divide into small groups and ask each group to make a "Family Friendship Hanging Mobile" with a clothes hanger, yarn, and art paper. Invite the children to draw scenes on art paper to show ways they think family friendships can be made stronger, then affix the scenes with yarn to the hanger. Hang the mobile for display over each group's work area and let volunteers tell what scenes of family friendship they elected to draw. Invite them to add additional scenes to the mobile as they wish on subsequent days.

Family Friendship Poems

Read aloud poems that reflect family friendships—positive, helpful, and humorous—to the children. Invite the children to chime in and repeat the words they know when you reread the poem aloud. As examples for read-alouds, you could select any or all of the following poems to read aloud from a contemporary collection entitled *Something Big Has Been Here* (Greenwillow, 1990), by Jack Prelutsky.

Poem Title	*Family Friendship*
"Happy Birthday, Mother Dearest"	Making breakfast for mother
"Life's Not Been the Same in My Family"	New infant at home
"My Brother Built a Robot"	Siblings use robot to clean room
"My Uncle Looked Me in the Eye"	Advice from a relative
"We Moved about a Week Ago"	Lack of friends due to family move

Ask children to look through the poetry books in the classroom to find additional family friendship poems to record in their family friendship journals. If appropriate, have them read favorite lines aloud to the group and record the poem's title on a chart with the heading, "Our Poems about Family Friendships."

Book Talks

Give brief book talks from books listed in the family friendship bibliography provided here and suggest some stories for further independent reading and browsing.

Book 1.10 *Snow Day* (19)

Ages:	6–7
Heritage:	European American
Goals:	To relate friendship to a family's activities
	To portray family friendship through artwork
	To contribute to the family by introducing a friendly game
	To reflect about ways to be better family friends
	To share what was learned through a variety of self-selected activities
Materials:	Copy of *Snow Day* (19), adding machine tape for a minimural, paper plates for family game, art paper for greeting cards, art paper or spiral-bound notebooks for stories

BOOK NOTES

Snow Day (Clarion, 1995), written by Barbara M. Josse and illustrated by Jennifer Plecas, is the story of an active young boy who goes outside early in the morning to play in banks of snow. His dog and the other family members join him for snowy-time fun—there is even a snow fight. Later, the parents, the children, and Zippy the dog go inside to wrap up in blankets and drink hot chocolate before a warm fire in the fireplace.

ACTIVITIES

Minitape Mural

Reread examples of expressive language in the story that reflect the family members as friends or express the fun the family has during this day of leisure. After listening to the excerpts, invite the children to make their own four-section minimural by folding lengths (12") of adding machine tape into four sections. Ask the children to record an excerpt of expressive language about the family's friendship on three sections of the tape and describe how they would use the idea to become a better friend to other family members. In the last section, ask children to write their own ideas for being a better friend to the family. Have them describe what their idea means to them.

Friendship Game

Introduce a paper plate game as a family friendship activity that the children can teach their family members at home and perhaps play at the next family gathering:

• Two family members sit facing one another about ten feet apart. Each member holds an end of a twelve-foot string in his or her hand.
• Punch a hole in a paper plate and slide the plate to one end of the string. On the direction "Ready, set, go," the two family members, still sitting, use just one hand to hold the string and jiggle, shake, and manipulate the string in order to cooperate and move the paper plate to the other end of the string.
• Family members can time their performance with a stopwatch and repeat the activity to beat their initial time. They also can form teams of two to outperform one another.

Place string, ruler, and paper plates at an activity center so children can measure a twelve-foot string. Have the children take the string and two paper plates home for their families.

Different Family Friendships

Talk about various kinds of family friendships after reading aloud other stories related to the topic (see bibliography). After reading, ask the children, "Who sees some friendships in this family? How could this family do a *better* job of building family friendships? How could we do a better job of building family friendships? What could each of us do as a family member?" Suggest that the children consider their families as an assignment and ask them to think of ways they can start to build stronger family friendships. If appropriate, list their ideas on a chart for future reference and group discussion.

Greeting Card

Have the children make a greeting card by folding art paper in half and writing one of their suggestions in it from the list in the previous activity. Encourage the children to ask for the family member's support in building stronger and more positive family friendships.

Friendly Child

Introducing incomplete sentences about friendship that allow more than one ending is a valuable exercise because it allows classroom friends to work together successfully. Write a simple sentence on the board or an overhead transparency and invite the children to work as partners and add to the sentence to make it longer. Example:

- The friendly boy played.
- The friendly boy and his dog Zippy played in the snow.
- The friendly boy and his dog Zippy played in the white snow banks.
- The friendly boy and his dog Zippy played in a snow fight with his family in the white snow banks.

Family Member as a Friend

Ask the children to participate in a discussion about ways a family member can be a friend to them. Write their responses on the board or on a chart. Invite them to think of a friendly act *they* can perform at home toward a family member and ask them to try it out after school. Tell them you will ask them what their friendly act was the next day at school and will want to know how they felt when they were being friendly toward someone in the family.

Family Journal

Have children decorate the cover of a spiral-bound notebook for their own family friendship journal. Or, have the children punch holes in art paper and bind inside pages together with ribbon or cord. Inside the journal, have the children complete several short projects about friendships. The children can draw a family friendship story in bordered frames similar to a storyboard, or retell a friendly event in a family story that they liked, or change the gender of a character in a family friendship story and rewrite the story to reflect the gender change. Additionally, they can read portions of a family friendship story to a family member and ask for his or her opinion, which can be recorded in the journal. Further, they can collect newspaper and magazine illustrations that reflect family friendships or write what they have learned about being part of a family friendship (or group of caring others) through this story and others they have read.

What I've Learned

Invite the children to share what they have learned about family friendships by completing some alternative activities that they can self-select. Examples include:

- Dioramas: Children can construct dioramas to show the most important information about family friendships they learned. Have the children display their dioramas and take questions from their peers.
- Dramas: Children can present brief dramas to explain what they have learned about family friendships.
- Journals: Children can reread and study everything they wrote or drew in their friendship journals. With this information, have the children summarize how much they have learned and then describe more specifically what they have learned.
- Murals: Children can illustrate the information they considered to be the most important on the mural paper. Have the children take questions from their peers.
- Points of view: Children can discuss, present, or write about the topic of family friendship from two different points of view.
- Posters: Children can prepare posters to describe the information they have learned. Have them display the posters and give a brief explanation of their reasons for selecting the information they did on the poster(s).
- Puzzles: Children can make crossword puzzles about family friendships and let others try to complete them.
- Reflections: In groups of four or five, children can describe what they learned about the idea of family friendships, what they were thinking during their reflections/thoughts earlier in the study, and how their reflections/thoughts have changed after hearing the stories about family friendships.
- Reporters: Invite the children to role-play a television newscaster and review the topic of family friendships as if they were on television.
- Scripts: Children can write a brief script on the topic of family friendships for a popular TV show and participate in the character roles on the program for a class demonstration.

2 Community, Neighborhood, and School Friendships

Book 2.1 *The Barber's Cutting Edge* (55)

Ages:	6–8
Heritage:	African American
Goals:	To relate friendship to a community worker
	To recognize African American History Month
	To recognize African Americans, their friendships, and their achievements
	To develop vocabulary related to the story through banners and friendship sayings
	To portray friendships in artwork
	To relate literature to community, neighborhood, and school friendships
Materials:	Copy of *The Barber's Cutting Edge* (55), writing board, chalk, magazines and newspapers, adding machine tape, butcher paper to make banners, chart to make collage, art paper for sketches

BOOK NOTES

The Barber's Cutting Edge (Children's Book Press, 1994) is written by Gwendolyn Battle-Lavert and illustrated by Raymond Holbert. It's about a visit to a local barbershop by Rashaad, an African American boy. Mr. Bigalow is known as the "best barber in town," and his customers can play checkers at a table or read books from a bookshelf. Rashaad tries to "stump" the barber by giving him difficult words to define in an amusing and entertaining exchange (a cutting edge). Mr. Bigalow keeps walking into his back room (perhaps to look in a dictionary for another cutting edge).

ACTIVITIES

African American History

February is African American history month sponsored by the Association for the Study of Negro Life and History, so invite children to recognize black Americans, their friendships, and their achievements not only during this month but all year long. To relate to the story of *The Barber's Cutting Edge,* arrange for the children to interview a barber in the community. Schedule a field trip so the children can observe the barber's workplace, record notes, make sketches of the work environment, and ask questions about the friendships (and contributions and achievements) he has made in the community. If appropriate, have each of the children autograph a pair of gloves to present to the barber as a symbol of being a "friendly hand" in the community. Back in the classroom, have the children identify other citizens who contribute to the community and make arrangements to establish new friendships with them through field trips.

Friendship Web

In the classroom, place the title of the book in the center of a chalk web on the writing board. Write some of the text's friendship words at the end of lines drawn from the web's center. Have children suggest descriptions, phrases, and even their own definitions for the words. Write in as much information as possible on the web. Let children know they can change or add to any of the information. Have children read/listen to *The Barber's Cutting Edge* again. Encourage the children to discuss and change any of the information on the web.

Friendship Banner

After adding information about friendship to the previous web, invite the children to work together as friends to make two-foot-long motivational banners about friendship using a roll of paper adding-machine tape. Elicit their ideas for slogans for the banners and write them on the board. Examples of slogans:

- We can smile and shake hands in the same language.
- Every day is a friendship day.
- Use a smile to be a friend.
- You can make friendships happen.
- Friendship is a LITTLE thing that makes a BIG difference.
- We're all part of Friendship.
- Tomorrow's friendship begins today.
- Have you been a friend today?
- Want a friend? Be a friend.
- Friendship works!
- There's nobody like a friend.
- Friendship is contagious.
- Friendship can change the day.
- A little friendship goes a long way.
- Friends . . . it's what is inside that counts.

Distribute sections of adding machine tape to small groups. Have the children write their slogan of choice and decide on accompanying drawings. Let them paint, draw with crayons, or use colored markers to highlight the slogan and artwork. Display in the classroom, school multipurpose room, or hallways, or give as a gift to another classroom.

Giant Collage

After completing the friendship web in the previous activity, invite the children to locate and cut out illustrations from magazines and newspapers that show friends in the neighborhood and workers in the community who could be future friends. Display their work in a giant collage labeled "Friendship" on mural paper in the classroom.

Friendship Charts

Have the children meet with a friend (or potential friend) in the classroom and read/browse through two additional books about friends in the neighborhood and the community. Ask them to locate and record friendship words from the books and compare the meanings of any friendship words they find. Have them write the friendship words in large, bold letters and cut out the words in "balloon" shapes. Let them paste the friendship words on several large "Friendship" charts for display in class.

Community Friends

Take the children on a community walk to identify business people who could become new friends in the neighborhood, just as the barber was a neighborhood friend in the story. The children can take a tape recorder to mention the places they see and record some facts about some of the businesspeople. After touring the area and returning to the classroom, ask the children which businesspeople they would like to know better as new friends and how they would begin a friendship. Write their suggestions on a class chart labeled "Ways to Begin Community Friendships." Invite them to put their friendship ideas into a friendly letter to a person in the community. If any of the children put their friendship ideas into action, have them report back to the group at a later date to tell how they initiated a community friendship.

Book 2.2   *Down at Angel's* (59)

Ages:	6–8
Heritage:	Bulgarian
Goals:	To reflect upon friendship with an elderly neighbor
	To identify friendship in actions such as gift-giving
	To perceive homemade and crafted gifts as valuable
	To suggest and record ways to meet new friends
	To appreciate the community and its history
Materials:	Copy of *Down at Angel's* (59), materials to make a handmade or handcrafted card or gift, art paper crayons, markers, paints

BOOK NOTES

Down at Angel's (Ticknor & Fields, 1994), written by Sharon Chmielarz and illustrated by Jill Kastner, is a story of two sisters who develop a friendship with an elderly neighbor, Angel, who is a widower and a woodcutter from Bulgaria. Angel is like a grandfather to the children and lets them watch him work as he carves tables, makes inlaid wood patterns, and listens to his favorite opera music. When Christmas comes, the girls and their mother prepare a gift of homemade sauces, preserves, and other foods. In return, Angel gives them a hand-carved table they had admired.

ACTIVITIES

Like a Grandparent to Me

Ask the children what these words mean to them: "Angel was like a grandfather to the two sisters." Write their responses on the board. Ask the children to share their own friendship experiences with a grandparent or an elderly person who seemed like a grandparent to them.

Gifts

Invite the children to plan a homemade or handcrafted gift that they could give to a grandparent or an elderly person who was like a grandparent to them. Have them sketch their ideas on square paper shapes cut to look like gift boxes. Have them complete their sketches by coloring a gift bow at the top of their drawings and addressing a small gift card. Encourage the children to take their artwork home and present it.

Greeting Cards

Invite the children to inscribe the gift cards to go with the drawings of their gifts. Read aloud the inscriptions on several commercial gift cards to give children ideas for what to write inside their cards. Give the children art paper and ask them to fold the paper in half to make their cards. Encourage them to write original inscriptions and to include words that tell the recipient why "you are a favorite grandparent" or "you are like a grandparent to me." Have them decorate their cards.

Friendship Guide

Ask the children to fold three pages of art paper in half to make a six-page friendship guide entitled "Making Friends in the Community." Have them write an action or behavior from the story at the top of each page with the beginning, "Making friends means . . ." (visiting one another, watching friends work and play, listening to music together, preparing a gift, exchanging gifts, and so on). Have the children write and tell how such actions will make them better friends. Ask the children to save the last page of the guide to describe in their own words what making friends means to them.

Guide to My Neighborhood

Discuss the people, objects, places, celebrations, and behaviors that make up the children's neighborhood. Ask them what newcomers might want to know about the neighborhood. Ask for suggestions to include in a guidebook for their neighborhood and write them on the board. Have children divide into small groups and make each group responsible for writing and illustrating a section of the book. Duplicate the book to be distributed to newcomers at the main office on the school grounds.

Community History Book

Engage the children in conducting research about the history of their neighborhood and compiling the findings in a booklet to be made available to children in class who are newcomers. Invite the children to choose a topic of interest for their research. Topics can include, but are not limited to, first inhabitants, survey of languages spoken, interviews with the elderly, community time line of events and changes, maps of past and present, contributions of different cultural groups.

Book 2.3   *The Flute Player: An Apache Folktale* (86)

Ages:	8 up
Heritage:	Native American
Goals:	To relate friendship to feelings for another person
	To relate friendship to caring actions
	To recognize friendship in folk literature
	To role-play showing friendship to others
	To develop and expand vocabulary related to the folktale
	To engage in conflict resolution through role-play
Materials:	Copy of *The Flute Player: An Apache Folktale* (86), selections of folk literature, music materials

BOOK NOTES

The Flute Player: An Apache Folktale (Flagstaff: Northland Pub., 1990), by Michael Lacapa, is the story of a young girl and a boy who plays the flute. They are attracted to one another during an Apache hoop dance and dance only with one another at the young people's social event, which is held once a year. The girl says that when she hears his flute, she will place a leaf in the river that runs through the canyon. The floating leaf will tell him that she likes his music. One day, the boy leaves on a long hunting trip, and the girl hears no music. She believes that he does not care for her anymore and is unhappy and despondent. She eventually becomes quite ill and dies. When the boy finally returns, he plays his flute for the girl, but no leaves float on the river. When the boy learns that the girl is dead, he disappears and is never seen again. The tale emphasizes that when the Apache people hear echoes through the canyon and see the leaves falling into the river, they know the girl still enjoys the music of the flute player.

ACTIVITIES

Friendship Stories

Ask the children to search for stories in which friendship, caring, forgiveness, and love are demonstrated by people of *all* origins. To encourage this search, display selections of folk literature from the Native American culture and others that the children find.

Have the children announce the stories they have read and record the titles and origins of the story's culture on a chart near a reading bookshelf in the classroom. The titles can be used as a recommended reading list for others in the room.

Friendship Chart

They care for one another.	They overcome anger and forgive.
African:	African:
Asian:	Asian:
Native American:	Native American:
The Flute Player	*The First Strawberries*
European:	European:
Other:	Other:

People are friends when:

They develop friendships.	They develop love for one another.
African:	African:
Asian:	Asian:
Native American:	Native American:
European:	European:
Other:	Other:

Also, have the children meet in pairs to decide (1) what music each can create with available materials in the room to enjoy their friendship together and (2) what each can say/do to communicate to the other that the music was liked and appreciated. Ask for volunteers to tell the whole group about their exchange.

Pantomime Roles

Break up the events of the story into short scenes so the children can role-play the parts. Assign several children to play the boy, others to play the girl, and still others to play their friends. Give such statements as: "You are the young flute player and you are going to approach the young girl because you like her. I want to see how many special ways you can show your feelings for her." Provide other statements to guide the children's actions related to these situations:

- A young girl and boy meeting at an Apache hoop dance. They dance only with one another at the annual social event.
- The young girl hearing his flute and placing a leaf in the river that runs through the canyon. The floating leaf tells him that she likes his music.
- The young boy leaving on a long hunting trip and the girl hearing no music. She believes that he does not care for her anymore and is unhappy and despondent. She eventually becomes quite ill and dies.
- The young boy returning and playing his flute for the girl, but no leaves floating on the river. When the boy learns that the girl is dead, he disappears and is never seen again.

Sharing Values

Ask the children to listen for values they share with the writers of poetry about Native American life as selected poems are read aloud. After listening, invite the children to work together to record their favorite poems on posters for display in the classroom. If appropriate, they can create a

Native American mask or an animal mask to hold in front of their faces when they are reading their favorite poems aloud. The poem can be written on the inside of the mask. Encourage the children to record their favorite lines of poetry that reflect their thoughts about values they have in common with Native American poets. Books to initiate such a listening/writing activity include the following:

Children's Books about Poetry of Native Americans

- Bruchac, Joseph, ed. *New Voices from the Longhouse: An Anthology of Contemporary Iroquois Writing*. New York: Greenfield Review Press, 1989.
- Bruchac, Joseph, reteller. *Four Ancestors: Stories, Songs and Poems from Native America*. New York: Bridgewater, 1996. (The four ancestors are earth, air, fire, and water and represent the headings of the sections for the stories, songs, and poems. Reteller's notes are included.)
- Bruchac, Joseph, and Jonathon Mondon. *Thirteen Moons on Turtle's Back: A Native American Year of Moons*. Illustrated by Thomas Locker. New York: Philomel, 1992. (Traditions about the moon from different tribes that are presented in poetic forms to emphasize nature.)
- Hirschfelder, Arlene, and Beverley Singers, eds. *Rising Voices: Writings of Young Native Americans*. New York: Scribner's, 1992. (Poems and prose by middle and high school children.)
- Jones, Hettie. *The Trees Stand Shining: Poetry of the North American Indians*. Illustrated by Robert Andrew Parker. New York: Dial, 1993. (Folk chants and songs identified by tribal group.)

After reading/hearing Native American poetry, have the children emphasize the values they have in common, as well as any cultural differences they note, by completing a Venn diagram on the topic.

Away with Friends

Have children visualize the flute player on his long hunting trip and research ways that he and his friends might have prepared their food, provided for shelter, and played games. How does this differ from what children and their friends do today for food, shelter, and recreation? Elicit their comments in a discussion and write their findings on the board in two columns: what the flute player did and what I do.

Invent a Scene

Encourage the children to invent a scene that *didn't* happen in the story but could have. For example, the children might suggest that the young girl does not become ill and die, but lives to greet the young boy when he returns from his long hunting trip. The children can improvise the meeting of the two upon the boy's return or pretend they are friends of the returning hunter and discuss their feelings about the boy's situation.

With Friends

Ask the children to imagine that they are a group of friends who went with the flute player on his hunt. Ask them what they would say to him when they all returned and found that his friend had died and what they would say to one another about what happened. Remind the children that this is a Native American folktale and that the things they say should be in keeping with the scenes. Further, ask them to imagine that they are friends who want to leave a rock or cave painting to record this event. Invite the children to participate in a brainstorming session about what to paint on the walls of a cave to tell this story to others.

Book 2.4   *Gracias, Rosa* (96)

Ages:	6–7
Heritage:	Guatemalan
Goals:	To relate friendship to a child's babysitter
	To role-play two people getting acquainted for the first time
	To recognize friendship with a gift
	To develop and expand vocabulary through friendship stories in English and Spanish
	To participate in a friendship game
Materials:	Copy of *Gracias, Rosa* (96), globe or world map, art paper, additional friendship stories, index cards

BOOK NOTES

Gracias, Rosa (Albert Whitman, 1995), written by Michelle Markel and illustrated by Diane Paterson, is a heart-warming story narrated by Kate, a young girl, who tells about her developing friendship with Rosa. Rosa, the new babysitter, is from Guatemala and doesn't speak much English. Kate is not sure that she likes Rosa. Rosa, however, gives Kate a gift—a cloth doll—and over time, the two develop a special friendly bond.

ACTIVITIES

A Friend's Homeland

Have the children look again at the illustrations in the book that show scenes of Rosa's homeland, Guatemala. If appropriate, locate Guatemala on a globe or world map. Have each child choose another child in class to role-play one or more of the scenes with the first child as Rosa and the other child, Kate. Have the two children trade roles so each can be Rosa and describe her homeland to her young charge—a potential friend.

Designed Doll as Gift

Invite children to design a doll as a gift that they would give a babysitter or another person with whom they were trying to begin a friendship. Distribute art paper and crayons for the designs. Have the children cut out their designs, paste the designs on the cover of a student-made greeting card, and write a note of friendship to a babysitter (or friend) on the inside of the card. Ask the children to give the friendship cards to the babysitter or friend.

Friendship Stories in Spanish

From the story, read the Spanish words aloud to highlight Rosa's culture and language. Ask the children what the words mean to them. As an aid, the words are defined in the context of the story and in the glossary, and the definitions can be read aloud. Ask the children to relate their experiences with Spanish words spoken by someone they know.

Have the children listen to another story about friendship in Spanish to increase their sensitivity to the friendship that Kate and Rosa developed. Discuss Kate's feelings when she discovered that Rosa did not speak much English. Have the children discuss the meaning of friendship conveyed by the illustrations or words in the story. Stories in Spanish about friendship can include the following:

- Broger, Achim. *Querida Ballena*. Madrid: Editorial Juventud, 1985. (This is a story about a friendship between a sailor and a whale that follows him home.)
- Cantieni, Benita, and Fred Gachter. *Elefantilo y Gran Raton*. Mexico City: Trillas, S.A., 1984. (This is a story about two friends who find out what the words *near* and *far* mean to them.)
- D'Atri, Adriana. *Asi Son Nuestros Amigos*. Madrid: Editorial Altea, 1977. (This is the story of two children, Clara and Enrique, and their friendship with others.)
- Heuer, Margarita. *Chipil y Macanudo*. Mexico City: Editorial Trillas, S.A., 1984. (This is the story of two friends who learn the value of friendship in spite of differences.)

Friendship Scramblers

Have the children write a word of their choice related to the topic of friends and friendship on the back of a small index card. Ask them to turn the card over and scramble the letters. Have the children put the cards together to make a friendship deck and play the game of identifying friendship words with partners. Some children may need to see the word first in its entirety on the front of the card, then turn the card over to note the scrambled letters and, next, write the word to identify a friendship word accurately.

Conversations

After reading the story aloud to the whole group, have the children improvise through skits what might have happened early in the story. In *Gracias, Rosa,* children learn that Kate was not sure that she liked her babysitter at first. Have pairs of children improvise the conversation that *might* have taken place between Kate and one of her friends when Kate was unsure about Rosa. Repeat the activity and have the children improvise a later conversation after Kate received the cloth doll and had developed a special friendship with Rosa.

Book 2.5   *Meet Danitra Brown* (71)

Ages: 7–9
Heritage: African American

Goals: To relate friendship to feelings
          To relate friendship to sharing
          To relate poetry to feelings about friends
          To participate in a friendly agreement situation
          To develop and expand vocabulary about friendships
Materials: *Meet Danitra Brown* (71), discarded T-shirts, markers,
           fabric paints, crayons, current newspaper, art paper

BOOK NOTES

Meet Danitra Brown (Lothrop, Lee & Shepard, 1994), written by Nikki
Grimes and illustrated by Floyd Cooper, is a collection of poems narrated
by Zuei Jackson about her friend, Danitra. The poems reflect moments of
friendship related to their thoughts and feelings about pride in their heritage,
future plans, their self-assurance, as well as some disappointments and pain.

ACTIVITIES

Moving Friendship Poems

Have children bring old or discarded T-shirts, which they should wear for
an activity called "Moving Friendship Poems." With markers, fabric
paints, or crayons, ask the children to record no more than four lines of poetry from *Meet Danitra Brown* on 12″ white adhesive-backed paper
squares. Have the children carefully remove the cover from the adhesive
side of the paper and place the poetry on the back of each T-shirt. Ask them
to make their poem lines "move" by wearing their shirts as they move during the school day. They can invite students in other classes to be their new
friends and to read their moving friendship poems during recess and lunch.
Before going home, have the children pin their poetry shirts to a clothes
line in the room to be displayed until the shirts are worn again.

Friendship Time Capsule

Have the children plan a "Friendship Time Capsule" and to think of several friends they have now and one or two friends they'd like to meet.
Have them draw pictures of their current friends and "hope-to-be" friends
and write the children's names along with their favorite lines of poetry at
the foot of the drawings. Place the materials in a plastic bag and bury or
hide the bag in a place where the children can rediscover it on the last day

of school and realize how their friendships have lasted or changed and what new friendships have been made during the school year.

Friendship Stamp

Have the children design a friendship stamp that shows a friend and friendly action. Engage the children in designing the stamps themselves and let them sketch and practice on newsprint first. Ask them to draw their final versions on art paper and re-create their friendship stamps on envelopes that will hold letters that they will write to their friends. Repeat the activity for Valentine's Day, so the children will have original friendship stamps for the envelopes for their valentines.

Newspaper Friendship Articles

Mention to the children that newspapers sometimes print features that highlight acts of friendship. Distribute pages of a current newspaper and ask the children to select a story that they think reflects an act of friendship. Let them share any information in the articles. Have children cut out the articles and paste them on pages to make a class booklet of "Friends in the News."

Friendly Agreements

Invite the children to participate in a compromise with another child at school sometime during the school week and report what happened back to the whole group. For instance, when a child's name is called during the morning classroom roll call, she can acknowledge her presence, then tell about her participation in a friendly agreement situation. Some teachers call this activity of incorporating the morning roll call with brief friendship reports "Friendship Roll Call" or "Show-and-Tell Roll Call."

Book 2.6   *Miss Penny and Mr. Grubbs* (66)

Ages:	6–8
Heritage:	European American
Goals:	To participate in puppet play about greeting a rival
	To develop and expand vocabulary related to literature
	To see friendship related to achievement

To design a friendship garden
To identify friendship/rivalry in pictures
Materials: Copy of *Miss Penny and Mr. Grubbs* (66), magazine
and newspaper pictures of friendly people that can be
grouped into categories, minibooklets

BOOK NOTES

Miss Penny and Mr. Grubbs (Aladdin, 1995), by Lisa Campbell Ernst, is
the story of two neighbors and rivals. Miss Penny's prize-winning vegetables from her garden make Mr. Grubbs green with envy. When the
mean-spirited Mr. Grubbs sabotages Miss Penny's crop with two hungry
rabbits, the kind-hearted woman learns that she has a talent for raising animals, too.

ACTIVITIES

Rival-Friend Finger Puppets

Have the children cut a short strip of white art paper and draw a face on
the strip to make a finger puppet to represent each of the two rivals. Have
the children wrap a strip around each finger and tape the end of the strip
so it will stay. Have them meet with a partner in class and let the pup-
pets tell one another how they would greet a rival, have a conversation
about what they like to do to get better acquainted, how they would say
hello and good-bye, and what plans they would make to be together
again.

Friends and Rivals

Write the words, "friends" and "rivals" on the board. Ask the children
what meaning the words have for them. Write their definitions on the
board in two lists:

friends   *rivals*

Discuss the definitions the children contributed and ask them to look
again at the illustrations in *Miss Penny and Mr. Grubbs* and to decide
which illustrations show the idea of friends/rivals. Ask them to tell how
they think the artist best showed friendship/rivalry in the illustration(s).

Friendship Garden

Invite the children to design their own friendship garden by moving around paper squares (2″ × 2″) with pictures of flowers that symbolize the longtime bond between the giver and receiver. If appropriate, distribute nursery catalogs or newspaper ads that show colorful pictures of flowers and let the children cut out and paste their selections in a garden design related to friendship. Some designs for gardens include flowers arranged in the shape of a heart, a face profile, a handshake. Here are some flowers and their meanings to discuss with children:

Flowers	Meanings
Forget-me-not	To remember
Daisy	Known for age-old game of pulling off the petals one by one and saying, he/she likes me, likes me not
Rosemary	Remembrance
Pansy	Thought
Rose	Delight
Gorse	Undying affection

If appropriate, have children plant flower seeds in paper cups to observe the growth of the plants and then give to a friend as a sign of their friendship.

Friendship Bouquet

Distribute nursery catalogs that show colorful pictures of the flowers on the previous list. Have the children sketch and color the pictures of flowers on art paper to make a bouquet, then compose a message they want to send to a friend. If they want to say "remember me," they can draw some sketches of forget-me-nots, for example. Have them tie a bow on the bouquet with yarn. Encourage the children to dedicate their artwork to their friends and offer the sketches as friendship gifts.

Rivals

Have the children browse through magazines, newspapers, catalogs, and brochures to locate pictures of children who might be rivals. Have them clip and paste the illustrations on writing paper. Engage them in writing what they could do to start a friendship with the child or children in the picture. What would each child say? How might each child be feeling?

What could each child do? What might have happened just before the picture was taken? After the picture was taken? Ask for volunteers to read their writings aloud to the whole group.

If the word Friend means . . . then the word Rival means . . .

Discuss expressions that include the word friend, friends, or friendship. List any examples offered by the students. Have the children select the most positive ones and make class banners to display in the room.

Book 2.7 *My Painted House, My Friendly Chicken, and Me* (53)

Ages:	6–8
Heritage:	South African, Ndebele
Goals:	To relate friendship to a visitor in a South African village
	To take the role of a "stranger-friend"
	To portray friendship with a class peer through dialogue
	To participate in working and playing together
	To suggest and implement ways to welcome a newcomer
Materials:	Copy of *My Painted House, My Friendly Chicken, and Me* (53)

BOOK NOTES

My Painted House, My Friendly Chicken, and Me (Potter, 1994), written by Maya Angelou and illustrated by Margaret Courtney-Clarke, depicts South African life in a small Ndebele village. It is narrated by eight-year-old Thandi, who starts her story with the words, "Hello, stranger-friend" and describes some events that happened to her people in their village.

ACTIVITIES

Greetings

Read Angelou's words aloud to emphasize a greeting to a "stranger-friend," as well as to describe the life of the Ndebele people. Discuss how they care about beauty and equate it to "good" and the differences between the friendly village in the story and busy town life. Ask the children to relate their own experiences in greeting stranger-friends and times when they, too, viewed beauty in the neighborhood or community as something "good."

Stranger-Friend Talk

Have the children choose someone in class to be their "stranger-friend" and have them meet in pairs to tell one another about their house (or a house they would like to have), the paint on or in it, and an animal companion they have (or would like) just as Thandi talked about her painted house and her friendly chicken. Repeat the activity and have each child choose another child in class who will play the role of a "stranger-friend."

Stranger-Friend System

Initiate a stranger-friend system and have the children go everywhere together with one stranger-friend from the classroom for a school day. Schedule a class meeting in the afternoon and invite the children to discuss the positive aspects and negative aspects of working and playing together in pairs.

Friendship Mural

With the whole group, have the children look again at the illustrations in the book—especially to see the Ndebele's geometric wall paintings created by the talented Ndebele people—and ask the children to discuss the friendliness of the people and life in the village as reflected in the wall paintings. What kind of wall paintings could they create to show their friendliness and acts of friendship in the classroom? Engage them in sketching their scenes of acts of friendship at school and use them to create a friendship mural for the classroom.

Stranger-Friend Chart

Ask them which words or pictures depict life in the village as friendly and fun. In what ways can they make their classroom friendly and fun for "stranger-friends"? Write the children's responses on a chart for future reference when a new student arrives in their classroom. Invite them to put their ideas into action to welcome each new "stranger-friend" in the class.

Stranger-Friend Greeting Cards

Ask the children to write original friendship greetings and draw their own friendship scenes for greeting cards to welcome each new "stranger-friend" to their class. Prepare the cards and save them to give to the next newcomer. Repeat the activity for a classmate who is ill and absent for several days.

Book 2.8   *The Pink Party* (94)

Ages:	6–8
Heritage:	European American
Goals:	To see friendship as something valuable
	To identify friendly actions in pictures
	To associate a favorite color with a friend and to develop minibooklets about friendships
	To recognize friendship scenes in the artwork of others
	To work with partners as friends and to participate in a friendship game
Materials:	Copy of *The Pink Party* (94), magazine and newspaper pictures of friendly people that can be grouped student-made minibooklets

BOOK NOTES

The Pink Party (Hyperion, 1994), written by Maryann Macdonald and illustrated by Abby Carter, is the story of two friends who both like the color pink. Lisa and Amy try to outdo one another in this often humorous depiction of one-upmanship. For instance, when Lisa gets pink shoes, Amy gets a pink lunch box. The one-upmanship turns into jealousy, but all ends well at a party when they realize that their friendship, not the color pink, is the thing to value.

ACTIVITIES

Favorite Colors Booklet

Ask the children to look again at the illustrations in *The Pink Party* and to recall the main color the illustrator was using in the book. Just as Lisa and Amy liked pink, have the children think of the favorite colors of their friends or suggest a color they think their friends might like. Ask them to imagine that their colors have shapes (perhaps pink is a cloud shape), to create their own "Favorite Colors" booklets with shape pages and sketch and color examples of objects in the colors they know their friends like. When completed, have them make a dedication page—This is a friendship book for my friend _____ because he/she likes the color _____. Have them present the booklets to their friends.

Recognizing Friendships

Give the children a collection of pictures taken from discarded magazines, newspapers, brochures, flyers, catalogs, and so on, with most of the pictures showing children interacting in a friendly way. Explain that the pictures show friends and friendships, but there will be *one or two* pictures that do not belong in the group showing friends. Have them look at the pictures and determine which ones *do* belong and *do not* belong in the group. Ask them to explain their reasons for placing a picture in the "friendly" group or the "unfriendly" group. Invite them to tell what changes could be made in the illustrations in the "unfriendly" group to make them more friendly.

Friendship Circle Game

Have children call off the numbers 1, 2, or 3 to identify themselves as the members of the group of ones, the group of twos, the group of threes. Have the children in each group hold hands in a circle and have a child in the middle select a friend as they sing the following words to the tune of "The Farmer in the Dell."

The good friend in the middle
The good friend in the middle
High-ho, the derry-o
The good friend in the middle

The good friend takes the second
The good friend takes the second
High-ho, the derry-o
The good friend takes the second

The second takes the third
The second takes the third

High-ho, the derry-o
The second takes the third

The third takes the fourth
(and so on through five friends)

New ending: The five children in the middle hold hands in a circle and invite the children on the outside circle to move inside. The five friends now move around the other children in the middle and all sing:

Our friends are in the middle
Our friends are in the middle
High-ho, the derry-o
Our friends are in the middle

Repeat the activity with different children assigned to different groups.

Cultures of Friends

Help the children diminish stereotypes they may have about the heritages of others by sharing stories of friendship from all cultures and reading stories aloud about the diversity of people who have contributed in a friendly manner to their communities. Invite the children to look for characters in books that reflect their own experiences, emphasizing that the characters could be from any cultural background. To begin, search for stories about ways children celebrate their birthdays. For example, two stories about children of Latino/Hispanic heritage who celebrate their birthdays are:

- Brown, Tricia. *Hello, Amigos!* New York: Holt, 1986. (A seven-year-old Mexican American boy celebrates his birthday in San Francisco.)
- Mora, Pat. *A Birthday Basket for Tia.* Macmillan, 1992. (Cecilia wonders what to give her great-aunt for her ninetieth birthday.)

With the children, develop a class chart to show the words for happy birthday in various languages, i.e., feliz cumpleaños, bonne anniversaire, buon compleanno, sto lat, and others.

Friendship Collection

Provide the children with magazines, newspapers, brochures, flyers, discarded greeting cards, and other materials with illustrations. Ask them to clip and make their own collection of ten pictures showing friends and friendships. Have them meet in pairs and explain to one another their reasons for selecting a picture for their friendship collection.

Friendship Party

Invite each child to meet with a class friend as a partner and list the types of parties to which they would like to invite their friends. They can include a come-as-you-are party, a housewarming, a baby shower, a holiday celebration, a birthday, and so on. Ask the children to work together and do the following:

- Write the type of imagined party the two children would like to have.
- Write the names of friends they would like to invite.
- Design an invitation that tells the type of party that is being given, the date, time, place, and who is giving the party.
- Role-play an imaginary telephone conversation in which a friend is invited to the party.
- Role-play a face-to-face conversation inviting a friend to the party who you just "ran into" at a store.
- Discuss what food and beverages the two children would serve to their friends at the party.
- Write a favorite recipe the two children would like to make for the party.
- Write the list of groceries the two would need in order to prepare for the party.
- Write a list of party games the friends would enjoy.
- Write a list of party decorations and favors the friends would enjoy.
- Practice introducing a friend to a newcomer at the party. For example, "Jim, I would like you to meet my friend, Laurie. Laurie, this is Jim."
- Have the two children imagine that they are invited to someone else's friendship party. Ask them to practice writing a note of acceptance (or decline).

Book 2.9   *Roxaboxen* (95)

Ages:	7–9
Heritage:	Multicultural
Goals:	To relate friendship to imaginary play

To suggest guidelines for being a friend
To relate friendship to sharing
To participate in a classroom friendship
To develop and expand vocabulary related to literature

Materials: Copy of *Roxaboxen* (95), newsprint, adhesive-backed
paper, heavy cardboard for cutout circles

BOOK NOTES

Roxaboxen (Lothrop, Lee & Shepard, 1991), is written by Alice McLerran and illustrated by Barbara Cooney. It is the story of a hill covered with sand, rocks, cactus, and wooden boxes that becomes an imaginary town for young Marian, her sisters, and their friends.

ACTIVITIES

Community Play

Have the children consider some of the objects found on the hill in the story and how the characters used their imagination to convert each object into something meaningful for playing together as friends. Ask them to consider what each of the following items could become during play with friends in an imaginary play town on a sandy hill:

Object	*Could be*
a. tin box filled with black pebbles	buried treasure, currency
b. street to the hill	winding river
c. stones	outlines of buildings
d. wooden boxes	tables, shelves
e. other	

Invite the children to relate the story to their own experience and tell of a time when they played with friends in an imaginary way.

Friendship Play Guidelines

Have the children suggest "guidelines" for being with friends by thinking of several rules they have now for their playtimes. Ask them to think of one or two rules they'd like to have in an imaginary town where they could play with friends. Have them make posters to illustrate the rules. Display the drawings on a chart or in a class book and make it available in a place where the children can refer to it as needed.

Friendship Coin

Have the children design a community friendship coin for Roxaboxen (or for their classroom) that shows acts of friendship—friends in action. Engage the children in designing the coins themselves and let them sketch and practice on newsprint first. Ask them to draw their final versions on adhesive-backed paper, affix them to discarded poker chips or heavy cardboard circles, and show their friendship coins to the whole group. Have children think of ways to use their friendship currency in the class, i.e., recognizing friendly words and actions by awarding their coins to others at the end of the day or at special times.

World of Play

The events in *Roxaboxen* really happened to the author's mother. With the assistance of her mother's childhood manuscript, the memories of relatives, and letters and maps from the former children who played at Roxaboxen, the author wrote about this imaginary world of play with community friends as if she had played there herself. The illustrator thought it was a tough assignment because she had to create a world of play out of something that wasn't there. In an art activity similar to the illustrator's challenge, invite the children to draw or sketch their ideas of a world of play—an imaginary town for friends—set in a location they know—perhaps a play area at school on the playground. Have them name their world of play and show their work to others in small groups so all will have an opportunity to talk about their imagined world of play for their friends.

Playground Roxaboxen

Invite the children to inhabit their own imaginary town of Roxaboxen and let everyone in the classroom play in an area marked off on the school grounds. The only requirement to enter the town is to be friendly. Mark off a selected area on the playground for the imaginary town of friends. Walk the site with the children, and after the children play in the imaginary town, discuss in class meetings the different ways they can make it special and safe and friendly:

- What do you want to name the town? How should we mark off the town (perhaps lines drawn in the dirt)?
- What natural object(s) could be used for money for the town?
- How should the town begin to grow (drawing lines in the dirt for streets, buildings, houses)?
- How could cardboard boxes be used (for tables, shelves, etc.)?
- Is a mayor (other officials) needed? How should they be elected?
- What shops can be added? Who wants to be the baker, owner of the ice-cream parlor?
- Does everyone want a car? What is needed to represent a steering wheel (paper plates)?
- Will there be a speed limit? Jail? Police officers?
- Does everyone want a horse? What is needed to represent riding a horse (discarded cardboard rolls from paper towels)?

Book 2.10   *Sweet Clara and the Freedom Quilt* (78)

Ages:	6–8
Heritage:	African American
Goals:	To see friendship as helping others in need
	To recognize the feelings of others
	To develop and expand awareness of the heritages of others
	To identify friendship in actions
	To develop a map of a nearby area where friends live
	To role-play being a friend to a newcomer
Materials:	Copy of *Sweet Clara and the Freedom Quilt* (78), materials to make a map, paper squares, markers, fabric, and fabric paints

BOOK NOTES

Sweet Clara and the Freedom Quilt (Knopf, 1993), by Deborah Hopkinson, depicts a young slave who works as a seamstress and dreams of freedom. Overhearing the talk of others escaping to the North gives her the information she needs to make a map of the area from quilt patches. When she uses the map and escapes to Canada, she leaves the quilt behind to guide others.

ACTIVITIES

Feelings

Review several scenes from the story with the children and discuss the feelings of the people in the illustrations—i.e., love and support of friends and family, the backbreaking work in the cotton fields, and the suffering of those who tried to run away. Have the children meet as partners to consider the following before they report back to the whole group on ways these problems might be resolved/softened through friendly acts:

- Have the children imagine they are together in the scene in the cotton fields. What are they seeing? Hearing? Touching? What are they feeling? How are they acting toward others? How are others acting toward them?
- Have each child tell about the problems that are not yet resolved in friendships between people who work in the fields and the land owners.
- Have each child tell about ways to soften the harshness of the situation through friendships and friendly actions.

Lucky

Ask the children what Clara's words mean to them when she reaches safety and says, "But not all are as lucky as we were, and most never can come." Have student-volunteers relate a time from their experience when they or someone in their family was lucky and they realized that others were not as lucky as they were.

Paper Quilt

Ask the children to design a map that shows the homes of their friends and turn the maps into a paper quilt made of paper squares to display in the room.

Friendship Borders

Ask the children to search for designs in informational books and reference sources that represent the cultural heritages of children in the classroom, such as the designs found on an African Kente cloth, a Navajo blanket, a Scottish tartan, a Guatemalan cloth, a Japanese kimono, an American quilt, a Mexican blouse or shirt, Indonesian batik cloth, Native American beadwork, and so on. Distribute narrow art paper strips (4″ ×

11 1/2″) and have them draw and color their interpretations of the designs for a bulletin board border. Ask them to record where they found their designs on the back of the strips, dedicate the border they created to a classroom friend, and sign their names.

Friendship Books

Invite the children to select a book about friendship from the class reading area or school library and to meet with children in class they don't know very well. Ask them to suggest the book to the other child as a gift of friendship and tell something about it. If appropriate, have the children read the suggested book and assist one another if needed. After the books have been read, have the children discuss what they *enjoyed* about the friendship story and about meeting with a classroom "newcomer" or a child in the class who they didn't know very well.

Clara's Sister/Brother

Have the children divide into groups. Ask one child to pretend that she is Clara's sister/brother and will be holding a meeting to show the quilt after Clara's escape to Canada. Ask the other children in the groups to play the role of people attending the meeting who have heard about Clara's escape and realize the quilt is a map. Encourage them to discuss their thoughts and feelings about Clara's act of friendship and about having a map to help them escape to the North. Repeat the activity, with other children taking the role of Clara's sister or brother.

Story-Ending Scene

In small drama groups, have the children imagine a scene with Clara after the story ends—perhaps a scene of her being welcomed in Canada. One child could play the role of Clara and the other children could be friends in Canada. What friendly words and actions could they offer to Clara? What are some items that Clara might need that they would give her in the name of friendship?

Book 2.11 *A Sled Dog for Moshi* (56)

Ages: 6–7
Heritage: Canadian Eskimo

Goals: To relate friendship to a newcomer in one's community
         To participate in a discussion and oral story about
            being friends
         To describe a friend's actions
         To role-play dialing 911 to get help for a friend
         To suggest and implement actions for being a friend
         To participate in creating a friendship story
         To give feedback to someone in a friendly way
Materials: Copy of *A Sled Dog for Moshi* (56), magazines,
         newspapers, illustrations of children

BOOK NOTES

A Sled Dog for Moshi (Hyperion, 1994), written by Jeanne Bushey and illustrated by Germaine Amaktauyok, is the story of Moshi, a Canadian Eskimo who wants a dog of her own, and her new friend from New York City. The two become lost in a snowy whiteout. During the chilling blizzard, Moshi becomes worried about her city friend, but she remembers what her father has taught her about surviving. The two friends are saved by Moshi's skills and her father's lead sled dog.

ACTIVITIES

Friend Who Helps

In the story, Moshi's skills saved her and her new friend during the blizzard, a potentially dangerous environment for the girls. Invite the children to tell of a time when someone they know used their special skills or abilities to help someone else in a dangerous situation. Ask them to describe some of the things they could do to help someone in an emergency. If appropriate, role-play dialing 911 to get help for a friend and reporting the details related to a particular emergency.

Friendship Alert

Ask the children to be on the lookout for someone who is by themselves at recess, lunch, or before school. Ask them to become a "friend of the moment" to that child. Have them suggest ways they can act friendly to a child who is alone at school and try out these actions during the school day. During a class meeting at the end of the day, have the children report back to the whole group to tell about their friendship actions.

Group Story

Divide the children into small groups—buzz groups for informal conversation—and give each child in the group an illustration that shows a child interacting in some way. Ask the group to create a friendship story aloud together that uses *all* the children shown in all the illustrations in the group. Ask two groups to meet together to listen to the stories told by the members of the other group. If appropriate, change groups again so the members can tell their stories to another group and hear a new story.

Partnership Drawings

Divide the children into partnerships and give each child a picture (taken from newspapers or magazines) of children working or playing. Have the child describe the picture to the partner, who can make stick figures from the other's description. Have the partners compare the original picture and the stick figure drawing. Let the second child make suggestions in a *friendly* way about what descriptive words and phrases might have helped him/her draw better stick figures. Have the children trade roles. Back in the whole group, invite volunteers to comment in a positive way on the *friendly* ways that suggestions were made and tell which suggestions they liked best.

Newcomer

Have each child select an illustration of a child from a magazine or newspaper and describe the child in the picture as if the child was a newcomer in the class or community. Let them choose a name for the newcomer and tell a short original story about what might happen to the child as a newcomer and what types of friends and assistance a newcomer might need.

3 Friendships around the World

Book 3.1 *All the Colors of the Earth* (118)

Ages:	6–8
Heritage:	Multicultural
Goals:	To relate friendship to children with different characteristics
	To appreciate descriptive words
	To recognize friendly traits in others
	To portray a friend's characteristics through artwork
	To participate in composing a directory of friends
	To relate literature to world friendships
	To develop and expand vocabulary through similes in literature
	To recognize friends' multicultural celebrations
Materials:	Copy of *All the Colors of the Earth* (118), self-adhesive paper, discarded T-shirts

BOOK NOTES

All the Colors of the Earth (Morrow, 1994), by Sheila Hamanaka, is a picture book with poetic words that describe children's characteristics in terms of nature and nature's creatures. For example, one child's hair is described as curled like a sleeping cat. Love for children is shown through words that describe rich, vibrant colors and tasty flavors. For instance, the author poetically expresses an appreciation and love for children of different heritages when she describes them as being the eye-catching, attractive colors of cinnamon, walnut, and wheat.

ACTIVITIES

Descriptions

Introduce this poetic book by asking the children if they ever felt like describing a friend's characteristics in terms of one of nature's creatures or colors or tasty flavors. Ask them which characteristics could be described in these terms and might be a good way to express their thoughts about friends. After a brief discussion, explain that we all know we can communicate our feelings through words, but another way is through descriptions in terms of nature's creatures or colors or flavors. Invite the children to listen to or read the poetic words again and consider ways that a friend's characteristics could be described in terms of nature instead of in ordinary terms.

Multicultural Buttons

Have the students celebrate a multicultural observance by drawing decorations that reflect a friend's characteristic on a button made of self-adhesive paper to wear during the school day. Encourage the children to draw one of nature's animals and to use the colors of nature to illustrate the friend's characteristic.

Friendship T-Shirts

Have the children write friendship poems on the empty space on the back of a discarded T-shirt (with a parent or guardian's permission, of course) as part of a friendship T-shirt survey. The main rule about space is no more than four lines of verse about friendship on the back of the shirt. Designs can be added. Have the students wear their T-shirts on a given day and ask other students at school what they think about the friendship T-shirts. Examples of survey questions are these:

- Did you notice the friendship poem on the shirt?
- Did you read it?
- What do you think about the friendship t-shirt?

- Do you feel that the poetry represents your friendships in any way?
- Do you like poetry or verses?

Have the students note the grade and gender of those interviewed. Tally the results of the survey to determine:

- Which grade and gender noticed the friendship poems most?
- Which grade and gender read the poems more often?
- Which grade and gender had positive thoughts about the friendship T-shirt?
- Which grade and gender said the verses represented their friendships?
- Which grade and gender indicated the most appreciation for poetry and verse?

Top Ten List

Invite the children to write a top ten list of likeable traits about a friend they have or would like to have. The children can list their ideas before they meet with others in small groups. In the group, have the children trade papers and ask them to introduce one another as "someone looking for a friend" who can then be described by the words from the list. A child introducing Jose might say: "I'd like you to meet Jose. He is looking for a friend who likes inline skating like he does."

New Friends

Provide the children with a list of the names of the group members on the left-hand side. Place headings across the top. Headings can include a favorite color, food, shirt, song, sport, academic subject. Ask the students to write the name of an item or sketch an item under each heading that they *think* relates to each student.

Next, divide the children into small groups and ask them to take turns and to ask the other class members in their group about a favorite color, food, piece of clothing, song, sport, academic subject, and so on. They can verify which of their original thoughts were accurate on the list by placing a check mark by the name of the items. Have them also discuss their insights into others in the group by identifying one of the items he or she has sketched or written for a particular child and explaining *why* they selected the items they did.

Directory of Friends

Provide the children with a list of the names of the students in the class. Invite them to tell about their heritage if appropriate and to identify the places on a map represented by relatives and ancestors. Ask the children to suggest what interests they have and ask them to write down the key words (or draw sketches) to remind them of the interests.

Name	Heritage	Interests
1.	1.	1.

Divide the children into small groups for discussion about what more they would like to know about one another as new and potential friends and what they would like to tell about themselves or the type of new friends they would like.

International Bulletin Board

Have the children research—then draw and color objects on paper that represent—multicultural celebrations of their friends. Ask them to cut out the objects and affix them to a mural entitled "My Friends' Multicultural Celebrations." Examples:

- Group 1: Hanukkah. Engage the students in drawing their interpretations of a menorah, scroll, dreidel, gifts, goblets, food, and amphora.
- Group 2: Kwanzaa. Have the students sketch and color different gifts, a mat, selection of food, and other symbols.
- Group 3: Cinco de Mayo. Invite the students to sketch and color a fiesta of food, flowers, Mexico's flag, piñata, pottery, sombreros, and fireworks displays.
- Group 4: Chinese New Year. Ask the students to draw and color dragons, hanging lanterns, firecracker displays, food, vases, and flowers.

Book 3.2   *Bed Bouncers* (120)

Ages:	5–7
Heritage:	Multicultural
Goals:	To relate friendship to friends around the world
	To develop a vocabulary web motivated by the story
	To develop and expand vocabulary related to literature

To recognize valued qualities and friendly actions of people around the world

Materials: Copy of *Bed Bouncers* (120), paper for journals, newspapers, writing paper for stories and class book

BOOK NOTES

In *Bed Bouncers* (Macmillan, 1995), by Kimberley Knutson, some children bounce so high on the bed that they fly into space. There, they meet multicultural bed bouncers from around the world and orbit Earth, as the children (of all colors and sizes) laugh and holler at the fun of it all. They return to the bedroom when a voice reminds them to stop jumping on the bed. They get under the covers and pretend they are sleeping.

ACTIVITIES

Bed Bouncer Says . . .

Outside on the playground, select five students (from different cultural groups, if possible) to be the friendly "bed bouncers" in this activity which is played like the game of "Simon Says." Have the children divide into five groups and line up in front of one of the bed bouncers. One at a time, each friendly bed bouncer gives a command such as "Friendly bed bouncer says take one step forward." The children follow any command that has the words *friendly bed bouncer* in it. They disregard any command that is given without the word bed bouncer. The first child to reach the bed bouncer who is giving the commands can be the new bed bouncer for continued play.

Friend in World News

Distribute copies of different newspapers and have the children choose one person in the world news that they would like to become friends with in some way. Ask the students to write down why they would like to develop a friendship with that person. Have them describe what the person did or what they noticed about that person that made them decide they would like to be a friend. Afterward, ask them to meet in small groups and read their work aloud to one another. Ask a volunteer in each group to keep a record of who was selected from the news, what they did, and some of the reasons the children wanted them as world friends. Have the volunteer report back to the whole group to determine what, if anything, the selected world friends had in common.

Friends in World News

From various newspapers and news articles from different locations in the world, discuss with the children a newsmaker's actions that show/do *not* show friendship. Write the list of actions of the newsmakers on the board under two headings—"Friendship" and "Not Friendship." Ask the children to read the lists and suggest several ways that the actions under the "Not Friendship" heading could be made more friendly.

Friendship Goals

Discuss with the children the idea of setting a goal to become a friend to someone new this week at school (perhaps someone whose family is from somewhere in the world other than the United States) and have them record their progress each day in a writing journal (writing paper stapled together). At the end of the school week, schedule a class meeting and ask the students to review their journals and tell what they did that week to build a friendship with someone new.

Give Me Five

Ask the children to pretend they could go anywhere in the world with one friendly partner they have worked with in class and to tell which five valued qualities they would want in the partner. Have the children draw an outline of their hand (as a hand of friendship), and on the outline, to list the qualities they value in a partner. Ask them to draw another outline of their hand and list five qualities that describe themselves. Ask them to meet with a partner and have both children read the two lists from the hand outlines to one another and discuss what they learned about friendship from doing this activity. Beneath the outline of one of the hands, ask them to write a "Hand of Friendship" summary about what they learned and give it to you to read aloud to the whole group during class meetings or other selected times.

Partner-Friend

Invite a community leader to class who has traveled worldwide to describe the things that help him or her develop friendships in their travels.

Invite the children to relate what they hear to their own experiences of making friends. After the speaker finishes, ask the children to write a brief story and title about the speaker's strategies and actions for developing friendships. Gather the stories together for a class book to read aloud and discuss.

Book 3.3 *Faraway Families* (24)

Ages:	7–9
Heritage:	Multicultural
Goals:	To relate friendship to diversity in all places
	To develop and expand vocabulary related to literature through friendship journals and diagrams
	To relate ways of caring and helping someone to children's experience
	To role-play a caring adult and a child who has a problem of some kind
	To initiate a friendship with someone who lives at a distance
Materials:	Copy of *Faraway Families* (24), board, chalk, writing paper for friendship journals

BOOK NOTES

Faraway Families (Silver Moon Press, 1995), written by Betsy Loredo and illustrated by Monisha Raja, offers five brief stories about the feelings children experience during change, a loss, or when family "friends" are separated and friendships are severed. Each of the stories features a child of a different heritage: African American, Jewish, Latino, Indian, and Vietnamese.

ACTIVITIES

Caring for Someone

With the whole group, discuss ways of caring and helping someone through a change in the family, a loss of some kind, or a family separation. Elicit suggestions for helping in these situations and write their ideas on the board. Ideas could include being a friend by making a gift of love (something the recipient likes) or sending a care package to someone; creating a family tree and mailing it to someone far away; drawing pictures and writing to someone back home about what is going on; or exploring a new area in another part of the world and meeting new people. Have the children relate the ideas to their own experiences of caring for and helping someone through a change in their family life.

Journal Writing

Encourage the children to write about helping others in a friendship journal (writing paper stapled together) and begin with the sentence, "I think I can be a caring person and help someone through a change, a loss, or a family separation because _____." Ask the children to write five more sentences using ideas they have about caring and helpful actions—especially when a person moves to another place—and how they could implement their ideas.

Facilitating Friendships

Ask the children to divide up into dyads, with one child playing the role of a caring adult and the other a child experiencing a change, a loss, or a separation from family members. Suggest the following experiences for the role-playing and, in a discussion, elicit the children's ideas about facilitating friendships. Write their ideas related to the following on the board, a chart, or an overhead transparency:

- The loss of a beloved brother or sister who is away (at college, in the military service, on a job)
- The divorce of parents
- A move to a new home in a new place
- A move to a new state (or country) for a time, leaving grandparents (or other family members) behind
- Some other situations suggested by the children

Ask the children to suggest other experiences for the role play and add their ideas to the list before they play their roles in the dyads.

Friendship Diagram

Before role-playing friends together, discuss any of the children's questions to provide information and to practice problem-solving. Consider distributing the following diagram of who, what, when, where, and why type questions to the children as a reference during the discussion and during their role-play. Copies of the diagram can be laminated before distribution and collected after each use to make it available for redistribution whenever role-playing is appropriate:

- *Who:* Who are you trying to be in this role-play?
- *What:* What are you doing and what could happen?
- *When:* When is this taking place?
- *Where:* Where are you?
- *Why:* Why are you here?

Additional questions you could ask include, What could a lonely child say to the caring adult? What could the caring adult reply? What facial expressions would the lonely child (caring adult) have? How might the lonely child feel when he or she experiences a change, a loss, or a separation from a family member? What actions would show the way(s) that the caring adult helped the lonely child?

Role-Play Intermission

Invite different partners to role-play being a lonely child and a caring adult. Have them role-play the general topic of world friendships through a particular event related to a change, a loss, or a separation from a family member.

- Have them change roles so each child can play both.
- Have them stop for an intermission during the role-play. Stop the children and ask them to write what they are thinking and feeling right at that moment of the role-play. To emphasize a world friendship theme, ask the children to write an entry on paper or in a writing journal about a long-distance friendship or to write what they learned about friendships scattered around the world from the role-playing. Invite them to record any friendly words and actions they observed during the role-play. After writing, invite the children to resume role-playing.
- Ask each pair to meet with another pair as an audience and role-play a scene depicting a friendship that extends to another place in the world.

Friendship Experiences

In the whole group, ask the children in what ways the role-playing stimulated their curiosity about maintaining friendships in other parts of the world or developing a friendship with someone far away. Ask, In what ways can we learn more about friendships with people in other countries? Elicit their experiences with world friendships. Have the children tell what they learned about caring for someone who is separated from family members. Finally, have them dictate or write brief sentences or paragraphs to tell what they learned from the role-playing about family friendships when family members have moved to other parts of the world.

Friendships at a Distance

Invite student volunteers to participate in keeping a friendship with someone who lives at a distance from them and report what they did to maintain the friendship. Perhaps they can become pen pals with a student in class who is moving away from the area. To incorporate the reports about friendship participation into the daily class schedule, consider having a morning classroom roll call each day. During the roll call, ask the children to respond to their names when called and report on what they would do (or on what someone they know does) to remain a friend with someone who lives at a distance.

Book 3.4   *Folks Call Me Appleseed John* (115)

Ages:	7–8
Heritage:	European American/Multiethnic
Goals:	To relate friendship to caring for others
	To realize cause and effect in friendships
	To develop and expand vocabulary related to poetry
	and literature
Materials:	Copy of *Folks Call Me Appleseed John* (115), board,
	chalk

BOOK NOTES

Folks Call Me Appleseed John (Doubleday, 1995), by Andrew Glass, offers a fictionalized first-person narrative about friendship and caring between two brothers as well as two cultures. Told by John Chapman, the story relates some experiences Chapman and his teenage half-brother Nathaniel had in Western Pennsylvania as they traveled from the east. The basis for the narrative is an out-of-print book, *Johnny Appleseed* (Peter Smith, 1954), by Robert Price. Price quotes William Gline, who heard the stories from Chapman's siblings. Chapman is a sensible young man, comfortable in the backwoods. On one adventure, John leaves Nathaniel sheltered in a tree to paddle his canoe to Fort Pitt to buy supplies. He pulls his canoe onto an ice cake to rest, falls asleep, and floats past the fort without realizing it. He finally returns weeks later to find that Nathaniel has been rescued from the cold by four friendly Senecas who had taught him to hunt small game with a bow and arrows. Map and biographical notes are included.

ACTIVITIES

Cause and Effect

Explain to the children that when one happening *causes* another happening (an effect), this can be called a cause-and-effect relationship and that sometimes cause-and-effect relationships affect friendships. Invite the students to identify a cause-and-effect relationship in this passage about the two brothers: *To rescue his brother, Appleseed pulls his canoe onto an ice cake to rest. He falls asleep and floats past the fort.* Ask, How could this happening (a cause) have affected the friendship between the two Chapman brothers? Ask the students to reread the story and read aloud any cause-and-effect sentences that relate to the friendship between the Chapman brothers or between the brothers and others.

Different Poems, Different Accounts

Reading poems aloud about Chapman written over time will allow the students to examine how this friendly man was viewed differently by poets writing at different times. For example, read aloud the poem "Johnny Appleseed" in *A Book of Americans* (Holt, 1986, all ages) to share descriptive words about Chapman, the man who loved apples, with the children. Emphasize Johnny Appleseed's world with additional words that describe his clothing—especially his buckskin bag—and the terrain he traveled—high peaks, valleys, and mountains—by reading the "Ballad of Johnny Appleseed," by Helmer O. Oleson, in *The Arbuthnot Anthology of Children's Literature* (Scott, Foresman, 1971, all ages). To give another account, you could select "In Praise of Johnny Appleseed," by Vachel Lindsay, in *Story and Verse,* compiled by Miriam Blanton Huber (Macmillan, 1946, all ages).

Character Diagram

As you read a poem aloud about Appleseed, ask the children to create a character diagram for him with the headings "friendly actions," "setting," "clothing," "travels," and other topics and add information they receive from listening to the poems. The diagram can be similar to the following:

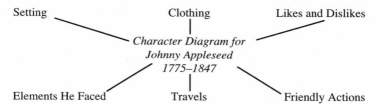

Setting   Clothing   Likes and Dislikes

Character Diagram for Johnny Appleseed 1775–1847

Elements He Faced   Travels   Friendly Actions

As you read aloud information from a poem, ask the children (age 8) to write facts under the headings on their own copies. For example, when the children hear the Benets' words from *A Book of Americans,* "He wore a tin pan on his white hair," they might write about the pan under the heading of "clothing." As you read aloud information from another poem about Appleseed, ask the students to prepare another character diagram with the same headings and add more facts. When the students hear Oleson's words of "Appleseed went plodding past high peak and mountain craig [*sic*]," they might write the fact under the heading of "setting." After two or more poems are read aloud, ask the students to discuss their lists to see if they reflect the major facts about Johnny Appleseed, his actions, his life, that were identified by the poets.

Two Poems, Two Diagrams

With the children, develop two character lists on the board to show information about friendship from two poems, and ask them to discuss the differences they hear when they listen to the poems. For example, they can suggest that they heard about the different ways in which Appleseed was portrayed and, if noted, the point of view of the poet(s), and what they learned about the friendship of this historical figure with others from the poems. They also can find similarities between the two poems and mention how the poets gave the children the opportunity to make judgments about Appleseed as a friendly figure.

Friendship with Native Americans

Read aloud several verses from the lengthy narrative "In Praise of Johnny Appleseed," by Vachel Lindsay, from *Story and Verse for Children*. Discuss what the children visualize during Appleseed's meeting with the Native Americans when they brought him magical trinkets, pipes, guns, beads, and furs. Invite the children to discuss the value of Appleseed's friendly actions from their points of view.

Apples

Reread aloud excerpts from a biography of Johnny Appleseed to establish a bridge to a study of apples, which represent a concrete example of Appleseed's friendship with others. Discuss and display informational books about the fruit and related topics. Engage the children in researching the history of apples, life cycles of apple trees, some problems with and solutions for growing and harvesting apples, as well as related economic principles from the books they find in the display or locate independently from the library. Complementary activities can include the following:

- Discovering more about the history of apples—especially recipes, games, natural history, and crafts related to them—from Paulette Bourgeois' *The Amazing Apple Book* (Addison Wesley, 1990, age 8).
- Supplying original words for the illustrated science lesson in the wordless book *The Apple and the Moth* (Pantheon, 1970, all ages) by Iela and Enzo Mari. In the book, the children will see a moth move through its life cycle stages of egg, caterpillar, cocoon, and adult, beginning with the moth's egg in the apple and ending with the next generation's egg in an apple blossom.

Caring for Someone

After reading aloud *Folks Call Me Appleseed John,* introduce a Venn diagram activity by having the children listen to another biographical book about Johnny Appleseed. After listening to the two stories, have the children suggest similarities and differences between the two portrayals of

Appleseed and his acts of friendship and record their suggestions on a Venn diagram. Have the children record their suggestions on the Venn diagram on paper to display in the room. Books suitable for this activity are the following:

- *Better Known as Johnny Appleseed* (Lippincott, 1950, ages 8–10), by M. L. Hunt. This story focuses on Appleseed as a humble man who was universally loved.
- *Johnny Appleseed* (Morrow, 1988, all ages), by Steven Kellogg. Kellogg's book is a biographical retelling of John Chapman, the gentle healer, who always carried apple seeds and was known to have a tame wolf as a companion. Sometimes, he dressed in ragged clothes and wore a cooking pot for a hat as he traveled through Pennsylvania, Ohio, and Indiana.
- *Johnny Appleseed* (Little Brown, 1990, ages 8–9), by Reeve Lindbergh. The author tells Appleseed's story of friendship with others in poetic rhyme.

Book 3.5 *Honi's Circle of Trees* (114)

Ages:	5–7
Heritage:	Jewish
Goals:	To relate friendship to selflessness
	To develop and expand vocabulary related to a legend with a character diagram
	To reflect on having a legendary character as a friend
	To write original stories of friendship
	To identify appreciated friendship traits
Materials:	Copy of *Honi's Circle of Trees* (114), board, chalk, chart paper, discarded shoes and boxes, index cards, overhead transparency

BOOK NOTES

Honi's Circle of Trees (Jewish Publication Society, 1995), written by Phillis Gershator and illustrated by Mimi Green, introduces Honi as an elderly legendary character who selflessly wanders across ancient Israel planting seeds of the dark evergreen carob trees to be enjoyed by generations to come. Honi comes to a village where a man remembers his rain miracle from years before and encourages Honi to take a rest. When Honi awakens from what he thought was a nap, he learns that seventy years have passed and is confused and upset. However, he soon discovers that he has been granted the extension of years so he can see his trees bear fruit. The story honors the Jewish holiday of Shavaos.

ACTIVITIES

For Generations to Come

In a discussion with the whole group, mention Honi's selflessness and that he planted the seeds for generations to come. Discuss ways of caring for and helping someone of a future generation just as Honi did when he planted the seeds of the carob tree. Write the children's ideas for helping someone in the future on the board. Have the children discuss ways they could put their ideas into actions.

Research

Out of friendship, Honi planted his seeds across ancient Israel for generations to come. Ask the children to divide up into groups of two to research the benefits of carob trees. Have the children report what they learned to the whole group and summarize each pair's findings on a chart, the board, or overhead transparency. Some of the benefits of the carob tree that the children might suggest are these:

- Offers shade—it is evergreen in hot countries and grows in the area around the Mediterranean Sea.
- Offers beauty—it has small flowers and looks like an apple tree.
- Offers food—the brown, leathery carob pods have sticky pulp that can be eaten by horses, cattle, and sometimes humans.
- Offers a symbol of history—carob was supposed to have been eaten by John the Baptist when he was in the wilderness.

Character Diagram

With the children, create a character diagram for Honi on the board with headings of setting, personality, and other topics and add information they learned from the story.

As you read aloud information from the story, ask the children to record facts under the headings on their own copies. For example, when the students hear the words, "rain miracle," they might write the fact under the heading "elements he faced." Using all of their diagrams, ask the students to discuss their suggestions to see if they reflect the major facts about Honi identified in the story.

Compare and Contrast

After reading Honi's story aloud to the students, compare his actions with the actions of John Chapman in *Folks Call Me Appleseed John* (Doubleday, 1995, ages 7–8), by Andrew Glass. Ask the children to join one of two groups to compare and contrast the two men as they hear the stories. Have one group listen for ways that Honi and Appleseed were alike and the other group listen for ways they were different.

After listening to the two stories, have the children suggest ways the two men were alike and different and record their suggestions on a Venn diagram on the board (one circle for Honi, one for Appleseed, with shared characteristics in the overlap area). Have the children record their individual compare-and-contrast ideas on a Venn diagram on art paper to display in a class booklet.

Carob Trees

If appropriate, reread aloud excerpts from *Honi's Circle of Trees* to establish a bridge to a study about carob trees, Honi's symbol of friendship. Introduce informational books about this evergreen tree and any related topics. Engage the children in researching, then reporting on, the history of carob trees, the tree's life cycle, problems with and solutions for harvesting the tree, which grows in the wilderness, and harvesting its long, ten-inch pods, as well as any related information gained from the books they locate.

Wanderer's Shoes

Invite the children to bring discarded shoes to symbolize the amount of walking that friendly wanderers such as Honi and Johnny Appleseed do. Ask them to paint objects on the shoes to represent the acts of friendship the wanderers performed on their journeys. If appropriate, have the children name the shoes (i.e., Appleseed's Friendship Activators) and glue them to shoe boxes as display items. To complete their wanderer's shoe exhibit, ask the children to write on index cards their original friendship stories from the shoes' point of view as the shoes accompanied their owners on the journeys. Have the children place the cards by the exhibits in the room.

Friends You Like

Ask the children, "Would you have liked to have Honi for a friend? Johnny Appleseed? What kind of friend would you like to have if you had wandered along with Honi or Johnny Appleseed?" List the children's responses (one who's humorous, one who likes me, one who stands by me, etc.) on the writing board or on an overhead transparency.

For a survey of the identified friendship traits, continue with the following: Provide the children with a copy of the list (or ask them to copy it down), then prioritize them in order of importance to a friendship. Ask the children to raise their hands as you ask about their responses related to the list on the board or transparency. How many wrote the numeral 1 by the first trait? How many wrote the numeral 2? 3? Write down the number of children who wrote 1, 2, or 3 by each trait. Discuss which traits were the most popular in the group and why the students think the traits are important in a friendship. Invite the children to show more of these traits in their friendships at school and have them volunteer ways they could do this.

Book 3.6 *The Peace Crane* (119)

Ages:	7–8
Heritage:	African American/Multicultural
Goals:	To relate the concept of friendship to a worldwide view of people
	To develop and expand vocabulary related to literature
	To portray an act of friendship and peace through artwork
	To participate in friendship groups
Materials:	Copy of *The Peace Crane* (119), art paper, crayons, markers, paints

BOOK NOTES

The Peace Crane (Morrow, 1995), written and illustrated by Sheila Hamanaka, emphasizes a worldwide view of the needs of people. An

African American girl folds her wishes for peace into a paper crane. Later, the peace crane visits her in a dream and takes her on a flight over farms, hills, and landscapes to see people and ways they care and show their benevolence. The flight of the bird takes the girl away from the violence of her world and allows her to see the goodness of people who want to be part of a caring Earth without weapons and acts of violence.

ACTIVITIES

Feelings in Symbolism

Go over the illustrations with the children to review the meaning of the words of the book in a visual way. Invite the children to show the impact of the words and the theme of peace on Earth on *their* thoughts through their own illustrations about friendship and peace in their daily lives.

Origami Crane

Show the children how to fold a paper crane. Distribute paper to the children and review the steps again. Just as the girl in the story folded her wishes for peace into a paper crane, encourage the children to write their wishes for world friendship and peace into the cranes they fold. If appropriate, have students read aloud their wishes before they fold them into the cranes. Collect the cranes, connect them with thread or string, and hang them from a coat hanger as a mobile for display in the classroom.

Mural: Goodness of People

Invite the children to volunteer incidents where they have seen the goodness of people who want to be part of a caring Earth without weapons and acts of violence. Ask them to suggest ways they can demonstrate their own goodness toward others for the day. In the afternoon, have students sketch what they have done for others and place the sketches on butcher paper for a mural entitled "Goodness of People."

Friendship Groups

Have groups of five children take turns reading pages from *The Peace Crane* and then discuss, write, or sketch one characteristic they discovered about friendship and peace. Have them use their sketches and ideas to make a poster that reflects their thoughts as a group about how to develop friendship and be a good friend, or how friendship can help bring about peace.

World Collage

Have the children look through magazines, newspapers, and brochures and cut out illustrations to prepare a collage that shows how they would interact as friends with others around the world. Perhaps they could select pictures of places to which they have traveled or places they have lived in the world. Have the children add words to the collage to describe how they could be friends with others in the world. If appropriate, audiotape some of the children who volunteer to tell about how they could be friends with others worldwide. Play the tape at a selected time—when students are getting ready for a class meeting, entering the room, leaving, working on art and friendship projects, and so on.

Friendships between Countries

With the whole group, discuss what countries (and people in countries) fight about. Do they think there would ever be a time when both countries could be right in a disagreement? Does the biggest country (strongest, one with most military resources) always win?

With the children, compare the idea of two countries fighting each other with the actions of a football game. To do this, first ask the children to offer some specifics of a football game and list them on the board:

Football Games	*Two Countries Fighting*
Two teams are playing.	
One team wins, one loses.	
Team players can get heated up.	
There are umpires and field judges.	

When there are several items on the list, ask which characteristics on it are similar to two countries fighting. List them under the heading "Two Countries Fighting." Discuss the similarities and differences found.

Book 3.7 *This Is the Way We Eat Our Lunch: A Book about Children around the World* (111)

Ages: 5–7
Heritage: Multicultural

Goals: To relate friendship to diversity and different cuisines

To develop and expand vocabulary related to poems and prose

To reflect on foods eaten by friends in different parts of the world

To record what was learned about multicultural friendships

To work with partners in a friendly manner

Materials: Copy of *This Is the Way We Eat Our Lunch: A Book about Children around the World* (111), samples of different foods, index cards, art paper, crayons, markers, paints

BOOK NOTES

This Is the Way We Eat Our Lunch (Scholastic, 1995), written by Edith Baer and illustrated by Steve Bjorkman, introduces children to foods such as curry, pita bread, rice, gumbo, couscous, Chinese dumplings and other foods from around the world. Each of the introductions features a particular location beginning with places in the United States of America, then moving on to Canada, South America, and so on. A map of the world highlights the locations. Types of cookery and a list of the dishes are included.

ACTIVITIES

Taste Testing

With the whole group, discuss some of the foods that represent different cuisines around the world. Ask for ideas on the scheduling of a food preparation time and taste testing for the group. Ideas could include tasting a new food and meeting the person who prepared it; creating a recipe card on an index card for a new dish and presenting it to someone at home; or drawing pictures of friends sampling the new food.

Cuisine Experiences

In the whole group, ask the children in what ways the information book stimulated their curiosity about foods and cuisines in other parts of the world. Ask for ideas on learning more about foods eaten by people in other areas of the world. Elicit their experiences. Discuss.

Recipe Cards

With children who have selected partners, visit a nearby library to locate cookbooks reflecting different cuisines. Have the children help one another search for and record recipes from different cultures on index cards. Back in the classroom, have the partners decorate the cards and present them as a gift in recognition of world friendship to someone at home.

Poetic Words

Read aloud poems to the children from *I Like You, If You Like Me: Poems about Friendship,* edited by Myra Cohn Livingston. Invite the children to pay particular attention to what the poems tell them about 1) what they expect of their friends; 2) differences between friendships with friends and friendships with siblings; and 3) honoring friendships that are multicultural.

Friendship Talks

Read a book from the "World Friendships" section of the bibliography. Discuss the book, the author's background, and the style of writing. Ask the children to use the information about the author to make a list of qualities that they think could make the author someone they would like to know—and possibly become friends with.

Understanding

Invite the children to complete an idea chart for the group with three columns: what I liked best, what I learned, and what I still want to know. Invite them to record how much they learned about multicultural friendships. Invite the children to refer to their graphs as references while they discuss: Now that we have thought about multicultural friendships, what will we do in the future related to friendships? Ask the children to complete the following statement with sketches or words:

I got a good idea about multicultural friendships. It was _____.

Food and Celebrations

While eating lunch is a daily event that can be shared by friendly children, celebrating holidays and noting the foods that are included is an annual event in December that could be enjoyed by children worldwide.

During the winter holiday time, you can invite the children to select a geographic place in the world and replicate one of the celebrating activities—including the preparation of food—for the others in the class. Ask the children to work with partners and select an activity—perhaps one related to a heritage they are interested in studying—and get involved in one of the activities from the following list:

Bulgaria: Ask the children to divide into small groups and to role-play a father bringing in a yule log for the fire during the winter holiday and the family members sprinkling him with corn kernels to signify health to all and a good harvest in the coming year.

Colombia: Invite the children to disguise themselves and role-play a winter holiday evening, when everyone disguises themselves and parades in the streets. When one guesses another's identity, the guesser claims a gift (an *aguinaldo*) from the one he or she recognizes.

Denmark: Invite the children to remember the birds as children in Denmark do by bundling sheaves of grain and placing them on every door for the birds' holiday dinner.

England: Ask the children to divide into small groups representing families and to role-play pulling a huge yule log inside the house. Each family member must sit on it and salute it before it is lighted to bring good luck to the family in the new year.

France: "Twelfth Night" pastry is made and a coin is hidden inside. A gold paper crown is given to the one who receives the coin, and that person "rules" for the evening. Have the children divide into small groups and role-play finding the coin and "ruling" for a short time.

Germany: Invite the children to make Advent calendars. Have them draw a Christmas scene with twenty-four numbered doors or windows (or trees or boxes that can be opened just like a tiny greeting card). Have them sketch tiny winter holiday scenes behind each opening (window, door, tree or box). When given as gifts to friends, the calendar gives the friend a tiny greeting card to open each day to reveal more winter holiday scenes.

Holland: Have the children fold a sheet of art paper in half. On the left-hand side, invite them to make large sketches of the wooden shoes filled with straw that Dutch children might leave on their windowsill for St. Nick's white horse. On the right-hand side, have them sketch the shoes the following morning—the straw is gone and the shoe contains candies and small gifts.

Mexico: Ask the children to divide into small groups to represent families and role-play a candlelit procession to neighbors' homes. When they are admitted to a home, they rejoice with dancing, singing, feasting, and the breaking of a piñata filled with candies.

Philippines: Invite the children to make wreaths and chains of colorful paper flowers to wear to celebrate the winter holiday.

Poland: For the holiday dinner, a Polish family always keeps one empty seat free at the table in case an unknown traveler should arrive. In the classroom, have the children decorate a chair or desk with holiday foods as an empty seat for any unexpected visitor (parent, grandparent, principal) during the holiday season.

Spain: Have the children fold a sheet of art paper in half. On the left-hand side, ask them to make large sketches of children's shoes filled with straw and carrots for the Wise Men's horses that Spanish children might leave outside. On the right-hand side, have the children sketch the shoes the following morning—when the straw and carrots are gone and the shoes hold gifts and candies left by wise man Balthazar.

II Stories and Activities for Children Ages 9–14

When I look at the future it's so bright it hurts my eyes.
—Oprah Winfrey, talk show host, actress, and child
protector advocate

Trust yourself. Think of yourself. Act for yourself. Speak for
yourself. Be yourself. Imitation is suicide.
—Marva Collins, educator

4 Family Friendships

Book 4.1 *All the Colors of the Race* (131)

Ages:	9–10
Heritage:	Multicultural
Goals:	To relate friendship to members of a biracial family
	To develop and expand vocabulary related to poetry
	To participate in role-play related to family friendship
	To reflect on the feelings of others
	To participate in an interview situation
	To compose free verse with others
Materials:	Copy of *All the Colors of the Race* (131)

BOOK NOTES

All the Colors of the Race (Lothrop, Lee & Shepard, 1982) is by Arnold Adoff. This is a sensitive collection of poems that describe a girl's feelings and thoughts related to her parents' biracial marriage. For example, the girl shares her thoughts about people getting over this "color thing" in her poem entitled "The Way I See Any Hope for Later" and suggests that people stop looking at how brown or tan a man or woman is and, instead, start loving one another.

ACTIVITIES

Role-Play

With the whole group, discuss ways of portraying the role of the girl and suggestions to stop looking at how brown or tan a person is and instead just liking one another in a friendly way. Write the students' suggestions and ideas on the board. Continue with one or more of the following:

- Ask the students to divide up into groups of two, with one student playing the role of the girl in the story and the other playing a student who wants to know about feelings associated with this "color thing."
- Ask the students to suggest experiences for the role-play and add their ideas to the list.
- Discuss the students' questions for information purposes and problem-solving before role-playing. The questions can be written on a diagram related to role-playing and used by the students as a reference for class discussion and role-playing events. Copies of the questions can be laminated before distribution to the students and collected after use.

What's your persona like?	Where are you?	Why are you there?
What do you look like?		What could happen?

Friendship Role-Playing Questions

How are you feeling?	What do you see?
What are you thinking?	What will you say?
How will you act toward the other person?	How can you make this friendship stronger?

Additional questions: What could the girl say to another student about the "color thing" and her hopes for a later time? What could the listening student reply? What facial expressions would the girl (listening student) have? How might the girl feel when she learns about the listening student's point of view? What actions would indicate that the listening student accepted the feelings of the girl?

Partners

Invite partners to role-play being a child and a parent to emphasize the general topic of family friendships through a particular event related to the story. Have them change roles so each student can play both roles. Later, stop the students and ask them to write what they are thinking and feeling. As part of the family friendship theme, students can be asked to record a favorite poem from the book on a page. Invite them to follow up by adding friendly words and actions they observed during the role-play. After recording the poem, invite the students to trade partners and resume role-playing with other partners.

Student Partners

Ask student partners to meet with another pair of partners and discuss ways the role-playing stimulated their curiosity about the feelings of people in different family situations, what their heritage is, and the love some children have for their parents and grandparents, homes, their original country of origin, and where they live now.

Back in the whole group, ask students in what ways the role-playing helped them learn more about friendships in families that may be different from their own. Elicit their experiences related to family friendships around the world. Discuss.

Written Words

Ask the students to discuss what they learned about a) the value of reading the poems of the girl and b) ways children show other family members that they appreciate and love them and where they live. Have students dictate or write brief sentences or paragraphs to tell what they learned about family friendship from the role-playing.

Free Verse

Invite the students to interview one another about the "color thing" and what hopes they have for the future. In what ways do they agree with the girl? Ask the students to take notes during the interview and use the notes to describe in writing how the other person feels about the "color thing."

Book 4.2 *Blue Skin of the Sea* (150)

Ages:	12–14
Heritage:	Hawaiian American
Goals:	To reflect upon friendship among family members

To recognize ways of working together
To take the role of different personas to write friendly
    letters
To acknowledge and appreciate differences in family
    friendships

Materials: Copy of *Blue Skin of the Sea* (150), board, chalk,
overhead transparency, paper for writing a friendly
letter, books about family friendships

BOOK NOTES

Blue Skin of the Sea (Delacorte, 1992) is written by Graham Salisbury. The story is set in the year of Hawaii's statehood in the village of Kailua-Kona, where Sonny Mendoza and his father, a fisherman, live. Sonny not only faces the dangers of the sea but the difficulties of facing a sixth-grade bully in a confrontation over a beautiful girl, and in just growing up as a teenager. Sonny's father is supportive of Sonny as he confronts his difficulties in growing up. When his father's fishing boat fails to return to shore on time, Sonny is afraid he has lost his father to the dangerous sea.

ACTIVITIES

Family Friendship

Ask the students what the words "family friendship" mean to them and write their responses on the board or overhead transparency. After reading excerpts about Sammy and his father from *Blue Skin of the Sea,* ask the students to list the kinds of things Sonny's father liked to do, and in contrast, things Sonny liked to do. Make a list of their suggestions on the board.

Ask the students to describe things they like to do for their families and why. Then have them write an advertisement asking for additional family friendships (perhaps mentioning the kinds of things they like to do for family members) and take it home to show to their families.

Letter Writing

Have the students trade letters written in the son's persona, read them, and then take the role of the father receiving the letter(s).

- In the parental role, have students write a response to the letter they each have and then return both letters to the original student writer.
- Have the original student writer return to the role of the son and read the parental letter. In the whole group, ask for volunteers to offer reasons why they would (or would not) take the offered parental advice.

Family Friend

Ask the students how it feels to have someone in the family with whom they can discuss their difficulties (as Sonny's father did), share ideas, and make decisions. Then ask the students how it feels to have someone in the family who is always the boss and decides what he or she should do. This might be someone who acts as if they own them. Ask the students how they can/cannot really be themselves with that person. Elicit from the students which of the two kinds of family friends they would prefer to spend their time with.

Differences in Families

Let each student select a book to read about family friendships from the bibliography in the back of this book or from another source. Divide the students into groups of five to read the books of their choice. Ask them to then discuss what they learned about differences in family friendships and appreciating them, and report back to the whole group what they learned.

Book 4.3 *Fighting Tackle* (134)

Ages:	9–11
Heritage:	European American
Goals:	To see providing for a sibling as a loving and friendly action
	To identify tension among friendly siblings
	To recognize ways of working together
	To participate in an interview
	To show family friendships through artwork
	To role-play imagined conversations
	To articulate what was learned about appreciating family friendships

To acknowledge special traits that make a good family
friend
Materials: Copy of *Fighting Tackle* (134), paper for interview
notes and letter writing, art paper for pictures

BOOK NOTES

Fighting Tackle (Little, Brown, 1994) is written by Matt Christopher
and illustrated by Karin Lidbeck. This book tells the story of Terry's
friendship and love toward his younger brother, Nicky, who has Down's
syndrome. Terry plays football and helps his brother practice for the
Special Olympics. When their father is injured in an accident, both Terry
and Nicky (not without some tension between them) work together to
help him.

ACTIVITIES

Sibling Interview

Invite the students to interview a parent or family member about a friendship with a sibling and a particular event when their friendship was very
evident. Have them take notes about the interview. Ask the students to
try their hand at visualizing the past event from their notes. To do this,
have them visualize the scene from their family's past and put their ideas
on paper. Ask them to refer to their notes to make the drawing as accurate as possible.

Describing a Family Friend

Ask the students to draw a picture to show how they would picture Terry
helping his brother practice for the Special Olympics. Beneath the picture, have them write a short description of what kind of family friend
they think Terry was.

Reflective Conversations

Ask the students to work in small groups of 4 (or 6 or 8) and respond to
several questions: How do you think the two felt when their father was
injured in an accident? How did what happened change them? Have the
students imagine that the two get together years later and they talk about

how they felt when their father was injured and tensions arose between them. Divided into pairs in the small groups, the students can role-play these conversations.

Learning from Families

Discuss the idea that there is something to learn about family friendships from every family. After the students have discussed this story, have them write a letter to the main character to mention specific events in the story that were valuable and important to the students. If appropriate, have the students read their letters to the whole group or in small groups and answer any questions asked by their classmates. Ask the students to conclude their presentations by reporting what they learned that helps them appreciate family friendships.

Being Special

Ask the students to write a description of a special character they admire from one of the stories about family friendships. Then ask them to compare this character's traits to their own traits by listing them in two columns. Have them trade lists with one another, read them, and return them to the original writer. Ask the students to write about the traits that make them special and unique in their families.

Peers

On the board, write the saying, "If you hide your feelings to keep a friendship, you may never have any." Ask the students to divide into buzz groups and informally discuss the saying, as well as any pluses and minuses of being pressured by friends. Back in the whole group, have the students offer suggestions to make a chart of strategies used by book characters to overcome the negative aspects of peer pressure.

Book 4.4 *Junius over Far* (142)

Ages: 9–11
Heritage: African American
Goals: To recognize intergenerational friendships
To develop and expand vocabulary through literature
To reflect on a grandchild's search for his grandfather

> To contribute to a "family friendship inventory"
> To contribute different words to a familiar musical tune
> To appreciate a family member's momentos—
>   photographs, letters, personal items
> To describe how they could be a better friend to
>   someone in the future

Materials: Copy of *Junius over Far* (142), chart paper for "family friendship inventory," writing paper to write new words to a familiar tune, art paper for sketches

BOOK NOTES

Junius over Far (Harper & Row, 1985) is by Virginia Hamilton. In the story, fourteen-year-old Junius goes looking for Jackaro, his grandfather, on an island in the Caribbean. Junius has a strong relationship with this family member and, through his actions, shows respect and love for his elderly grandfather.

ACTIVITIES

Junius

Ask the students to find and read excerpts from the story concerning things Junius did to search for his grandfather. Elicit from the students their comments about events that make the story interesting (uninteresting). Ask the students to imagine what they would do in a similar search to make Junius more real to them. Ask for volunteers to read parts of dialogue by Junius in the same way they think he would say the words.

Friendship Inventory

Friendships with elderly family members, such as the one Junius had with Jackaro, can be recorded on a "family friendship inventory." To develop an inventory, invite the students to each name a family member and the achievement most remembered and record the information on a class chart under the heading, "Family Friendship Inventory."

Song about a Friend

Ask the students to consider the questions, "What's a family friend?" and "What does it take to be a family friend?" Engage the students in listing several of their family friends and, next to each one, have them write down what makes that person a friend to them. Ask them to select one of their family friends and make up words to a familiar tune about that friend. If appropriate, the students can write new words about the friend to the tune of *Yankee Doodle*. For example, original lyrics to the tune might begin: "Grandson Junius searched quite far/ For Jackaro, his granddad . . ."

Momentos

Friendships with elderly family members—such as Junius' friendship with his grandfather—can be remembered with all sorts of momentos— photographs, letters, personal items. Invite the students to sketch a momento related to an elderly family member (or other person) with whom they had a friendship. After they sketch the momento, ask various students to volunteer and show the drawings of the memorabilia to the whole group or members of a small group.

Search

Ask the students what they think it would be like to be a fourteen-year-old searching for his or her grandfather. During this discussion, establish that a fourteen-year-old could have many problems on a search of this kind. Write the problems mentioned by the students on a list on the board and ask them if they have read or heard any stories in which these same problems were encountered by a teenage character. What acts of friendship did the character need to help combat these problems? What friendship actions did the character appreciate? Take time to hear about the stories they have read.

First Five Pages

Ask the students to record a saying (phrase, sentence) related to friendship from this story. Describe how the meaning of the words could help them be a better friend to someone in the future.

Book 4.5 *Knots on a Counting Rope* (147)

Ages: 9–11
Heritage: Native American
Goals: To show appreciation for an elderly family member

To recognize achievements of others

To recognize intergenerational friendships as family friendships

To recognize that a person's name can symbolize their achievements or contributions

To reflect on family friendships

To take the role of news reporters

To develop and expand vocabulary related to literature

Materials: Copy of *Knots on a Counting Rope* (147), art paper for designing a family tree, paper for interview questions, writing board, chalk, writing paper for stories

BOOK NOTES

Knots on a Counting Rope (Holt, Rinehart & Winston, 1987) is by Bill Martin Jr. and John Archambault. In this story, Boy-Strength-of-Blue-Horses, a blind boy, asks his grandfather to tell him over and over the story of the night he was born. His grandfather poetically tells the boy that he was born during a howling windstorm and when he made his first cry in the world, the wind stopped its howl and the storm was over. As the boy matures, he teaches his horse to run the trails and to race. As the boy gains self-confidence, he prepares to compete in a horse race.

ACTIVITIES

Respect in a Name

The boy in this story was named in accordance with a meaningful prediction in his Native American family. Mention to students that this practice draws attention to the achievements of family members or elderly people. Ask them to give each person in their family a new name that shows respect and reflects an achievement or contribution made by the person. If appropriate, have the students design a family tree on paper and write in the new names for the family members.

Improving Friendships

Have the students discuss the following in informal buzz groups:

• If you could change one thing in your family to make more friendships (or stronger friendships), what would it be?

- In what way is this change something you could actually help accomplish?
- How would you begin to make the change toward friendship really happen?

Boy-Strength-of-Blue-Horses

Ask the students if they have wondered how people got their names and ask why they think the boy in the story was given the name of Boy-Strength-of-Blue Horses. Invite the students to suggest other names that might be suitable for the boy. Record their suggestions on the board. Ask them which name might be most suitable from their point of view. Encourage them to suggest other possibilities and to include some names that might not be obvious.

Reporting on Friendship

Tell the students that they are to play the role of news reporters who have been sent to interview the boy and his grandfather about the race. Have them make a list of questions they will ask the boy and his grandfather in order to find out about the relationship between the two and why the boy was motivated to race. Have the students take the imagined answers from their questions and write a news story about the boy and his friendship with his grandfather. Have the students include the basic *w*'s in the news story: *who, what, when, where* and *why*.

Friendship Events

Ask the students to recall events in the story and list their suggestions on the board. At the top of the list, write the heading "Family Friendship Events." Then, review the items on the list and ask the students to make deletions, one by one, until there are only three main events remaining that reflect the friendship between the boy and his grandfather. Invite the students to think of some descriptive words that tell the way the events were written and write those words in a second column.

List the suggested descriptive words next to the events on the board. Have the students imagine what would have happened to the friendly relationship if one of the events had *not* happened. Have them write how the story would be different without one particular event. Ask them to read aloud their results with partners in class.

Book 4.6   *My Daniel* (135)

Ages:	9–11
Heritage:	European American
Goals:	To see an elderly family member as a loving friend
	To note friendly actions and reflect upon feelings
	To recognize intergenerational friendships
	To write a friendly letter
	To role-play a dinosaur fossil hunter
	To act as a friendship planner
Materials:	Copy of *My Daniel* (135), board, chalk, paper for a partner chart, writing paper for a friendly letter, note paper for recording group decisions, art paper for designing a friendly environment

BOOK NOTES

My Daniel (Harper & Row, 1989) is written by Pam Conrad. In the story, eighty-year-old Julia Creath Summerwaite shares memories of her brother's work as a dinosaur hunter with her grandchildren when she flies to New York to visit them. During a family field trip to the Natural History Museum, her grandchildren learn about great-uncle Daniel from Nebraska—his love for fossils, his search for a dinosaur skeleton, and the competition among paleontologists when he searched for fossils.

ACTIVITIES

Fossil Hunting

Ask students whether they ever go fossil hunting with friends and, if so, invite them to tell about the experience. Ask any student who has found some artifacts to tell how big the items were, where they were found, and some interesting details about how being with a friend or friends helped in the search. Elicit comments from students about how it feels to share the excitement of a find with friends or, if they have never hunted for bones, how they think it would feel.

Friendly Explaining

With students, discuss the idea that sometimes *important* details can be left out when a friend explains how to do something—perhaps how to search for dinosaur bones—to another friend. Have the students meet with friends as partners in class and talk about experiences they have had trying to learn how to do something from someone else when they did not have all the facts they needed or when the information was incorrect. Back in the whole group, ask volunteers to give their examples.

Rivalry

Write the word *rivalry* on the board and ask the students what the word means to them. Mention to students that the author used some examples about rivalry among the competitive dinosaur bone hunters in the story. Have them identify an example of such rivalry in the story. Ask them how the word *rivalry* is explained through the story in various ways. Have the students fill in a chart on the board with some information about rivalry, with one column for the page number of the example and another column for their explanation.

Discuss any questions that the students have and then ask them to work with partners to make a partner-chart for the term *friendship*. After completing their charts, have students meet with another partnership to discuss their findings with questions such as: From your point of view, were friendship events clearly explained? Were friendship events explained in too little or too much detail? What are some friendship events we would like to know more about?

Friendly Letter

Ask the students to imagine they went on a dinosaur bone hunting trip with friends. Elicit their comments about the following questions:

- How did you get the equipment you needed?
- In what ways did you find dinosaur bone hunting easy to do? Hard to do?
- Did you find any dinosaur bones?
- Did you have a good time?

Then, ask the students to write a friendly letter to someone to tell them about their dinosaur bone hunting trip with friends. Encourage them to use their imaginations to write about whatever they wish could be true on their imaginary trip.

Group Decisions

Ask the students to imagine they are paleontologists with Daniel during his difficult times with other dinosaur bone hunters of the past and to plan a friendly environment for their work. Have them discuss information with classroom friends in small buzz groups of 5 or 6 relating to the friendly environment they would like to have to work in as paleontologists. Here are some examples of things the students can ask one another about:

- How could paleontologists work together in friendly ways?
- How could paleontologists conduct their searches in friendly ways?
- What laws (or professional ethics), if any, might be needed?

Ask the groups to select a recorder/reporter to relate what they decided back to the whole group.

Friendship Planners

Ask the students to imagine they are friendship planners and can completely re-create their part of the globe by planning and designing friendly environments for their home, neighborhood, and world. Have them collect information from their school friends about what kind of friendly environment they would like. Here are some examples of things the students can ask others about:

- How could people live in friendly ways?
- How could people play in friendly ways?
- What would people-friendly buildings (and workplaces) look like?
- How could people work and sell their products in friendly ways?
- How could people make friendly decisions?
- What laws, if any, would be needed?

Book 4.7 *Partners* (153)

Ages:	9–10
Heritage:	European American
Goals:	To see the resolution of conflict of interest
	To identify tension among siblings

To recognize ways of working together
To reflect on the feelings of others
To role-play being friends and partners in a
    "business"
To contribute writing and art to a friendship journal

Materials: Copy of *Partners* (153), art paper for Venn diagram,
              posters, and sketches; writing paper for journals

BOOK NOTES

Partners (Simon & Schuster, 1995) is written by Karen Waggoner and illustrated by Cat Bowman Smith. This is a chapter book about a conflict of interest between Jamie and his older brother, Gordon. The brothers raise mice, and Jamie wants to sell them as pets, while Gordon wants to sell them as snake food. Jamie has to figure out a way to get out of the partnership without upsetting his brother.

ACTIVITIES

Conflict of Interest

Invite the students to relate their own experiences with conflicts of interest with a sibling. Do they know anyone like Jamie? Like Gordon? In what ways have they felt like Jamie? Like Gordon? What happened? Was the conflict resolved in some way? How?

Feelings

Invite the students to consider the feelings of the two brothers and respond to the following:

Feelings about mice as pets	Feelings about mice as snake food
Feelings about the partnership	Feelings about the partnership
Friendly Feelings	Friendly Feelings
Unfriendly Feelings	Unfriendly Feelings
Friendliest actions	Friendliest actions

Have the students draw a Venn diagram and write their responses about the brothers in the circles. Feelings common to both brothers can be written in the intersection of the two circles.

Partnership Posters

Ask the students to pretend that they are in a partnership with a friend. The two of you are raising mice (just like the boys in the story) and you want to sell them. Ask them to plan what they would put on signs for houses or apartment buildings or yards to attract customers. Have them think up unusual ways to catch people's attention and to buy their mice. If appropriate, let the students look through newspapers and magazines to get an idea of ways other advertisers have used language to sell a particular product. Have them prepare posters to persuade others to buy their product.

Friendship Journal

Invite the students to decorate the covers of a spiral-bound notebook to reflect what the word *friendship* means to them. Tell them the notebooks are to be their friendship journals and ask them to write what they have learned about their own friendships with a sibling through the story in *Partners*.

Futuristic Friendly Images

Have the students reread their friendship journal notes and draw a picture of their own original images of the brothers as partners in a futuristic friendly family environment.

Book 4.8   *The Song and Dance Man* (130)

Ages:	9–11
Heritage:	European American
Goals:	To see an elderly family member as successful and achieving
	To note a family friendship
	To recognize intergenerational friendships
	To remember an elderly family member through momentos
	To display knowledge about a selected elderly family member
Materials:	Copy of *The Song and Dance Man* (130), art paper for sketches, an item from a family's past, notepaper

BOOK NOTES

The Song and Dance Man (Knopf, 1988) is written by Karen Ackerman. In this story, the grandchildren persuade Grandpa to go to the attic, get out his tap dancing shoes, his top hat and cane, and perform his old-fashioned vaudeville song and dance routine.

ACTIVITIES

Personal Items

Friendships with elderly family members can be remembered by their favorite personal items. Invite the students to sketch a personal item owned by an elderly family member (or acquaintance) with whom they have (or had) a friendship. After they sketch the item, invite the students to show their drawings to the group and talk about the sketches. Encourage them to tell what meaning the item has for them.

Family Faire

Friendships with family members can be remembered with a classroom activity, "Ye Olde Family Faire," that the students plan. To do this, ask them to describe in a unique way a selected elderly family member with whom they had a friendship. For example, the students can do the following:

- Wear old clothes or carry items like tap shoes, straw hats, and parasols.
- Prepare foods that have been favorites for years—lemonade, popcorn, and hot dogs.
- Use old photographs to make a slide show.
- Play records or tapes of music of years past.
- Display homemade crafts—knitted items, toys, quilts.
- Give brief biographical sketches of family members and the friendships they enjoyed.

Curiosity

With the students, discuss the idea that the author has a main character, the song and dance man, in this story of family relationships and that the reader sees that character mainly through the eyes of another character.

In this story, the author used the children watching their grandfather as a strategy to make the reader curious about him. Ask the students what the children did in the story to make them

- Wonder about the man's friendship with other song and dance people
- Believe that grandfather liked being an entertainer
- Believe there are unanswered questions about the song and dance man

Momentos

Ask the students to ask someone in the home about any family member's momentos that they can write about to help someone else understand and appreciate that possession. Invite the students to draw the momento to accompany their writing.

Book 4.9   *Toning the Sweep* (144)

Ages:	11–14
Heritage:	African American
Goals:	To appreciate discovering more about one's heritage
	To appreciate documenting the present for the future
	To compose miniscrapbooks to document their homes and friends
	To reflect on one's feelings when moving out of a home
	To acknowledge the importance of knowing one's heritage
Materials:	Copy of *Toning the Sweep* (144), board, chalk, paper for miniscrapbooks, art paper for pictures

BOOK NOTES

Toning the Sweep (Orchard, 1993) is written by Angela Johnson. It offers a theme of discovering more about one's heritage. When Grandmother leaves her desert home, Emily, an African American teenager, uses a video and records her grandmother's friends and documents her home for future memories. In doing so, she learns more about her heritage.

ACTIVITIES

Moving Away

Have the students imagine that they are going to leave their homes as Grandmother did; they will leave friends behind and will want to document their surroundings for future reflection. Ask them in what ways they could document their homes and surroundings. Write their suggestions on the board. Have them establish which suggestion would appeal to them most and *why* it is appealing.

Miniscrapbooks

Engage the students in making miniscrapbooks to document their homes and friends for the future. Remind them to devote one page per topic — one page for each friend, one for each room of the home, one for family pets, and so on.

Ideas

With students, discuss how they would express in a picture *only* feelings or ideas about leaving their home — perhaps an abstract presentation. Working as partners, have the students select one idea or feeling to portray in crayon. Have the partners informally meet with other partnerships to present their results.

Memories

Ask the students if they ever think of a former house or surroundings or ever have other pleasant memories or dreams about happy experiences they have had in a former home. Invite volunteers to discuss the events they enjoy remembering. After some discussion, mention to the students that sometimes our memories are so detailed we could almost paint colorful pictures about the thoughts. Invite the students to imagine they are painting their own memory scenes of a former home and have them discuss what they would put in the painting.

Heritage

Ask the students to find parts in the story that show how Emily, an African American teenager, learned more about her family heritage. Ask the students how they think she felt about her grandmother leaving her desert home. Have the students discuss the importance of heritage from their point of view: In what ways is heritage important to a person?

Book 4.10   *Totem Pole* (143)

Ages:	9–11
Heritage:	Native American
Goals:	To see a totem as a way to record memories
	To appreciate the traditions of others
	To develop and expand vocabulary through literature
	To reflect on ways a totem could represent family happiness, sadness
	To record a family's memories
	To make a totem collage
Materials:	Copy of *Totem Pole* (143), art paper for totem sketches, discarded ice-cream containers, pipe cleaners for designs

BOOK NOTES

Totem Pole (Holiday House, 1990) is written by Diane Hoyt-Goldsmith. The story takes place in the Pacific Northwest. A Native American wood carver and his son carve a 40-foot totem pole, a tradition to record memories of their people. The totem pole is to be a symbol of their family, tribe, and clan. They make carvings not only to remember family members but to record important events. They know that, in the past, their ancestors even carved events from their people's legends on just such a pole. They look forward to a celebration when the totem is finished and ready to show to others.

ACTIVITIES

Father-Son Feelings

With the students, look at the illustrations and talk about how they think the family members in the pictures feel. How did the family members feel when they created the design of the totem pole? Do the totem poles talk? Do they tell stories? What might a totem say? Ask the students to suggest ways that the totem could represent family togetherness, happiness, sadness, and so on. If they were to design their family's totem pole, what designs would they choose to represent these things?

Events

Ask the students to record family events important enough to place on a totem pole. Have students list the events, then decide on images that would represent them. Ask them to sketch their ideas.

Pipe Cleaner Designs

Engage the students in designing a family totem pole on paper to record their family's memories using the images they sketched. Distribute pipe cleaners to the students and ask them to make a totem design of their choice with the pipe cleaners. Ask the students to place the designs on the stage of an overhead projector and then tell about the meaning of each. Have the students place the designs on the left-hand side of a sheet of art paper and record what meaning each design has for them in a right-hand column.

If appropriate, have the students re-create their designs on the outside of empty ice-cream containers taped on top of one another to simulate family totems.

Different Totems

With students, discuss different kinds of totems and the family life of the people who made them. Engage the students in finding information and illustrations about totems that interest them and about the people who made the totems. Have the students describe aloud what they learned in the whole group or small groups.

Totem Collage

Invite the students to make a totem collage for their families using pictures from newspapers, magazines, flyers, brochures, and catalogs. The pictures can represent the families' interests and activities. Ask the students to talk and write about the totems they created.

Book 4.11   *Water Ghost* (148)

Ages:	9–11
Heritage:	Chinese
Goals:	To relate friendship to an intergenerational relationship
	To relate friendship to community friends
	To develop and expand vocabulary through poetry and literature
	To retell a story and reflect on what was read
	To empathize with a book character and to create a friendship experience for the main character
	To contribute to a "Bill of Family Friendship Rights"
Materials:	Copy of *Water Ghost* (149), board, chalk, writing paper, pencils or pens

BOOK NOTES

Water Ghost (Caroline House/Boyds Mills Pr., 1995) is written by Ching Young Russell and illustrated by Christopher Zhong-Yuan Zhang. Set 50 years ago in China, ten-year-old Ying is raised by her loving yet firm grandmother, Ah Pau. Ying wants to raise some money and bargains with her cousin Kee for help. In a bittersweet episode, Ying is accused of theft, but an orphaned, disabled classmate eventually is exposed as the real thief and commits suicide. Ying feels guilt over the sad experience and spends the money she earns to buy a chicken that the classmate's needy grandmother is trying to sell.

ACTIVITIES

Caring Experience

Discuss the story and have students respond to Ying's act of caring for the orphaned, disabled classmate and her family. Did they notice any influences on Ying of other characters in the book that might have affected her actions toward the classmate? If so, what did they notice? Ask the students to identify a family member or caring other who has inspired them to care for others. If appropriate, have them record their own caring experiences (real or imagined) in a brief story. Ask them to illustrate their stories and share them with a small group.

Realizations

Have the students dictate or write three things that they now know about this family and its friendships in China 50 years ago that they did not know before they heard/read this story. Record their ideas on the board. Elicit from the students similarities between their families and the family in China years ago.

Diamante

Encourage the students to write a diamante poem about Ying caring for the lost classmate, and her grandmother's attempt to sell the chicken and earn money. Review the features of the diamante poetry form with the students:

- It is a seven-line poem.
- The first line is a noun (i.e., Ying) and the seventh line is a noun (perhaps the word "caregiver" to complement [or contrast with] the noun in line one).
- The second line has two adjectives related to the noun (hard worker, classmate).
- The third line has three verbs ending in *ing* or *ed* (loved, accused, acquitted).
- The fourth line has four nouns or a phrase that complements the first noun (feels guilty over death).
- The fifth line has three participles to relate to the noun in line seven (feeling, buying, giving).
- The sixth line has two adjectives that relate to the noun in line seven (considerate, thoughtful).
- The seventh line is a noun that complements (or contrasts with) the noun in line one (caregiver).

With words suggested by the students, a group-composed poem might look something like this:

Ying

hard worker, classmate
loved, accused, acquitted
feels guilty over death
considerate, thoughtful
caregiver

Opinions

Invite the students to think about whether or not they always agree with or have the same opinions as their family members. Help students see that differences of opinion in a family are natural, because no two people think alike. Ask the students to identify details in the story that show that Ying and her family members had the same/different opinions. Invite the students to discuss why the family may have had differences of opinion and to use information from the story to support their responses.

Maturity

Ask the students what they think it means when Ying *matures* (and grows in wisdom about her relationship with others). Write their suggestions on the board. Have them locate the definition of maturity in a dictionary and compare their interpretations with the dictionary definition. Discuss any differences. Ask the students to find examples from the story that showed that Ying matured and developed better family relationships during the story.

Bill of Family Friendship Rights

Engage the students in getting a feeling for friendship "rights" in a family environment by discussing what rights they feel they have. Ask them to suggest a proposed "Bill of Family Friendship Rights" that would have been useful to the story's main character:

- The right to choose one's own friends
- The right to be respected
- The right to make more and more friends each day
- The right to be friends with everyone

Ask them to copy the Bill of Family Friendship Rights and check off the rights they consider most important from their own points of view.

Proposed Bill of Rights

Have the students prioritize each proposed right and record the results on the board in graph form.

5 Community, Neighborhood, and School Friendships

Book 5.1 *Backyard Rescue* (191)

Ages:	9–11
Heritage:	European American
Goals:	To discuss how friendship can be strengthened/weakened
	To identify friendly actions toward others
	To role-play events about friendship from literature
	To compose an accordion-folded friendship booklet
	To record what is valued in a friendship
	To demonstrate friendly ways to talk with others
	To participate in meeting a new friend
Materials:	Copy of *Backyard Rescue* (191), notepaper for skit, strip of adding machine tape (25″ long), drawing and writing utensils, art paper for cutout profiles of faces, clear plastic straws, the yellow pages

BOOK NOTES

Backyard Rescue (Tambourine, 1994), written by Hope Ryden and illustrated by Ted Rand, is a story of two friends, ten-year-old Lindsay and Greta, an animal lover. Greta, who has family financial problems, leads Lindsay, whose family is well-off, into a commitment toward animals and animal rescues. Unfortunately, local laws get in the way of the girls' caring for animals. Their friendship, however, becomes stronger as they face civil disobedience together.

ACTIVITIES

Both Sides

Divide the students into groups of equal number (four, six) to consider playing the following scene related to the story:

> Lindsay and Greta, animal lovers, are caring for animals in their yard when law officials appear to state that local laws prohibit what the girls are doing in a residential area.

Have the students prepare a brief skit about what might be said and done. The skit can include an opportunity for the girls to tell their point of view and the officials to tell theirs. Then, both sides make suggestions about how this can be resolved. Each skit developed in the groups can be presented to the whole class.

Friendship Booklet

Ask the students to fold a strip of adding machine tape (25″ long) into five sections to make an accordion-fold booklet. Have them consider the essence of this friendship story by drawing or writing about each of the following on one of the pages:

- Title and author page.
- The "Who" page: Who were the main characters in this friendship story? (Students can draw or write a response.)
- The "What Happened" page: What was one of the main friendship actions that happened in the story?
- The "When" page: When did this friendship story take place? Long ago? In the future?
- The "Where" page: Where does this friendship story take place?
- The "Why" page: Why do you think this friendship became stronger?

Have the students decorate the pages as they wish with scenes of friendship. Display the booklets in a reading area so others can browse through the interpreted material about friendship.

Reasons for Valued Friends

Invite the students to think of their favorite friend and write ten reasons why they value that friend. Ask the students to read the reasons aloud and make a list of their values on the board, chart, or overhead transparency. Tally the number of students who mentioned each value, then ask the students to figure out which similar qualities they value in friendships. Make a graphic web on the board to show the similar qualities.

Talking Profiles

Ask the students to think about how they talk with their friends at home or at school. Ask for volunteers to give examples to the whole group of the way they talk when they are playing with friends and to use cutout paper profiles of heads on the overhead projector. Invite them to join with partners and place cutout profiles of two faces on the overhead as a focus for showing others how they talk with their friends. If appropriate, the lower jaw of each profile can be cut off and glued to a clear paper straw so the student can manipulate the jaw up and down while talking. The students can imagine that they are in situations similar to those in the story or similar to those described below and role-play talking with their profiles on the overhead in front of the group.

- You are in a pet store with one of your friends and your friend turns around suddenly, causing you to knock over a pet food display. The store manager appears and asks you and your friend to come into the office. What friendly language could you use with your friend? With the pet store manager?
- You and your friend are caring for animals in your backyard when law officials appear to tell you that local laws prohibit what you are doing in a residential area. What friendly language could you use with your friend? With the law officials?
- You realize that one of your friends has family financial problems, as Greta did in the story. You realize that your family is well-off, as Lindsay's family was. What friendly language could you use with your friend when the cost of something comes up in your relationship?

In a follow-up discussion, have the students review the friendly language used in the situations and describe which actions and words were appropriate from their point of view.

Different Friends

Invite the students to form groups of four or six and to join groups whose members they do not know very well. In the groups, ask the students to pair up and tell something about themselves to their partners. Have them make sketches or line drawings to remind them of what the other student is saying. Next, have each student introduce the partner to the whole group as an act of friendship. They can show their sketches or line drawings and refer to the artwork as reminders for the introduction. After the introductions are made, have the students discuss what they liked best about talking with someone they didn't know very well.

Diversity

Have the students meet in small conversational groups and distribute copies of the yellow pages to them. Ask the students to use the pages as reference material to identify diverse people who serve the community in their area and who the students might be interested in meeting. Have the students take notes on the discussion and report back their findings to the whole group. Ask the students to write headings (Diverse People, Occupations, Needs Met) on their note-taking sheets before they collect information from the yellow pages.

Book 5.2   *The Best Friends Book: True Stories about Real Best Friends, Fun Things to Do with Your Best Friends, Solving Best Friend Problems, Long-Distance Friends, Finding New Friends and More!* (168)

Ages:	9–14
Heritage:	Multicultural
Goals:	To recognize ways friendship can be strengthened/weakened
	To identify friendly fun things to do with a best friend
	To find new friends nearby and far away
	To meet a new friend
	To reflect on what friends do together
	To compose a friendship motto

To prepare a friendship calendar
To work with friends in a "business"

Materials: Copy of *The Best Friends Book* (168), paper for secret code and letter, scrapbook, adhesive-backed paper, calendar

BOOK NOTES

The Best Friends Book: True Stories about Real Best Friends, Fun Things to Do with Your Best Friends, Solving Best Friend Problems, Long-Distance Friends, Finding New Friends and More! (Free Spirit, 1994) is written by Arlene Erlbach, with photographs by Stephen J. Carrera. This book begins with first-person stories about the pluses and minuses of having (and being) best friends. It also offers advice for meeting new friends and activities that friends can do together.

ACTIVITIES

New Friends

Assign the students to teams so students can work with someone they don't know very well as partners to do one or more of the following:

- Develop a secret code that only the two of you will know how to decode.
- Start a "new friends" scrapbook and make decisions together on what could be placed in the scrapbook.
- Write a "new friend" letter to one another.
- Plan a small party that you would like to give for your new friend. Ask the teacher if you can have a "small parties" afternoon so you two can enjoy a small party, as well as a whole group friendship party.
- Interview one another and try to learn more about your "new friend," his or her likes or dislikes, interests, hobbies, crafts, favorite colors, and so on. Write your interview questions before you begin.
- Make lapel buttons from adhesive-backed paper that read, "Today my new friend was _____."
- Make a map of the classroom to show where the friends have their desks in the room. Prepare a second map to show how the classroom furniture could be rearranged so the two friends could be closer together.

Values in Friendship

To involve the students in reflecting about friendships, ask them to think about the friends they have and what activities they do together. Ask them to use the following checklist of "characteristics" they value in a current friendship: fun, popularity, power, adventure, companionship, status, other.

Being Right

Ask the students if they have heard the saying, "Be sure you're right, then go ahead." Discuss ways the students can be sure they are "right" in their friendships. To help them reflect upon this, ask them to write down the strong points of a friendship they have before deciding that the friendship is "right." Ask volunteers to read aloud their thoughts.

Friendship Motto

Discuss the meaning of the word *motto* with the students—a motto sums up a guiding principle of a person or group. Ask the students, "Knowing what you do about your friendships, what motto would you write for your friendships?" Have the students write one or more friendship mottos and illustrate them. Ask for student volunteers to read their words aloud and display the accompanying illustration.

Friendship Calendar

With students, discuss the preparation and display of a friendship calendar for the class. Elicit ideas from the students and have them divide into groups to prepare their contributions—birthdays, special dates, observances, celebrations—for the calendar. The students can print out their names and birthday dates and place it in the correct blank for the month. They can add friendship events, multicultural celebrations, pictures, birth dates and contributions of famous people from different cultures, important historical dates related to the history of different groups, and quotations, if they wish.

Evenings at School

Talk with the students about ways they can request that the school be open at night and on weekends as a place to meet their friends, other students, and some caring adults and to develop friendships with people in the neighborhood and the community. What do they think of the idea of having a program—perhaps called "Right Track Camp"—on Saturdays at the school for tutoring students in algebra and other subjects? How could they help their friends in such a program?

Jobs at School

With students, discuss ways they can tag along with someone who works at the school and learn the characteristics of that particular job. In what ways could they shadow what the workers at school do and get acquainted with the worker and others?

Popcorn People

In addition to learning the work others do at school, invite the students to be budding entrepreneurs together as friends and play the role of a popcorn business person. Suggest that they start their own popcorn business at school, just as others in the community have their own businesses. Have the students brainstorm at recess and during the lunch hour. What would they need to begin the business? Who would their customers be? Encourage them to think through the materials and supplies that would be required, the money that would need to be raised to start up the business, the bookkeeping, the proposals that would have to be presented to school and city officials, and any permission from the school or community that could be requested.

Book 5.3   *Darnell Rock Reporting* (183)

Ages:	9–12
Heritage:	African American
Goals:	To see how friendship affects decisions
	To identify a goal to reach with a best friend
	To find new friends nearby
	To reflect on being a do-good kid
	To write a business letter of advocacy
	To communicate in a friendly way
	To be a friend and help another in locating information
	To record why a best friend is valued
	To recognize others for their acts of friendship
Materials:	Copy of *Darnell Rock Reporting* (183), art paper for maps, writing paper for stories and letters

BOOK NOTES

Darnell Rock Reporting (Delacorte, 1994) is written by Walter Dean Myers. The story is about a boy who changes from a do-nothing thirteen-year-old city kid to a do-good kid through friendships. Darnell Rock hangs out with his friends called the South Oakdale Corner Crew and does nothing. Faced with poor grades, misbehavior, and the principal, Mr. Baker, who threatens to call Darnell's parents, Darnell decides to join the school newspaper staff. Looking for a story that others will read, Darnell meets and befriends a homeless man, Sweeby Jones, who served in the Vietnam War with Darnell's father. Sweeby motivates Darnell to write an editorial suggesting that unused basketball courts be turned into community gardens instead of parking lots, as proposed by city planners. The city paper runs the story and interviews Darnell, who speaks before the city council.

ACTIVITIES

Unused Courts

In the story, Darnell wants unused basketball courts to be turned into community gardens. Have students imagine that one of the school's basketball courts is to be turned into a garden for the community. Walk with the students to the court so the students can inspect the location with the purpose of sketching a map of the court's location for an imaginary city council. In the classroom, have the students refer to their sketches to draw a map of the location of the court and to write a business letter to the imaginary city council advocating another use for the court.

Maps and Stories

After the students have sketched their maps of the location of the basketball court, ask them to write a brief story for a class friend/partner and describe the location of the court *without identifying its exact location on the map.* Have the students trade their maps and stories so others can decipher what the map and stories depict. When the maps and stories are returned to their owners, have students give friendly feedback to one another concerning what helped or hindered them in identifying the exact location of the court on the map.

Success

Ask the students to name persons in the community who they admire and think are successful and enjoy being successful—perhaps it is a real-life Darnell who has campaigned for community gardens. Write the names on the board. Ask the students to select one of these people and write a brief description of why the person appeared successful to them. Ask for volunteers to read their descriptions aloud to the group and to tell why they would like that person for a friend.

Courts into Gardens

Ask the students to find examples in the story that show how Sweeby Jones, who served in the Vietnam War with Darnell's father, and Darnell helped one another and were friends. Ask them to imagine what plans Darnell had to consider in turning the unused basketball courts into gardens. If appropriate, have students work in teams of two on a diagram using paper and crayons or colored pencils to show how a basketball court could be turned into a community garden.

Suppose

Invite the students to imagine that they want a library book on developing a community garden and want their friends to help them. In teams of two, ask them as friends to tell one another how they could locate a book on the topic of gardening. Back in the whole group, invite volunteers to report on their helpful suggestions. Emphasize some of the following:

- You could use a card catalog which lists books on various subjects in the library.
- You can find your key word, *gardening,* on the cards, since key words are listed on the cards in alphabetical order.
- You can find your subject on a computer file on a computer in the library. Books on the subject will be listed electronically.
- Others suggested by the students.

Treasured Friend

Have the students, working independently, reflect on their most treasured friend and write ten reasons why they value that friend. As a group, ask the students to read their lists aloud and tally their entries to see the extent to which they value similar things in their friendships. Ask the students to summarize with a statement that best describes the friendship that they share with their treasured friend.

Friendly Student of the Week

During a class meeting on Friday afternoon, invite the students to write on slips of paper the names of the person they thought was the most friendly during the previous school week. Create a special section on a display board to feature the student or students selected.

Book 5.4   *Fifth Grade Fever* (173)

Ages:	9–10
Heritage:	European American
Goals:	To recognize how friendship affects decisions
	To identify a goal to accomplish with a best friend
	To create a personal friendship motto
	To design a seal or coat of arms to represent friendships
	To write friendly letters to others
	To identify a person in the community who exhibits friendship
	To design a poster acknowledging friendship
	To participate in a school and community buddy system
Materials:	Copy of *Fifth Grade Fever* (173), milk cartons for mail boxes, art paper for sketches, poster board

BOOK NOTES

Fifth Grade Fever (New York: Dutton, 1955) is written by Michele Granger. The author focuses on friendship in this entertaining story about two friends, Marty and Nina, who decide wholeheartedly that they want to be the teacher's pets for the school year. Their new teacher is Mr. Truesdale, who is young and handsome. Their competition is Beverly Bridges, who has been the teacher's pet every year so far, and their obstacle is that the two don't like studying or doing their homework.

ACTIVITIES

Personal Friendship Motto

Ask the students to think about how Marty and Nina acted in their friendship and how they themselves want to act. Have the students create a personal friendship motto for Marty and Nina and then create a personal motto for themselves and write it on a length of art paper (4″ × 11″). Have the students sign their work and display the art in the room.

Friendship Coat of Arms

Sometimes, words and pictures can be brought together to make a seal or a coat of arms for a family. Have the students design their own seal or coat of arms to represent their friendships. Encourage them to depict what they like or value in their friends on the coat of arms.

Class Express

Have the students make "Class Express" mailboxes from empty milk cartons to facilitate writing to friends in class. Ask them to suggest three friends in the classroom to whom they will correspond in a friendly way by mailing letters or postcards or sending drawings and poems. Next to the names, have the students write about (or sketch) the qualities they like that makes that person a friend. Have them affix the list to their mailboxes. As they enter or leave the room for recess or lunch, encourage them to mail their letters to one another by placing their mail in the boxes. At the end of the school day as they leave the room, encourage them to pick up their mail on the way out the door.

Friendship Reading

Have the students, in groups of four or five, take turns reading pages from a book listed in the "community friendships" portion of the bibliography in the back of this book. After reading, engage them in discussing, writing about and sketching one quality they identified in a character who exhibited friendship toward others. Have the students make posters to reflect their thoughts on how to be a good friend in the community and display the posters in the classroom.

School Community Pals

In cooperation with another teacher and class, engage the students in sending unsigned letters and sketches about themselves to a "community school pal." Encourage them to tell how they can demonstrate friendship toward the school and the community pal, what topics they like to talk about, what sports they like to play, what they like to watch on TV, and so on. As an alternative, repeat the activity with in-class pals using personalized mailboxes.

Buddies

Encourage the students to be a part of a community buddy system on the school campus. Invite them to go everywhere with one buddy for a full school morning. Use the afternoon for a class meeting to talk about the pluses and minuses of working and playing together in pairs during the morning hours.

Trust

Discuss with the students, how they can learn to trust someone they are unfamiliar with in their neighborhood or community. What is it that they feel they need in order to develop trust? In what ways is this a problem to be resolved? How can it be resolved?

Book 5.5   *I Gave Thomas Edison My Sandwich* (182)

Ages:	9–10
Heritage:	European American
Goals:	To recognize friendly actions
	To role-play Thomas Edison and a fourth-grade boy
	To develop and expand vocabulary related to poetry and prose
	To contribute to free verse
	To develop "friendship rules"
	To describe what a friendship with a famous person might be like
	To research acts of friendship by a historical figure

Materials: Several copies of *I Gave Thomas Edison My Sandwich*
              (182); paper and pencils for writing poems;
              newspapers, travel brochures, and magazines; pages for
              student-written book; copies of the Inupiat's list of
              values, called the Ilitqusiat

BOOK NOTES

I Gave Thomas Edison My Sandwich (Albert Whitman, 1995), written by
Floyd C. Moore, with illustrations by Donna Kae Nelson, focuses on the
nostalgic reflections of an eighty-seven-year-old man. Floyd remembers
when his fourth-grade class went to the train station in Iron City, Tenn.,
to see the celebrity train carrying William Taft, Henry Ford, and Thomas
Edison. The elderly gentleman recalls standing on his lunch pail to see
over the grown-ups in the crowd and that Thomas Edison teased him
about standing on his ham sandwich. Floyd responded that the sandwich
was made of souse. Edison said he had not thought about souse in a long
time or had such a sandwich. When the train started to pull out, Floyd
gave his sandwich to the conductor to pass on to Edison—a quick gesture of friendship.

ACTIVITIES

Role-Playing

Have the students role-play different situations related to a friendship in
the community, neighborhood, or at school. Mention that their purpose
in role-play will be to defend a point of view of the value of friends, to
argue for or against something—i.e., giving your sandwich to someone—
to make a decision about a friendship, or to come up with a solution or
plan for making new friends or patching up a broken friendship. if appropriate, before the students begin, share the acronym AH! BAN CADS
to help them remember the roles that follow:

- "A" is for an authority figure who espouses the value of friends and
  friendship (can be role-played as a principal, parent, church pastor, or
  priest, with the students in the role of group members listening to the
  authority).
- "H" is for the helpless or the less fortunate (role-played as someone
  who is unable to share food with someone else).

- "B" is for a "best friend" (role-played as the best friend of Floyd at the train station and the students as the rest of the crowd who overhear the conversation between Floyd and the friend).
- "A" and "N" are for an advocate who's negative (role-played as a challenger to the ideas of Edison or Taft or Ford or to the idea of giving food away).
- "C" is for one of the crowd (role-played as a member of the crowd at the train station).
- "A" is for an absentee (role-played outside the main drama as a newspaper reader from another town who reads about the incident when the students take the roles of townspeople of Iron City, Tenn.).
- "D" is for someone who dislikes celebrities (role-played as the leader of a small, nearby group that dislikes the celebrities, with the students in role as the crowd who likes the celebrities).
- "S" is for a specialist outside the action (role-played as a town historian who records events, with the students as townspeople who have witnessed the event); or a supplemental person on the edge of the event (role-played as the engineer of the train or one who prepares sandwiches at a local shop).

After demonstrating the various roles, ask the students to work with partners to take one or more of the roles themselves. Have them play out a scene, then switch roles. Ask for volunteers to play their situation for the whole group.

In a role-playing situation, in front of the whole group ask the students in the audience to take the roles of members of observation teams to collect information about the different feelings that are shown by the main "actors." Encourage the students in the audience to observe the actors carefully and take notes on how many times feelings are expressed and in what ways.

After the role-playing, ask each student in the audience to report how a certain "actor" reacted and showed his or her feelings. As a further activity, help the students tally their information on a chart to show how many times signs of friendship or unfriendliness were demonstrated in the role-playing. As a follow-up, invite the students to check the accuracy of their "report" on the chart with the information each student received *independently*. Point out to the students that when social scientists do this they call it "checking the reliability" of their observations.

Floyd and Edison

Invite the students to write free verse poems in two voices to show Edison's and Floyd's thoughts during the meeting at the train. Example:

Floyd	*Edison*
I am nine years old.	I am forty years old.
I live in Iron City, Tenn.	I live _____.
I traveled to the train station.	I traveled on the celebrity train.
I was with my fourth grade class.	I was with William Taft and Henry Ford.
I gave my sandwich to Edison. (Other by students)	I _____.

Engage the students in reading aloud the two-voice poem as a choral reading.

Evidence of Friendship

Ask the students to read or listen to the story again to find evidence of Floyd's appreciation of friendship. Invite the students to meet with partners to write a collaborative paragraph about Floyd's gesture of friendship in the story. Back in the whole group, take a quick survey of the partners to determine how many are in favor of giving their sandwich away as a brief gesture of friendship and how many are not. Record the results on the board. Ask volunteers to read their paragraphs aloud to the rest of the class.

Friendship Rules

Divide the students into groups of four or six and ask them to consider developing some "friendship rules." Ask for volunteers in each group to be a recorder and a speaker for the group. Write on the board the following topics the groups should consider in their group discussion:

- Give five examples of friendship rules that you know about. Write a list.
- In what ways have you seen friendship rules get broken?
- Why do you suppose each friendship rule was made?
- Rank each entry on the list of rules according to #1 (most important) to #5 (least important). How important is each rule relative to the others from your point of view?

- What rule would you add or delete from the list?
- What are some consequences for breaking each rule?

Back in the whole group, ask the recorder in each group to read their list of friendship rules and the speaker to explain the consequences for breaking rules that were discussed.

Playing Detective

Invite the students to identify details related to the friendship of a famous historical figure affiliated with the student's community or state. For example, students in Tennessee could research details related to Thomas Edison, since he visited the area on the celebrity train. Ask the students to develop brief paragraphs about famous people who contributed to the community (the nation, the world) without naming the person in the descriptions. Have the paragraphs read aloud and invite other students to listen for details to identify the historical figure. Ask students to recall the point at which they could identify the figure and their contributions and to note any details similar to those of another historical person.

Famous Person

Ask the students to write brief paragraphs to describe what a friendship might be like with a famous person in the community, region, or state and to trade papers with another student. After the receiving students have read the paragraphs, ask them to identify the people described, explain their contributions to the community, and to read the details that helped them identify the person.

Book 5.6   *If You're Not from the Prairie . . .* (163)

Ages:	9–11
Heritage:	European American
Goals:	To reflect on ways friendships are made
	To see friendships in a prairie setting
	To participate in an interview
	To develop and expand vocabulary through literature

Materials: Copy of *If You're Not from the Prairie . . .* (163), letter-writing materials

BOOK NOTES

If You're Not from the Prairie . . . (Atheneum/Simon & Schuster, 1995), written by David Bouchard, is a portrayal of a young boy of the prairie. The boy and his dog play in a prairie setting of fields, farms, and country roads. Their friendship activities are told in rhythmic verse that gives a feeling for the wind, dirt grit, sunburned skin, and chapped lips suffered by those who live on the prairie. In the dry season, the boy walks in a creek bed in solitude. In the winter, the boy and his friends have a snowball fight in front of a large country home and ride the school bus in a winter blizzard. At the end, the concept of change and time passing by is shown with the boy as a grown farmer.

ACTIVITIES

Community Friends

With students, review the book's illustrations a second time and invite them to respond to these questions:

- Who in the prairie setting could become community friends? How would you initiate a friendship with a community worker?
- Why do you think there is such a variety of jobs on a prairie?
- Why do you think a prairie family does not do these different jobs all by itself?
- Do you think that the people who do these special jobs have unique abilities for their work? Why or why not?

If I Were a Friend . . .

Invite each student to reflect on the words, "If I Were a Friend of _____ (community worker), I would . . ." Ask each student to select one prairie worker and dictate/write what the student might experience during one or two days with the worker on the job. Have the child explain why the worker's job is important and ways it meets people's needs. Have the students illustrate their writing with sketches of the worker doing the job in a prairie community.

Interviewing

Ask the students to interview a community friend about his or her job. Have students prepare questions for the interview and write them on the board. They should focus on meeting people's needs, the work environment, and safety. Write them in diagram form on the board:

work environment	job that is done	safety
	community worker	
people's needs		other

After the interviews, have volunteers report on what they learned from the community worker about the job and meeting people's needs.

Without a Title

With the students, read aloud (or silently and independently) additional stories of community friendships to introduce different workers and jobs and to provide basic knowledge about meeting people's needs. For each story read, ask the students to take notes about ways that community workers help provide food, water, shelter, clothing, and transportation. The note-taking sheet, *without a title,* could resemble the following:

Notes

food
background information:

water
background information:

shelter
background information:

clothing
background information:

transportation
background information:

After each story is read and the notes are taken, have students meet with partners to review their notes, share information, and make additions or deletions. Back in the whole group, have the students suggest information from their notes to place on a similar note-taking sheet replicated on the board, a chart, or an overhead transparency. Ask the students to explain the reasoning behind their suggestions. Have them suggest a title for the chart that summarizes the information gathered during the activity.

Grandparents

Ask the students to interview a grandparent or an elderly relative or friend to learn more about a time in their childhood when they lived in a different environment—perhaps the prairie—and ways they formed friendships. Have the students write their interview questions before they begin; one or more of the questions should relate to a friendship that was initiated. Ask them to report what they learned about friendships back to the whole group.

Friends

Discuss ways the students can make new friends in their neighborhood or community. How would this be different from or the same as finding friends if they lived on the prairie? Record their ideas in two lists on the board.

How could the students find new friends in school, church, homes, and neighborhood organizations in each of the locales? In an urban area, what do they think of the idea of fathers and other adult males maintaining safety by walking the streets in pairs in the morning as students arrive at school and in the afternoon as students depart? Discuss the idea that one purpose of the walkers would be to talk to kids who might be in trouble and give them a number to call to get in touch with a caring adult. In what ways could fathers and others contribute to the friendliness and safety of the prairie environment?

Book 5.7   *An Island Far From Home* (167)

Ages: 9–13
Heritage: European American
Goals: To see how friendship can be strengthened through communication
           To see stereotypes fade through letter-writing
           To see how respect can turn into friendship

To identify one's personal characteristics
To write to someone as a pen pal
To show respect for others
Materials: Copy of *An Island Far From Home* (167), letter-writing materials, art paper

BOOK NOTES

An Island Far From Home (Carolrhoda, 1994) is written by John Donahue. This is a story of a twelve-year-old yankee boy, Joshua Loring, and a fourteen-year-old confederate soldier who is a prisoner on nearby George's Island. Joshua's uncle, in charge of the prisoners on the island, tells Joshua about the young prisoner, who is scared and alone, and asks Joshua to write to him. Barely recovered from his grief over the death of his father, a doctor in the Union Army, Joshua at first rejects the idea of writing to a hated confederate. He later decides to write one letter. The prisoner writes back and soon their stereotypical views of one another fade as a respectful relationship grows through subsequent letters.

ACTIVITIES

Friendly Letter

Discuss with the students the idea of writing a letter to an unknown person about the personal characteristics you have that would help contradict any stereotypical view of your affiliations that he or she might have. Engage the students in drafting such a letter.

Personal Communication

Have the students work more on the letter written in the previous activity and sign the letter as "anonymous." Read it and provide feedback if appropriate for the group members.

SchoolEx

Arrange with a teacher in another class to match up each other's students so each has a "SchoolEx" pen pal to write to during the school day. Have each student send letters or artwork about themselves to their anonymous SchoolEx pal. Have students assume that the anonymous recipient might have a stereotypical view of the letter-sender, and encourage the students to describe their personal characteristics so the receiver can get to know them. Encourage students to write about or draw subjects they like and to tell what they like to do for work and play.

Respect

Have the students make "respect" paper ribbons with their names on it. Have them mark it each time they show respect for others and others show respect for them. Ask the students to suggest ways to give and show respect (one way is to say "thank you" and "please") and to list their suggestions on the board. Display the ribbons at the end of the day and ask the students how it felt to get respect and show respect to others during the day. Ask how others responded to shows of respect.

Anger Management

With older students, introduce a videocassette about dealing with anger (perhaps the one entitled *When Anger Turns to Rage* [Sunburst Communications, 1995][1] for ages 9–14). The focus of the video is multicultural, mixed-gender students who get involved in realistic situations in which anger occurs. After seeing such a video, emphasize the value of anger management skills and invite the students to relate what they learned to their own experience. When might anger management skills have helped them or someone they know?

Book 5.8   *The Lancelot Closes at Five* (193)

Ages:	9–13
Heritage:	European American
Goals:	To recognize how friendship can be strengthened through adversity
	To tell about having his/her feelings changed by another person/new friend
	To reflect on a time when a secret was told by a "friend"

---

[1] 39 Washington Ave., Pleasantville, NY 10570.

To identify what friends have in common
To suggest ways to show respect to others
To record qualities that could make an unknown person
    a new friend
To write a friendly letter
To develop a new friendship in the community

Materials: Copy of *The Lancelot Closes at Five* (193), writing
           paper

BOOK NOTES

The Lancelot Closes at Five (Macmillan, 1976) is written by Marjorie W. Sharmat and illustrated by Lisl Weil. Hutch, a health food fanatic, and Abby, his friend, spend the night in the Lancelot, the model home of the new housing development in which they live. When the newspaper writes about the unusual vandalism at the home, several confess to spending the night there. The two friends realize that a sock with Abby's name on it was left behind and could tie Hutch and Abby to the scene of the crime at the house.

ACTIVITIES

Give Me Five

Mention to the students that Hutch and Abby probably felt nervous and anxious when they discovered they had left evidence that could link them to the crime at the model home. Point out that it was normal for the two to have "roller coaster" feelings and that it is normal for students to have their own ups and downs about feelings. As an activity, ask the students to give you five (show five fingers in hand held up) if they feel good. Invite students to give you four fingers if they feel OK, three fingers if they feel bad, etc. Follow these steps for the "Five-Minute Give Me Five" activity. The purpose of this activity is for students to realize that it is OK to be friendly and to talk about how they feel (and why). You will want them to notice if any of their feelings change after being around another person who could become a new friend.

- Ask the students who held up five fingers and two fingers to go to the right side of the room. The members of one group should pair up with members of the other group.

- Have the students who held up four fingers and three fingers go to the left side of the room and pair up in the same way.
- Let them all know it is OK to be friendly and to talk about how they feel and why during this "Give Me Five" activity. Set a time limit of five minutes for conversation.
- Back in the whole group, invite volunteers to tell how their feelings changed when around another person who could become a new friend.

Responsibilities

Have the students imagine that they were friends of Hutch and Abby and told Hutch a secret and that he told it to Abby and some other people. Discuss the feelings they had when they discovered the secret had been revealed. Talk about the following with students and ask them to respond individually in their journals:

- How would you feel if Hutch told your secret?
- Would you tell Hutch how you feel?
- What would you say to Hutch?
- Do you think keeping a secret is a friend's responsibility?
- What other responsibilities do you think friends have?
- What responsibilities related to friendship do you take on that make others trust you?
- How do you know when someone trusts you?

Respect

Discuss the implication in the story that Abby and Hutch respect one another. Ask the students to select one friend they respect and have them write a brief account of what the friend first did or what they first noticed about the friend that earned their respect. After the students have written their accounts, ask them to read them aloud and analyze them in small groups. To start the analysis, have the students list the qualities of their friends on the board, a chart, or an overhead transparency. Have them identify what the friends have in common. The group analysis, written by a volunteer, can include one paragraph that describes what the friends they respect have in common and a second paragraph that describes what the students learned about themselves from this friendship analysis activity.

Showing Respect

With the students, prepare a list of ways to show respect for others. Have the students make a mark every time they show respect, i.e., saying "please" and "thank you" and "may I" and so on. Engage the students in writing a closing sentence on the list about how they felt while showing respect for others and how others treated them in return.

Author as Friend

Read a book from the "Community, Neighborhood, and School Friendships" section of the bibliography for grades 4–8 at the back of this book. Discuss the book, the author's background from a resource such as "Something About the Author," and the writer's style of writing. Ask the students to make a list of qualities based on the information that might make the author a friend of theirs. If appropriate, engage the students in writing a friendly letter to the author in care of the publisher.

Caring Students

Discuss things the students can do with friends (new and old) to give something back to their neighborhood or community. How can they develop new friendships and help others in the schools, local hospitals, medical clinics, dentist offices, senior citizens homes, and neighborhood health organizations? What do they think of the idea of getting school credit for the hours they contribute helping out in the community?

Book 5.9   *The Potato Man* (179)

Ages:	9–10
Heritage:	European American
Goals:	To recognize a kind/unkind statement
	To show appreciation for an individual's uniqueness
	To write an original short story about a community member's contributions
	To demonstrate ways to show friendship to others
	To suggest and implement friendly alternatives for unfriendly actions

To write suggestions for improving relations with others
To suggest ways to sit down with others, listen and talk
    to them, and ask what they feel and why
To recognize ways people deal with anger
Materials: Copy of *The Potato Man* (179), chart paper, writing
    paper for short stories

BOOK NOTES

In *The Potato Man* (Orchard Books, 1991), written by Megan McDonald and illustrated by Ted Lewin, Grandpa tells stories to his grandchildren about a fruit and vegetable seller driving a horse-drawn wagon in his childhood community. After a confrontational beginning, Grandpa recalls he learned to appreciate the seller.

ACTIVITIES

Appearance

Grandpa tells his grandchildren that when he first caught sight of the Potato Man, the fruit and vegetable seller in his childhood neighborhood, he thought the man's face was as lumpy as a potato itself. Ask the students to consider the remark as a kind/unkind statement. Invite them to substitute other comparisons that are more appreciative of individual uniqueness. *Examples:* The Potato Man's face looked as comfortable as a favorite pillow. The Potato Man was as_____.
Write the suggestions on a chart for display in the room.

Language

Grandpa tells his grandchildren that the Potato Man loudly yelled his call, "Abba-no-potato-man" in the neighborhood and that's why the students named him the Potato Man. Invite the students to think about how they could have found out the man's legal name and learned about some of his community contributions. (In the story, the children's mother explains that his name was Mr. Angelo and he had lost his right eye fighting in the Great War.) In what ways could the students have met Mr. Angelo and become better acquainted with him? Have the students write an original, brief story and title about how they think Mr. Angelo might have contributed in the Great War.

Actions

Grandpa tells his grandchildren that some of the children in the neighborhood yelled at Mr. Angelo when he came around and chased his wagon. Some local boys threw cinders at the back of the wagon. When some potatoes fell off the wagon, grandpa and another boy took them and roasted them. Mr. Angelo saw the boys and told their parents, and the boys were punished. At the end of the fruit and vegetable season, when the first light snow was falling, the Potato Man returns and gives Grandpa a round, red pomegranate, all nice and shiny, and tells him Merry Christmas. Ask the students what meaning the gift had. What action could Grandpa take in response? Instead of Mr. Angelo performing an act of friendship first, what could the boys have done to show friendship first? Invite the students to tell of times when they were the first ones (last ones) to show friendship. Challenge them to be the first ones to show friendship in at least one situation during the upcoming week and encourage them to report what was done back to the group.

Alternatives

Have the students suggest the unfriendly actions of the young boys toward the Potato Man in the story and list them on the board. Have students suggest friendly alternative behaviors and list them on the board:

Actions of Boys	Friendly Alternatives
a. Yelled at Mr. Angelo when he came around	a.
b. Chased his wagon	b.
c. Threw objects at the wagon	c.
d. Took produce	d.

To relate the story to current times, ask the students to write a brief paragraph describing an unfriendly action they saw and include any friendly alternative(s) that would have made the situation better.

Kindness

This is a story about eventual kindness in a historical period, centering on a fruit and vegetable peddler who seemed frightening to the neighborhood students. Invite the students to reflect on situations in which someone seemed frightening to them and to suggest acts of kindness that might make the situation less threatening. Invite them to act kindly in a seemingly frightening situation, if it arises.

The Man's Return

Grandpa told his grandchildren that the Potato Man returned the next spring and every spring after that for as long as he could remember growing up on his neighborhood street. The relationship improved between the students and the peddler, and Grandpa even bought the biggest pumpkin ever seen from Mr. Angelo. Invite the students to write their own suggestions for improving relations with the Potato Man. What could they have done if they had been there?

Sit-Down Talker

With students ages 13–14, discuss excerpts from *Crews* (Harcourt Brace, 1993) by Maria Hinojosa, with photographs by German Perex. In the book, Hinojosa recorded talks with gang (crew) members who deal with street violence in today's environment. During the conversations, some crew members said they wanted someone who would sit down and talk to them, someone who will ask what they feel and why, and someone who would listen to them, no matter what the answers were. What suggestions do the students have that might fulfill the crew members' requests?

Anger

With students, watch a video about ways to cope with anger such as *Anger: You Can Handle It* (Sunburst Communications, 1995,[1] grades 7–8). While watching the video, ask the students to look and listen for constructive ways to deal with anger, as expressed by an African American teen. If appropriate, divide the students into three groups and ask each to focus on a specific segment of the video. In the segment titled "Triggers," have a group listen for examples of how people react to different triggers; for the segment titled "Anger Styles," have a second group listen for various ways people deal with anger; for the segment "Taking Action," have the third group listen for specific suggestions for dealing with anger. After seeing the video, have members from each group tell what they learned about dealing with

---

[1] 39 Washington Ave., Pleasantville, NY 10570.

anger that, if mastered, would free them to make more new friends in their lives.

Crews

With students ages 13–14, discuss additional excerpts from *Crews* dealing with violence on the streets and ask them what they think has changed. In her recorded talks with gang members, Hinojosa's conversations revealed that, in some areas, there were no street groups called gangs—they were called crews and posses. Discuss the need to be aware of others and their beliefs, with questions such as these:

- Do you know any groups of kids who hang out together and call themselves something other than a gang?
- What do you know about crew members who look out for one another so they can get respect on the street?
- What ways are you aware that some groups fight over colors and others over territory?
- Are you aware of crews that become violent to protect what is theirs?
- Do you believe that if you are by yourself in a certain crews' area, chances are you'll get rushed or robbed—that something will happen to you?
- What suggestions do you have related to avoiding dangerous groups?

6 Friendships around the World

Book 6.1 *Arctic Hunter* (216)

Ages:	9–14
Heritage:	Inupiat/Eskimo
Goals:	To recognize that providing for others is a sign of maturity
	To record friendly actions in text and illustrations for a student-published book
	To write free verse poems in two voices
	To compare one's values with the values of others
	To find evidence of the value of friendship in literature
	To role-play an Eskimo song duel
	To write a collaborative paragraph
Materials:	Several copies of *Arctic Hunter* (216); paper and pencils for writing poems; newspapers, travel brochures, and magazines; pages for student-written book; copies of the Inupiat's list of values, called the Ilitqusiat

BOOK NOTES

Arctic Hunter (Holiday House, 1992) is by Diane Hoyt-Goldsmith, with photographs by Lawrence Migdale. It is the story of ten-year-old Reggie, an Inupiat boy who lives with his family above the arctic circle. In the spring, the family journeys across an ice floe to reach their spring camp on Sadie Creek. Reggie goes on a seal hunt and stays in the boat while the men stalk seals on the ice. When a seal comes close to the boat, Reggie seizes the opportunity to capture his first seal. Then, in friendship, Reggie gives his seal to an elderly woman so she can feed her family with its meat during the long cold days of winter in the coming months.

ACTIVITIES

Reggie's Story

Ask the students to work with partners and rewrite Reggie's friendship story in their own words. Additionally, have them locate and cut out illustrations of the story's setting in newspapers, travel brochures, and magazines. Ask them to collaborate on which pictures should be used to accompany their text and where the pictures should be inserted. Have them complete their story versions by placing the illustrations on the pages and composing their own glossary and index, as the author did.

REGGIE'S THOUGHTS

Invite the students to see Reggie as a contemporary of theirs in today's world and ask them to write thoughts from the perspective of Reggie, who sees the seasons and supplies food for his family, and from the perspective of students, who do those same things today. Ask the students to read their two-people reflections aloud to others in pairs. Then, have volunteers read their thoughts aloud to the whole group. Example:

Reggie	*Name of Student*
I am ten years old.	I am _____ years old.
I live above the arctic circle.	I live _____.
Winter days are long and dark.	Winter days are _____.
Summer is always light.	Summer is _____.
I travel on ice floes.	I travel _____.
I captured my first seal.	I _____.
I gave the seal to an elderly friend.	I _____.
(Other by students)	(Other)

Reggie's Values

As a whole group, ask the students to suggest valued qualities of a friend/friendship and list their suggestions on the board. Ask the students to use their list of values as a reference for friendship and return to the story to find evidence of these same values (such as giving food to others) in Reggie's story; then list the page number next to each value.

Eskimo Song Duel

Invite volunteers to role-play an Eskimo song duel—an activity in which words are mightier than swords when a friendship breaks down. In this song duel activity, adapted for the classroom, the students can join with partners as verbal opponents. An aspect of the other's school life, past or present, can be mentioned with the student's permission using humorous words of wrongdoing, mockery, mimicry, dancing, burlesque, or irony. (Note: in an authentic Eskimo song duel, any aspect of the other's life can be seriously attacked with words, insults, taunting, and innuendo.) Each partner in the duel is required to listen to the other's "song" (or narrative tale) of wrongdoing and may respond with their own tale of wrongdoing only when the singer says "break the point." A "break point" occurs when the teller is tired, wants time to think of more words, or has no more to say. Have the students take time to write down some of their humorous ideas about wrongdoing before they begin their word duels and to include where they want to say "break point." Discuss the rules of the duel with the students and ask for volunteers to perform the first duel:

- Each must listen to the other's humorous remarks about wrongdoing without showing anger.
- Each must perform without showing anger.
- A response from the listener can be given only at a stated "break point."
- A duel is performed in front of an audience (usually members of the local Eskimo community).
- The outcome is determined by the audience's response to the songs/ tales, and favors the participant who listened and performed without showing anger. Set a brief time limit in the classroom and, if appropriate, invite the students to give written feedback as part of the audience response.

With the students, analyze the role-playing and have the students suggest reasons why the Eskimos would prefer a song duel to a fistfight as a community custom when a friendship breaks down. What are the benefits of such a custom? What are the drawbacks? Write the students' responses in two columns on the board.

Word Duels

Invite the students to meet with partners to write a collaborative paragraph on why word duels could or could *not* be used at school when friendships break down. Back in the whole group, take a quick survey of the partners to determine those in favor of using word duels and those against. Record the results on the board. Ask volunteers to read their "for and against" paragraphs aloud to the rest of the class.

Turn It Around

Discuss ways the students can turn their life around by developing new friendships, as Reggie did with the elderly woman, and have them reflect on a motto relating to developing new friendships—"Turn it around: Start your right track friendship journey now." Ask for their suggestions for implementing the motto during the next school day/week. In small groups at the end of the day/week, have them describe what actions they took.

Book 6.2   *The Flame of Peace: A Tale of the Aztecs* (219)

Ages:	9–14
Heritage:	Multicultural
Goals:	To relate friendship and peace to other cultures and time periods
	To develop and expand vocabulary through literature
	To research details about friendship in a selected culture
	To participate in an interview
	To suggest and implement ways to build friendships
	To record what life would be like without hostilities
	To recognize cultural heritages in the community
	To show how art can enhance the idea of friendship and peace

Materials: Folk literature entitled *The Flame of Peace: A Tale of the Aztecs* (219), writing paper, world map, opaque projector, board, colored chalk, stars, flags, art materials for dioramas, masks, murals, papier-mâché ingredients, maps, collages

BOOK NOTES

The Flame of Peace (Harper & Row, 1987) is adapted by Deborah Nourse Lattimore. It is a story borrowed from an Aztec myth about young Two Flint of Tenochtitlan, who honors his dead father by going on a far-reaching quest. His goal is to return with a new flame of peace from the hill of Lord Morning Star. On his quest, Two Flint faces the challenges of several demons, including the cloak of forgetfulness in the shape of Lord Smoking Mirror and some chattering bones in the form of Lord and Lady Death. Finally, he reaches the hill and receives a reward of fire from Lord Morning Star. When Two Flint returns home, the flame glows bright in Tenochtitlan to mark an end to fighting and war.

ACTIVITIES

Culture

To help develop the students' further appreciation for the value of peace in this culture, have them research the Aztec culture and pay special attention to details related to friendship in the customs, religion, and rituals.

Good and Bad

After the students have read or heard the myth, ask if they can think of any of the characters in the myth who could be considered "good" and "bad" at the same time. Discuss their opinions about the characters. For example, in what ways could Two Flint of Tenochtitlan be considered both good and bad? Lord Morning Star? The cloak of forgetfulness in the shape of Lord Smoking Mirror? Chattering bones in the form of Lord and Lady Death? Ask the students to document descriptions in the book that would cause the students to consider the character either good or bad. In what ways would they want (not want) Two Flint to be a new friend?

World Myths

Encourage the students to interview their parents, grandparents, other family members or elderly friends to find out where they came from geographically and to determine if any have heard the myth of *The Flame of Peace* or a similar story about putting an end to fighting and to war. Demonstrate how to project a world map on the board with an opaque projector so the students can locate where their relatives are from on the map with colored chalk, stars, flags. Tape mural paper on the board so the world map shows on the paper and have the students outline the world map on the paper. Ask the students to write his or her account of the interview and display it as part of a border around the map.

Myth Heritage

Invite the students to research names representing different cultures in their community through the yellow pages of the local telephone book. Guide their research with questions such as, How many business persons are listed under names that represent Asian Americans, Latino-Hispanic Americans? How many restaurants serving ethnic foods are there? What are the types of ethnic foods listed? How many doctors under the entry "Physicians" in the yellow pages have identifiable ethnic names?

Have the students write a summary of their research findings and describe their conclusions about the contributions of people from different cultural heritages in their community. Ask the students to use their summaries to predict which businesspeople may be linked to the Aztec culture and, thus, may have heard the story of *The Flame of Peace* from friends or relatives. Have the students decide if their findings about the various cultures in their area surprised/did not surprise them. Ask them to describe ways to build friendships with people of different cultural heritages in their community.

Flame of Pax

Discuss with students the meaning of the word "peace" (from the Latin *pax*), which means a pact or agreement. Incorporating the meanings offered by the students, discuss the idea that the flame of peace could symbolize the end to fighting and war through its bright glowing flame. The bright flame could stand for the sunrise of a "new day" and, thus, a new beginning for the people. This could also be a time for quiet harmony and public order and to end hostilities between those who have been at war or in a state of civil disturbances. Invite the students to consider and record (from their point of view) what a day of quiet harmony and public order without hostilities would be like for a fatherless Aztec boy—especially Two Flint of Tenochtitlan. Invite volunteers to read their essay aloud to the group.

Brainstorming

In the myth, Two Flint of Tenochtitlan honored his dead father by going on a far-reaching quest to return with a new flame of peace to mark an end to fighting and war. With the students, consider ways to end "fighting and war" among their peers and record their responses on a graphic web on the board with the words "friendship" and "peace," written in the center. Talk about what can be done to develop new friendships and to make the old friendships last. Draw lines that radiate from the center of the web to such headings as

- What are some of the problems that make finding friends difficult for the students?
- What problems might break up friendships that the students have?
- What can students do to make their friendships last?
- Why do students feel the need for friends and friendships?

World Friendships

Engage the students in a unit of study about the achievements of people worldwide who have been important to the causes of world peace and friendship. Ask them to relate this to their own neighborhood and suggest the names of local peacemakers and peacekeepers who could visit the classroom and talk about the contributions of immigrants to the community in achieving peace and developing friendships.

Art Enhances Friendship

With students, discuss how art can enhance the idea of friendship and peace, e.g., Picasso's *Dove of Peace*. Invite the students to express what they have learned about friendship and peace—perhaps information gained from their research about Aztec culture—in an art form to share with others in the class. Transformations can include covers for reports, dioramas of peacemaking or peacekeeping scenes, masks of noted figures, murals picturing friendships and scenes of peaceful events, papier-mâché figures of people or sculptures of symbols of peace, or collages made of pictures, words, maps, poetry, or small objects for a 3-D textured presentation.

Book 6.3   *The Middle East in Search of Peace* (221)

Ages:	9–14
Heritage:	Multicultural
Goals:	To recognize a mitzvah as a good deed or act of kindness
	To see kindness as an element of friendship
	To see caring contributions as a way of "repairing the world"
	To participate in a "friendship" discussion
	To suggest and implement ways children can keep multicultural friendships going
	To recognize cultural folk tales and fairy tales that emphasize friendship
Materials:	Copy of *The Middle East in Search of Peace* (221), writing paper for note-taking, foods for a Middle Eastern meal, selection of folktales

BOOK NOTES

The Middle East in Search of Peace (Millbrook, 1994), by Cathryn J. Long, is a fair and evenhanded overview of the disputes among the people in the Middle East. The disputes include the role of water and oil, the beginnings of self-rule in places such as Jericho, and the political role of outside governments. The development of the contemporary conflict and the steps that are being taken to achieve peace are discussed. It includes a full-color photograph of the historic handshake between Yitzhak Rabin and Yasir Arafat.

ACTIVITIES

Friendship Discussion

Invite the students to pair up with someone in the group they don't know very well and meet with them as partners in the classroom. Additionally,

- Ask the students to talk and listen to one another to learn something personal about each other's lives—a brief anecdote from the person's life story.
- Hold a face-to-face discussion about their thoughts on friendship and continue listening to begin a friendly relationship.
- Back in the whole group, ask volunteers to talk about meeting as partners. Encourage the students to tell why they chose the partners they did, what it is like to be a member of a particular multicultural group, ways students put themselves in the other's place, and how it felt.
- If appropriate, ask if anything is keeping them from believing the other person's story. What if the life story is true? How would that make you feel? What if your idea of life is wrong? How would you feel? What would the other person's life story mean to you then?

Another's Feelings

Ask the students to think about how they can feel what another person feels; ways they can help a multicultural friendship begin one-on-one; ways one can accept all parts of himself or herself—even the unconscious part that denies the feelings of others; ways they can acknowledge the other person's life story; and ways they can keep the momentum of multicultural friendships going.

Parents

Invite a parent who was born in the Middle East to visit the class to tell about his or her homeland as they remember it. Ask the students to listen for information related to childhood experiences, arriving in the United States, and life in America for a newcomer. Have the students take notes and use them to record a life story of the visitor. Ask them to meet in groups to plan ways to write these stories together.

Friends Eating Together

With the students, plan and prepare a simple meal from a country in the Middle East—perhaps rice and vegetables that represent a particular dish. During the meal, read aloud excerpts from *Eating and Cooking Around the World: Fingers Before Forks,* by Erich Berry (Day, 1994).

Similar Tales, Different Cultures

Ask the students to read a fairy tale that comes from the Middle East, a newcomer's country, or the culture of a classroom visitor that emphasizes friendship in various ways. The following versions of the story of Cinderella exemplify how various cultures treated Cinderella's friendship with others, her godmother's friendliness, the consequences of being unfair toward a family member, and so on.

CHILDREN'S BOOKS ABOUT CINDERELLA

Africa
- Fairman, T. "Omutugwa." In *Bury My Bones But Keep My Words: African Tales for Retelling.* New York: Holt, 1992. Ages 9–12. Africa.
- San Souci, R. D. *Sukey and the Mermaid.* New York: Four Winds, 1992. Ages 9 up. West Africa & Caribbean.

Asia
- Coburn, J. R., adapter with T. C. Lee. *Jouanah: A Hmong Cinderella.* Illustrated by Anne Sibley O'Brien. New York: Shen's, 1996. Ages 5–8. Southeast Asia and Cambodia.
- Louis, Ai-Lang. *Yeh Shen: A Cinderella Story from China.* Ill. by E. Young. New York: Philomel, 1982. Ages 9–10. China.

Vietnam
- Clark, A. N. *In the Land of Small Dragon.* New York: Viking, 1979. Ages 9 up. Vietnam.
- Vuong, L. D. *The Brocaded Slipper and Other Vietnamese Tales.* Reading, Mass.: Addison-Wesley, 1982. Ages 9–11. Vietnam.
- Garland, S. *Song of the Buffalo Boy.* San Diego: Harcourt, Brace Jovanovich, 1992. Ages 12 up. Vietnam.

Europe, England, Ireland
- Climo, S. *The Irish Cinderlad.* Illustrated by L. Krupinski. San Francisco: HarperCollins, 1996. Ages 8 up. Ireland.
- Philip, N. "The Twelve Months." In *Fairy Tales of Eastern Europe.* New York: Clarion, 1992. Ages 9–10. Czechoslovakia.
- Nimmo, J. *The Starlight Cloak.* New York: Dial, 1993. Ages 9–10. Ireland.
- Stell, F. A. *Tattercoats.* New York: Bradbury, 1978. Ages 9 up. England.
- Grimm, The Brothers. *Iron John.* New York: Holiday, 1994. Ages 9–10. Germany.

- Delamare, D. *Cinderella*. San Diego: Green Tiger Press, 1993. Ages 9–11. Russia.
- Afanasyev, A. *Vasilisa the Beautiful*. New York: Macmillan, 1970. Ages 9–10. Russia.
- Mayer, M., reteller. *Baba Yaga and Vasilisa the Brave*. New York: Morrow, 1994. Ages 9–10. Russia.
- Winthrop, E., adapter. *Vasilisa the Beautiful: A Russian Folktale*. San Francisco: HarperCollins, 1990. Ages 9–10. Russia.

Middle East
- Lewis, N., reteller. *Stories From the Arabian Nights*. New York: Holt, 1987. Ages 10 up. Arabia.

Pacific
- De La Paz, M. *Abadeha: The Philippine Cinderella*. San Diego: Pacific Queen Pub., n.d. Ages 9–10. Philippines.

The Americas
- Boucher, C. *Fanny's Dream*. Illustrated by M. Buehner. New York: Dial, 1996. Ages 8–11.
- Cole, B. *Prince Cinders*. New York: Putnam, 1988. Ages 9 up. United States (male Cinderella).
- Davenport Films. *Ashpet: An American Cinderella*. Davenport Films, 1991 (Rt. 1, Box 527, Delaplane, VA 22025). Ages 10 up. United States.
- de Wit, D., ed. "Little Burnt Face." In *The Talking Stone: An Anthology of Native American Tales and Legends*. New York: Greenwillow, 1979. Ages 9–11. United States.
- Haviland, V., ed. "The Indian Cinderella." In *North American Legends*. New York: Collins, 1979. Ages 9–11. United States.
- Hooks, W. H. *Moss Gown*. Clarion, 1987. Ages 9 up. United States.
- Martin, R. *The Rough-Faced Girl*. New York: Putnam Group, 1992. Ages 9 up. United States.
- Murphy, S. R. *Silver Woven in My Hair*. New York: Aladdin, 1992. Ages 9–11. United States.
- Pollock, P. *The Turkey Girl: A Zuni Cinderella Story*. Boston: Little, Brown, 1996. Ages 5–8. United States.
- San Souci, R. D. *The Talking Eggs*. Illustrated by author. New York: Dial, 1989. Ages 9–10. United States.

Students can gain a great deal of information about the value of friendships in other cultures through various versions of "Cinderella." Additionally, they may hear/read a selected tale, get together in writing groups, and write/draw what they learned. If the students prefer to sketch, they can form illustration groups and create pictures to "read" aloud to others. The students also can collect information about places that are important to the cultural group, the special language or vocabulary noted, and the friendship events that reveal the values of those who told the tale. If appropriate, have the students meet in small groups to plan a "reader's theater" presentation of a tale they selected to emphasize the value of friendships in the story.

Celebrations

Have the students in small groups read stories aloud of friendships that are set in a particular country being studied. Engage them in acting out a scene about a friendship set in the selected country. Additionally,

- Invite the students to work independently and research ways that various occasions in a selected country are celebrated.
- Invite the students to work with partners and make a relief map of the country or make a diorama of a scene of friends attending a particular celebration, holiday, or observance in a selected country being studied.
- Ask the students to read poetry about friendships. Engage them in writing an original brief poem about a friend and what his/her friendship means to the writer.

Book 6.4 *On the Wings of Peace* (213)

Ages: 10 up
Heritage: Multicultural
Goals: To recognize various issues related to peace
To commemorate the anniversary of the bombings of Hiroshima and Nagasaki
To acknowledge the dangers of nuclear proliferation
To suggest ways to bring friendship and peace into their lives
To compose a research paper
To keep a log of the research process
To take the persona of a newcomer from another part of the world

Materials: Copy of *On the Wings of Peace* (213); transparency;
              overhead projector; paint, chalks, or colored pens and
              markers for drawings and sketches; photocopied clock face

BOOK NOTES

On the Wings of Peace (Clarion, 1995) is a presentation coordinated by Sheila Hamanaka. The book contains the contributed work of more than 50 artists and authors of children's books that relate to the subject of peace. This coordinated collection commemorates the anniversary of the bombings of Hiroshima and Nagasaki and also discusses the dangers of nuclear proliferation. Royalties are donated to peace organizations.

ACTIVITIES

Illustrations of Peace

Discuss what meaning several selected illustrations in the book have for them. To begin, ask for comments on the illustration by Leo and Diane Dillon showing multicultural children riding on the back of an oversized white dove of peace that carries an olive branch in its beak.

Peace in the World

In this collection, each story and poem is about an aspect of peace. After reading a selection of the students' choice aloud, ask, "What can we do to help achieve peace in our lives?" Ask the students to make suggestions about what they can do to spread peace—perhaps in the world. List their suggestions on a transparency for the overhead projector. Ask them how they could implement their ideas.

Symbols of Peace

Ask the students to creatively interpret a symbol of peace. Some students may want to write poems and short stories about peace; others may want to sculpt symbols of peace; and still others may want to use paint, chalk, or colored pens and markers to prepare drawings and sketches. For another example, some student volunteers can research the topic of the dove and the olive branch as peace symbols and have them report what they learned back to the class.

I Would Like to Know . . .

Ask the students to make a list of three things they want to know related to friendship and peace around the world—e.g., I would like to know how a friend my age in Japan lives with his or her family; what a friend in _____ would be like; how the story of the dove as a symbol of peace started.

Introduce the students to the idea of using a "research" clock, a photocopied clock face that identifies the steps in writing an "I Would Like to Know . . ." paper. The clock face can become a log for the students to record dated entries describing the process they are involved in at particular times—all culminating at "twelve o'clock." Recording their research process around the face of the clock, the students also can include their notes from research reading or interviewing. A teacher can emphasize that the clock log can become part of the students' final report, if appropriate. The steps in turning the face of the "research clock" into a research log are as follows:

- Stating the question (problem) and reasons the students selected the question (perhaps record this at 1:00)
- Getting acquainted with the benefits of using reference materials and listing ways to get information through teacher talks, librarian demonstrations, visits to the library, etc. (perhaps record this at 2:00 and 3:00)
- Recording dated entries of the process the students are involved in (perhaps record this at 4:00, 5:00 and 6:00)
- Reading notes, planning a written presentation in paragraphs, and including an alternative way of presenting the information in an interesting manner (perhaps record this at 7:00, 8:00, and 9:00)
- Writing a summary (perhaps recorded at 10:00 and 11:00)
- Sharing with others a summary that tells the importance or significance of the study of the questions including personal feelings, ways to use the information in the future, ways the information will lead a student to other inquiries (perhaps recorded at 12:00)

Pretend

Invite the students to pretend to be someone from another part of the world (past or present) who has arrived in the classroom. For instance, how might the new student react to being a friend in today's world? What would they think of the lack of friendship shown on the daily news broadcasts? How would they react to such acts as carjacking, purse snatching, and other hostile acts? Students may write a diary page for the person and include speculation about the person's reactions related to a topic or situation that interests them.

Book 6.5 *People of Peace* (202)

Ages:	10–14
Heritage:	Multicultural
Goals:	To recognize a promoter of peace in the world
	To research life stories of people of peace
	To recognize words related to friendship and peace found in America's governmental documents
	To turn words of peace and friendship into actions
	To participate in an interview
	To create a self-check chart to show what was learned about friendship and peace
Materials:	Copy of *People of Peace* (202), writing paper for interview questions, board and chalk, chart or overhead transparency

BOOK NOTES

People of Peace (Millbrook, 1994) is by Rose Blue and Corinne J. Naden. This book includes biographies of eleven peaceful figures. The life stories include Andrew Carnegie, Woodrow Wilson, Ralph Bunche, Jimmy Carter, Desmond Tutu, Oscar Arias Sanchez, Betty Williams, and others.

ACTIVITIES

Individual Inquiry

Invite the students to further investigate the lives of leaders of peace and friendship. After their inquiries, have students choose at least three interesting events in the peoples' lives related to peace and role-play interviews that might have taken place about the events. Have the students write the questions they would ask before role-playing the interviews and, after, record the interviews into interview stories. The stories can be read aloud, discussed, and placed in a binder on a bookshelf for student reference.

Documents

Read aloud several excerpts from the Declaration of Independence, the Preamble to the Constitution, and the Bill of Rights and have students select two or three phrases that they think relate to the meaning of friendship and peace. Have the students explain what meaning the phrases have for them. Write their words on the board, a chart or overhead transparency. Ask the students what they could do in keeping with the spirit of the phrases to develop friendships in their own lives.

Phrase	*Actions Related to Friendship*
a. Value diversity	a. Cooperatively develop projects to help others
b. Safeguard freedom	b. Speak out when another's freedoms are threatened
c. Contribute to the welfare	c. Cooperatively assist those in need

Ask the students to select one of the actions to implement in their own lives and to explain their choices. Schedule a class meeting to discuss what must be done.

Friendship, 1841

Provide the students with a copy of selected words from a person of peace, such as the following from Ralph Waldo Emerson's essay on friendship (1841), and delete every fifth word. Ask the students to incorporate words that make sense to them in the material. Examples of selected sentences are:

A friend is a person with whom I may be sincere. Before him (her), I may think aloud. I am arrived at last in the presence of a man (woman) so real and equal that I may drop even those undermost garments of dissimulation, courtesy, and second thought, which men never put off, and may deal with him (her) with the simplicity and wholeness with which one chemical atom meets another . . . (A) friend is a sane man who exercises not my ingenuity, but me.

Have the students record sentences with their word choices in a brief friendship essay of their own and below each sentence give examples of ways they could implement the action in the sentence(s). Example:

A friend is a _____ with whom I may be _____.
My actions:

Have the students read the sentences aloud and discuss their actions.

Interviewing

With the students, select an angle for interviewing a person about the topic "People Who Are Peacemakers." One angle might be "People Who Are Peacemakers in Our School." Students could interview people at school who they see as peacemakers—other students, the principal, teachers, secretaries, coaches, librarians, maintenance people, cooks, the nurse, bus drivers, and so on. Engage the students in the following:

- Have the students list the people they would like to interview and the questions they want to ask.
- Make a tape recorder available so students can ask their questions on tape and listen to their questioning techniques as they play it back. Encourage the students to revise their questions after taping.
- Have the students make arrangements for the interviews.
- Further interest the students in the idea of interviewing by reading aloud excerpts from *Anastasia's Chosen Career* (1987) by Lois Lowry.
- Conduct the interviews with note-taking materials.
- Using their notes, have the students write their interview stories. Encourage them to mention at least one interesting event in the interviewee's life. Have them trade stories with another student to elicit feedback about the writing.
- Have them consider feedback about the story and make revisions. Place revisions in a three-ring binder entitled "Interviews with Peacemakers" and make the stories available for student reading and browsing.

Self-Check

Engage the students in compiling self-check charts (which can be placed in a portfolio) to show what they learned about friendship and peace from their interviews with people who are peacemakers.

Self-Check Chart for Interviews
✔ for satisfactory progress

_____ I listed the names of people I would like to interview.

_____ I wrote the questions I wanted to ask.

_____ I asked my questions on tape.

_____ I listened to my questioning techniques and played back the tape.

_____ I made revisions to my questions after taping.

_____ I made arrangements with the interviewee for the interview.

_____ I used note-taking materials.

_____ I wrote an interview story.

_____ I mentioned at least one interesting event in the interviewee's life.

_____ I traded stories with another student to elicit feedback about the writing.

_____ I considered feedback about the interview story and made revisions.

_____ I placed my revision in a three-ring binder entitled "Interviews with Peacemakers" so my story could be read by others.

Observe the students and keep anecdotal records. Review the students' self-check charts to document the progress of those who practiced interviewing techniques.

Book 6.6   *The Sleeping Lady* (205)

Ages:	9–14
Heritage:	Alaskan
Goals:	To retell a modern day folk legend of war and peace
	To recognize an explanation for snowfall and the formation of Mount Susitna
	To recognize the value of living in harmony with nature and one another
	To recognize the value of peace, love, and the consequences of war
	To write free verse poems
	To participate in conflict resolution
	To document evidence of the values of peace in literature
Materials:	Several copies of *The Sleeping Lady* (205), paper and pencils for writing poems, newspapers, travel brochures, magazines, pages for student-written book

BOOK NOTES

The Sleeping Lady (Alaska Northwest Books, 1994) is retold by Ann Dixon, with illustrations by Elizabeth Johns. It explains Alaska's first snowfall and the formation of Mount Susitna, known in south central Alaska as "The Sleeping Lady." In a village, peace-loving prehistoric giants face the dilemma of how to confront a group of attacking warriors who threaten their homes. The consequences of war are contrasted with peace and love. It seems that long ago, peaceful prehistoric giants lived together in their village in harmony with nature and one another. When warriors appear, the giants must cooperate together to confront the warriors who threaten their homes and peaceful ways. Related to this confrontation is the "how and why" part of the tale that explains Alaska's first snowfall and how Mount Susitna was formed.

ACTIVITIES

How and Why

Reread aloud the part of the legend that explains the reasons for Alaska's first snowfall and have students explain in their own words how Mount Susitna was formed and later became known as "The Sleeping Lady."

Harmony

Reread the entire legend aloud and ask the students to listen for examples of living together in harmony. Have them write a brief paragraph with partners about one of the following aspects of the story and what it means to them: cooperation, decision making, living together in harmony, love, peace, or war. Have the partners take turns reading their paragraphs aloud to the whole group.

Giants vs. Warriors

Have the students divide into groups of six or eight. Half the students in the group can take the roles of the peace-loving giants and the other half can take the roles of the approaching warriors. The two subgroups can create a brief drama scene together. Ask the subgroups to consider the following situation for creative drama:

> In a prehistoric village in Alaska, one of the giants returned from a long walk
> and said that he had seen a large group of warriors heading toward the

giants' homes. The warriors appear at the top of a nearby hill and make threatening motions. Four warriors approach the giants. Four giants walk out to meet the warriors. The warriors tell what they want and their reasons for confronting the giants in a hostile way. The giants tell how they have overcome these problems in their peaceful community and tell the warriors their favorite "giant" sayings (such as, "A friend who's big is a friend indeed) and talk about the peace-loving behaviors or rules they have in their lives.

Have the two subgroups meet to decide what to say and to create the scene. Have the subgroups trade roles and re-create another scene so both groups can play the roles of the giants. Ask for groups to volunteer to present their scenes to the whole class.

Ask the students to think of a fight they had with one of their friends. What was it about? How was it resolved? In contrast, ask them to think of a time when they had fun with one of their friends. From these two situations, which friend do you remember the best and why? Which time do you remember the best and why?

Rewrite the Story

Ask the students to work with partners and rewrite the story of the Sleeping Lady—especially the resolution of the conflict—in their own words. Have them locate and cut out illustrations that show an Alaskan setting from discarded newspapers, travel brochures, and magazines. Furthermore, ask the students to collaborate on which pictures should be used to accompany their text and where the pictures should be inserted. Have them complete their versions by placing the illustrations on the pages as the illustrator did.

Dialogue

Invite the students to imagine one of the peace-loving giants as a contemporary of theirs in today's world and ask them to write some dialogue to show differences between the way the giant might perceive peace, love, the consequences of war, and the importance of living in harmony with one another and in the way the students see those same things today. Have two columns (one for giant and one for student) and write under each phrases like "Peace is _____" and "Consequences of war are _____."

Peaceful Values

Ask the students to dictate or write a list of the peaceful giants' values as a reference list and return to the story to find evidence of those values.

Next, ask the students to return to the list and check any of the giants' values that are similar to their own.

Book 6.7   *Summer of My German Soldier* (211)

Ages:	13 up
Heritage:	European American/German
Goals:	To recognize a good deed or act of kindness
	To see kindness and compassion as elements of friendship and love through literature, videos, and films
	To engage in a self-selected topic of inquiry related to friendship
Materials:	Copy of *Summer of My German Soldier* (211), schedule for time line; selection of friendship novels; and writing paper for taking notes; reflection writing, analysis, compare-and-contrast paragraphs, creative writing, quick writes, and synopsis writing

BOOK NOTES

Summer of My German Soldier (Kar-Ben, 1993) is written by Bette Greene. In a small town in Arkansas, Patty Bergen, the twelve-year-old daughter of a department store owner, sees herself as awkward. Her parents fight and are mean to Patty. The Bergens' black cook, however, loves Patty and cares for her. Living in a compassionless home, Patty gives what she lacks—compassion—to Anton, a good-looking, well-educated German prisoner of war who lives in a prison camp near town and shops at her father's store. A friendship develops. When she later sees him running down the railroad tracks, she offers him the safety of a special hide-out room over the garage. When Anton is captured, Patty's part in his escape is discovered. She is arrested, sent to reform school, and thinks ahead of the time when she will be released and can leave her family.

ACTIVITIES

Friendship Mini-Unit

Discuss friendship as a topic of a mini-unit to be studied and discuss various genres (novel, play, biography, short story, essay, poetry) and writing styles or readings related to the topic. Mention that the topic can cross into other areas of the curriculum—i.e., English, social science, science, art, and so on. Show the students a graphic web of the friendship mini-unit on the board and then engage the students in joint decision making about the following:

- With students, decide on a time line for the unit (3 weeks, 6 weeks, etc.). Introduce an appropriate novel as the core reading for the friendship unit and assign parts to be read outside of class.
- As a whole group, introduce the shorter pieces of reading using different reading approaches such as read-arounds, individual silent reading, and student choice. For example, "A Rose for Emily" by William Faulkner could be selected for a group read-around or independent reading.

Videos and Films

Ask the students to take notes about videos and films they see in the study such as *Love Story, Barefoot in the Park,* or *Harold and Maude,* or ask them to identify music they relate to the theme of friendship. The students can use their notes to engage in reflection writing, analysis, compare-and-contrast paragraphs, creative writing, quick writes, and synopsis writing about friendship and love.

Inquiry

Ask the students to select a topic of inquiry, such as courtship/marriage celebrations in other cultures, historical romances or how some romances affected political issues, views of courtship/romance, or poetry on friendship/love/romance.

Illustrations

Have the students collect illustrations from newspapers, magazines, brochures, and catalogs that reflect the theme of friendship/love/romance and display them in the room.

Music Videos, Speakers, Reader's Theater

Engage the students in one or more of the following related activities:

- Have the students debate the pluses and minuses of love/romance/friendship music videos shown on television.

- Invite guest speakers, perhaps a local romance writer, to the class.
- Have the students read selected scenes from *Our Town* by Thornton Wilder or *Antigone* by Sophocles as "reader's theater" pieces.
- Assign independent reading from which students can select according to their interests. Have them report back in small groups to tell what they learned about love and friendship from their reading in the mini-unit. Choices could include: *Buried Alive: The Elements of Love* (Fletcher), *The Color Purple* (Walker), *Gone with the Wind* (Mitchell), *A Patch of Blue* (Kata) and *The Sound of Waves* (Mishima).

Book 6.8   *Tell Me a Mitzvah: Little and Big Ways to Repair the World* (226)

Ages:	9–11
Heritage:	Jewish/multicultural
Goals:	To recognize a mitzvah as a good deed or act of kindness
	To see kindness as an element of friendship
	To see caring contributions as "repairing the world"
	To develop and expand vocabulary related to literature
	To suggest and implement acts of kindness
	To take part in compromise — agreeing on answers
	To write a paragraph about kindness and friendship for a class notebook
Materials:	Copy of *Tell Me a Mitzvah: Little and Big Ways to Repair the World* (226), board, chalk, transparency, overhead projector, writing paper

BOOK NOTES

Tell Me a Mitzvah: Little and Big Ways to Repair the World (Kar-Ben, 1993) is written by Danny Siegel and illustrated by Judith Friedman. The book profiles twelve people who have made kind contributions toward "repairing the world," or *Tikkun Olam*. They are common people performing uncommon acts: a woman who collects and distributes shoes to those who need them, a man who gathers pennies for the homeless, and some farmers who give part of their harvest to feed the hungry. Yiddish and Hebrew terms are included in the text.

ACTIVITIES

Meaning of Kindness

Write the word *kindness* in the center of the board and ask students to suggest as many words as they can that relate to kindness to make a word web on the board. Write their suggestions on the board around the word in the center.

Ask the students to suggest actions they have seen or heard about that relate to the words on the board. To compare the students' suggestions, read aloud the dictionary definition of kindness. Have students copy the word web in their friendship journals and, near each key word, write the kind and friendly actions they have performed that relate to the word.

What Can I Do?

In *Tell Me a Mitzvah,* each story is about a common person performing an uncommon act of kindness and is followed by a page titled, "What Can I Do?" Ask the students to give their own specific suggestions for what they can do to spread kindness in the world. List their suggestions on a transparency for the overhead projector. Ask them to identify which ones they could implement and challenge them to do an act of kindness during the school day/week.

Uncommon Kindness

Ask the students about some of the common people they know who have performed uncommon acts of kindness. List the names on a transparency for the overhead projector. How can these people be recognized by the students? Record the students' suggestions. Who can follow in the footsteps of these kind people?

Kindness Record

Ask the students to record daily some of the kind acts they have performed or have seen or heard were performed by others. Elicit the students' suggestions daily and, at the end of the week, tally the actual number of acts of kindness the students have offered. Invite them to suggest ways they can increase that number.

Agreeing on Answers

With the students in small groups, ask them to select a facilitator (leader) and a scribe (recorder). Distribute copies of questions for a group discussion in an informal buzz group. Sample questions are:

- In what ways could you live without friends or kindness in your life?
- Why do you think people feel the need to have friends or to be friends? To be kind to others?
- What are some of the problems that make being kind to others difficult? That make finding a friend/being a friend difficult?
- What are some of the actions that could break up a friendship?
- When would you want to make a friendship last?
- What could you do to make a friendship last?

Have the students in groups read the questions, individually write a response to each one, then discuss each question in turn. Encourage the group to agree on one answer for each question and have the scribe write the group answer.

Back in the whole group, ask each group's facilitator (leader) to read each answer for each question and record the information on the board. After the answers have been announced, have each student write a paragraph about what kindness and friendship mean to him or her.

Have the students take their paragraphs back to the small groups and read them aloud. Group members should be encouraged to tell which part of the writing they liked best and make one suggestion for strengthening the writing of the paragraph. Have the students rewrite their paragraphs and place their revised work in a class notebook. Put the notebook in an area where class members can read it.

Glossary

Ask the students who know the Yiddish and Hebrew terms in the book to work together and prepare a glossary of the terms to make the book more user friendly to non-Jewish children.

Middle East Study

Focus on the Middle East and Middle Eastern Americans by writing the words *Middle East* in the center of the writing board and asking the students to dictate all the words that he or she relate to the term. Write their suggestions in a graphic web format. After preparing the web as a group, have the students prepare a web individually. Ask them to keep the web so they can examine it at the end of the study to see what more they have learned. Engage students in the following:

- Ask students to decorate the room by locating folktales, fiction, reference books, maps, pictures, and other items of interest related to the Middle East. Take time to use the materials as focal points in discussion.
- Read aloud a folktale from the Middle East. After hearing this story, ask the students to relate any information about the Middle East that they gained from the story. Record their contributions on a class chart or on the board. Emphasize acts and words of friendship and peace.
- Invite the students to a Middle East activity center, where students can study concepts from social studies, math, and literature through task cards that involve students in such activities as:
  (1) Writing letters to one another as friendship pals to share information about people, objects, and places of interest in the area being studied. Enclosures in the letters can include:
     - Reproducing the area's flags with paper or cloth
     - Drawing posters to advertise facts about the area—perhaps the best known historical figure, architectural structure, geographic feature, tree, flower, bird, food, coat of arms, flag, and so on
     - Developing a "line of time" to show the history of the area beginning with its first habitants
     - Writing a book report about a book set in some part of the area being studied
     - Sketching a map of a selected area with cities, roads, rivers, etc.
     - A summary of a favorite fairy tale from the area
  (2) Working with partners to write original tales. After the students have written their tales, have them "published" in a book. Place the book in an area where others can read it.

III Bibliography

All humanity is one undivided and indivisible family.
—Mahatma Gandhi

7 More Multicultural Friendship Stories for Children Ages 5–8

FAMILY FRIENDSHIPS

1. Adoff, Arnold (1973). *Black Is Brown Is Tan*. New York: HarperCollins. Ages 6–9. Heritage: Multiethnic.

This is a story, poetically told, about a loving biracial family and the caring grandmothers, both maternal and paternal, who share happy family activities with their two grandchildren and the parents, a black mother and white father.

2. Bogart, Jo Ellen (1996). *Gifts*. Illustrated by Barbara Reid. New York: Scholastic. Ages 5–7. Heritage: European American.

This story shows the warm relationship between a granddaughter and her grandmother as the years go by. Grandmother travels to various places and offers to bring back gifts for her granddaughter each time. Her granddaughter asks for imaginative items, such as a piece of the sky, a memory, a rainbow to wear, and so on. The story is filled with smiles and hugs between the two.

3. Bunting, Eve (1994). *A Day's Work*. Illustrated by Ronald Himler. New York: Clarion. Ages 5–8. Heritage: Mexican American.

Bunting gives readers an intergenerational friendship story about a grandson's testimonial to his grandfather, newly arrived from Mexico to live with his daughter and her son. The grandson, Francisco, believes his grandfather, Abuelo, is a fine man and convinces an employer to hire him, even though his grandfather doesn't know English yet.

4. Bunting, Eve (1989). *The Wednesday Surprise*. New York: Clarion. Ages 5–8. Heritage: African American.

Offering a warm happy mood, this story is about Anna, a young girl, and her grandmother as they both work on a present for Dad's birthday. This is a present

177

that only the two of them can give to Dad: Anna teaches Grandmother to read. Creatively, the two are persistent and persevere each day as they work together, and Grandmother develops her new reading skills at Anna's instruction. They both surprise the girl's father when Grandmother reads for Dad for his birthday.

5. Byars, Betsy (1996). *My Brother, Ant*. Illustrated by Marc Simont. New York: Viking. Ages 5–8. Heritage: European American.

A caring older brother describes the ways that his younger brother, Ant (short for Anthony), a preschooler, is a pest. Young Ant wants his brother to get rid of a monster under the bed, to read "The Three Little Pigs," and to help him write a thank you note to Santa six months late. In return, Ant later causes his brother some anxiety when he adds his own creative spelling to his brother's homework.

6. Catalanotto, Peter (1995). *The Painter*. Illustrated by the author. New York: Orchard. Ages 5–7. Heritage: European American.

A young girl narrates this story about the warm father-daughter relationship in her loving family. The girl's father, an artist, shows how he cares for her as they cook breakfast together, read the comics in the daily paper, and dance to their favorite music. At times, the father is busy in his studio, and the girl leaves him alone to do his work. Later, the girl joins him at the end of the day and paints as he does. The final pages show her artwork, with her comments on being a painter, too.

7. Cazet, Denys (1995). *Dancing*. Illustrated by the author. Musical score by Craig Bond. New York: Orchard. Ages 5–7. Heritage: European American.

The warm father-son relationship in this story helps a young boy overcome his jealous emotions about his new baby brother. When he leaves the house in anger, his father joins him outside on the front steps. His father sings a song about the boy, the new baby, and the moon, to reassure the boy he is still loved. His musical analogy is that the moon shares the sky with the stars (even a rising star that resembles a new baby's face) and all the heavenly bodies are together as they dance through the sky. Singing the song, the boy and his father also dance under the moon and the starlit heavens. Music for the song is included.

8. Coerr, Eleanor (1986). *The Josefina Story Quilt*. New York: Harper & Row. Ages 5–8. Heritage: European American.

Coerr's story describes how family events can be memorialized with a quilt. On a covered wagon trip, a young girl, Faith, wants to take along her pet hen, Josefina. Faith's father sets up the condition that the pet hen would have to go if she caused trouble. Well, Josefina does cause some trouble, but, fortunately, she also helps — she cackles and warns the family of robbers and is hailed as a feathered heroine. When Josefina dies of old age, Faith creates a quilt that illustrates the hen's story.

9. Flournoy, Valerie (1985). *The Patchwork Quilt*. New York: Dial. Ages 5–8. Heritage: African American.

In a contemporary setting, this story shows the value in making a quilt, an activity that brings the intergenerational members of an African American family together as they recall the events related to the fabric remnants. As they assemble the pieces, the family sees that the completed quilt tells their family's "history." Making the quilt together enabled the family members to show one another love and respect for one another.

10. Galbraith, Kathryn O. (1995). *Holding onto Sunday*. Illustrated by Michael Hays. New York: McElderry, Simon & Schuster. Ages 5–7. Heritage: African American.

Galbraith's chaptered story is about the warm relationship between Jemma, a young girl, and her father. Sunday, whatever the weather, is considered a special day for the two of them to share experiences together. One rainy Sunday, Jemma and her father visit the Natural History Museum for their own version of a dinosaur hunt. While touring the exhibits, Jemma is startled by the fierce expression of the tyrannosaurus rex and her father reassures her with a comforting hug. At the end of the outing at the museum, they return home, where Jemma's grandmother waits for them.

11. Goble, Paul, reteller (1988). *Her Seven Brothers*. Illustrated by the reteller. New York: Bradbury. Ages 7–8. Heritage: Native American/folk literature.

A Cheyenne girl journeys northward to the land of pines to find seven brothers she has never seen. She finds her brothers' tepee, gives them a gift of clothing, and is taken in and cared for by them. One day, the chief of the Buffalo nation asks for the girl's hand in marriage but the brothers refuse to let her go. Rebuffed, the chief threatens to return with his Buffalo people and kill them. To avoid the threatening Buffalo stampede and to save his siblings, the youngest brother shoots an arrow in the air and makes a pine tree appear. As the tree magically grows upward, the girl and her brothers climb it. The youngest brother shoots arrow after arrow into the sky so they all can climb upward away from danger, toward the stars. When they jump down onto the prairies of the sky, they form the Big Dipper, and to this day, one tiny star represents the smallest brother, who always walks near his sister.

12. Goldin, Barbara Diamond (1995). *Night Lights*. Illustrated by Louise August. New York: Harcourt Brace. Ages 5–6. Heritage: European/Jewish.

An older sister and younger brother spend the night in the family's sukkah, a small temporary hut covered with tree branches that is built during the Jewish fall harvest festival in celebration of Sukkot. The two children help their parents decorate the hut and eat a family meal inside of it. When the children get ready for bed, Daniel has trouble sleeping because he hears unfamiliar sounds during the night. Lovingly, his sister reassures him and tells him that the light of the moon and stars can be his night-light.

13. Guback, Georgia (1994). *Luka's Quilt*. New York: Greenwillow. Ages 6–8. Heritage: Hawaiian American.

This story highlights intergenerational love and friendship. Luka and her grandmother have quarreled because the traditional plain Hawaiian quilt that her grandmother is making for her does not have the large beautiful flowers that Luka wanted. After a sulking time, they declare a truce, and Luka returns to make flower leis and Luka's grandmother makes a colorful fabric lei to help heal Luka's hurt feelings.

14. Howard, Elizabeth Fitzgerald (1991). *Aunt Flossie's Hats and Crab Cakes*. Illustrated by James Ransome. New York: Houghton Mifflin. Ages 5–8. Heritage: African American.

Intergenerational relationships and traditions are the focus of this story about an extended African American family. Every Sunday, Aunt Flossie entertains her two nieces by letting them look through her wondrous hats. As the girls anticipate what's to come, their aunt tells them a story about each hat, with the tale (some humorous) placed in a different setting — including a Baltimore fire, a postwar parade, and a nearby pond.

15. James, Betsy (1995). *Blow Away Soon*. Illustrated by Anna Vojtech. New York: The Putnam Group. Ages 5–7. Heritage: Native American.

The warm friendship between young Sophie and Nana, her grandmother, is the focus of this story. When Sophie says she doesn't like the wind blowing at night in the desert, her grandmother promises to help her. The next day, the two walk together along the cliffs and in the desert canyons so Sophie can collect treasures from the land (sand, grass, a feather, an ancient shell). She helps her grandmother build a small stone altar (a place to offer treasures to the wind) that her grandmother calls the blow-away-soon. The two talk about how the wind helps the life cycle of every living thing, and Sophie's relationship with her grandmother deepens as she begins to appreciate how nature changes.

16. Jeffers, Susan, reteller (1983). *Hiawatha*. Illustrated by the reteller. New York: Dial. Ages 6–9. Heritage: Native American.

This is a story of intergenerational love and friendship. It is based on stories of an actual Onondaga chief and is woven together with other tales from Indian folklore found in Henry Wadsworth Longfellow's poem, "The Song of Hiawatha," written in 1855. Near the shores of Gitche Gumee, Hiawatha is raised by his loving grandmother, Nokomis, daughter of the moon, and is always watched over by his dead mother's spirit. Nokomis nurtures him and teaches him many things about nature. He learns about every bird and beast, their language, their names, and their secrets. He talks with the beasts when he meets them and calls them Hiawatha's brothers.

17. Johnson, Tony (1985). *The Quilt Story*. New York: The Putnam Group. Ages 6–7. Heritage: European American.

Abigail, a small pioneer girl, receives a lovely quilt made for her by her mother. Throughout her life, Abigail takes the quilt with her as she travels and treasures it wherever she goes. When Abigail marries, she keeps the quilt and gives it to her little girl. Abigail's daughter sits on her mother's lap, comforted by the quilt just as Abigail was comforted by the quilt on her mother's lap years earlier.

18. Jones, Rebecca C. (1995). *Great Aunt Martha*. Illustrated by Shelley Jackson. New York: E. P. Dutton. Ages 5–8. Heritage: European American.

To get ready for a visit by her Great Aunt Martha, a young girl must pick up her toys and take a bath. She notices some changes going on—that the family shops for special food, such as prune juice, fish, and spinach, instead of pizza and pretzels. When Aunt Martha arrives, the girl says the conversations are about people she doesn't know. Family life changes still further when Aunt Martha needs her rest and everyone must be quiet. There is no television, no music, and the dog is put in the garage when it barks. The next day, however, the early morning quiet is disturbed by music, and the family finds Aunt Martha dancing in her sneakers, keeping time with her cane, and asking for her favorite—pizza.

19. Jossee, Barbara M. (1995). *Snow Day*. Illustrated by Jennifer Plecas. New York: Clarion. Ages 6–8. Heritage: European American.

This is a story of an active young boy who goes outside early in the morning to play in the snow drifts. His dog and the other family members join him for some snow-time fun, which leads to a snow fight. Later, the parents, the children, and Zippy the dog go inside to wrap up in blankets and get warm. They all enjoy a drink of hot chocolate before a warm fire.

20. Kinsey-Warnock, Natalie (1989). *The Canada Geese Quilt*. New York: Cobblehill/E. P. Dutton. Ages 7–8. Heritage: European American.

Kinsey-Warnock offers a theme about a grandmother's determination to live in this extended family story. In Vermont, a granddaughter sketches the wild geese flying overhead, and the geese become kindred spirits to her ailing grandmother and influence her grandmother's will to live.

21. Kroll, Virginia (1995). *Sweet Magnolia*. Illustrated by Laura Jacques. Watertown, MA: Charlesbridge. Ages 6–8. Heritage: European American.

Denise visits her grandmother, a wildlife activist for creatures in the Louisiana bayou. There is a warm and affectionate relationship between the two as they explore the swamps and its wildlife and enjoy the taste of Cajun food. After Denise rescues a small bird, names it, and cares for it, she learns how hard it is to return a loved creature back to the wild.

22. Kurtz, Shirley (1991). *The Boy and the Quilt*. New York: Good Books. Ages 5–6. Heritage: European American.

Kurtz's story is about a young boy who sees that his sister and mother are going to make a quilt, and his mother tells him that he can help, too. The boy considers his contribution to the family project very important. He claims ownership of the family's quilt. The boy says that it's *his* quilt now, and the story ends with instructions about how to make a simple quilt with a child.

23. Lagercrantz, Rose and Samuel Lagercrantz (1984). *Brave Little Pete of Geranium Street*. Illustrated by the authors. New York: Greenwillow. Ages 6–9. Heritage: Multiethnic.

Pete wishes he was big and strong but he is four years old and scared of the bullies who live nearby on Geranium Street. He dreams of standing up to the bullies, who delight in frightening him, and is convinced that a magic cake would make him strong and brave. When his grandma finally brings him one, he takes one bite and then runs after the teasing children. Impressed by his actions, they become friends with Pete and never chase or tease him again.

24. Loredo, Betsy (1995). *Faraway Families*. Illustrated by Monisha Raja. New York: Silver Moon Pr. Ages 7–9. Heritage: Multiethnic.

This collection of short stories focuses on nurturing adults. Each story features a caretaker—a supportive adult who helps a child work through his or her loneliness in a family situation. Additionally, each story includes a child of identifiable ethnicity as the main character who faces a loss or change. As examples, the story situations consider a child's feelings when a loved sibling is away from home, when a family member is left behind, when the family moves, when parents divorce, and when a family relocates to a totally new area.

25. McMillan, Bruce (1995). *Grandfather's Trolley*. Illustrated by the author. New York: Candlewick. Ages 5–7. Heritage: European American.

This is a story about the friendly companionship and love between an elderly man and his granddaughter. Set in the summer in the early 1900s, Grandfather is a trolley motorman and always saves a seat in the last row for his granddaughter. She loves the open-sided car and always rides to the end of the line with him. Of course, on the way back, she sits up front next to him, where the warm wind blows her hair and makes her eyes close tighter.

26. Mahy, Margaret, reteller (1990). *The Seven Chinese Brothers*. Illustrated by Jean and Mou-sien Tseung. New York: Scholastic. Ages 5–8. Heritage: Asian/folk literature.

In this Chinese family, seven brothers look alike but they each have a different power that they use to help one another. In a confrontation with the emperor, each brother is sentenced to a deadly consequence, but is saved by another brother, who takes his place and, with his power, escapes the punishment. For example, when the third brother is sentenced to be beheaded, the fourth brother, who has bones of iron, takes his place and escapes the beheading. When a brother is sentenced to drowning, he is replaced by another who has the ability to drink huge amounts of water and escapes the drowning.

27. Medearis, Angela Shelf (1995). *Annie's Gifts*. Illustrated by Anna Rich. New York: Just Us Books. Ages 5–8. Heritage: African American.

Medearis' story is about the impact of parent reinforcement and support. A young girl, Annie, soon realizes that her natural abilities—her gifts—are different from those of the other family members, but equally important. Everyone in the family loves music and plays a musical instrument, but Annie lacks the ability to play an instrument even though she takes lessons and tries hard. In support of Annie, her parents praise her talent for writing poems and drawing beautiful pictures.

28. Miles, Miska (1971). *Annie and the Old One*. Illustrated by Peter Parnall. Boston: Little Brown. Ages 7–8. Heritage: Native American.

Miles' story is about the natural evolution of destiny, seasons, and time. A young girl, Annie, lives on a Navajo Indian reservation with the Old One, her beloved grandmother, her parents, and a herd of sheep. She learns that when the new rug being woven is completed, her grandmother will go back to Mother Earth—a loss Annie wants to prevent. To keep her grandmother with her longer, Annie resorts to unweaving the rug each night. When she is caught by her grandmother, the two talk, and Annie finally realizes that her grandmother—and other humans—are part of the earth and all things on it.

29. Mills, Claudia (1992). *A Visit to Amy-Claire*. Illustrated by Sheila Hamanaka. New York: Macmillan. Ages 5–7. Heritage: Asian American.

Rachel, a young Asian American, looks forward to a visit to see her older cousin, Amy-Claire. Arriving at Amy-Claire's house, Rachel becomes jealous when she sees her relative as a rival and feels isolated from the older girl. Later when things improve, Rachel sorts out her feelings of rivalry and talks about them with her cousin.

30. Moon, Nicola (1995). *Lucy's Picture*. New York: Dial. Ages 5–7. Heritage: European American.

Lucy has a special relationship with her blind grandfather and wants to make something special for him. When her classmates paint, she asks her teacher if she can instead make a collage of soft velvet for hills, shiny blue material for a lake, and some twigs, sand, and feathers. When school is out, her mother and grandfather meet her, and Lucy gives him a textured picture he can "see" with his fingers.

31. Moore, Elaine (1995). *Grandma's Smile*. Illustrated by Dan Andreasen. New York: Lothrop, Lee & Shepard. Ages 5–7. Heritage: European American.

In the fall, Kim and her grandmother harvest the biggest and best pumpkin in the patch. In a spirit of fun, they prepare to enter it in the jack-o-lantern contest at the local fall festival. The two support one another, and Kim carves the pumpkin and uses her grandmother's smile as a model.

32. Murphy, Elspeth Campbell (1995). *The Mystery of the Dancing Angels*. New York: Bethany. Ages 7–8. Heritage: European American/multicultural.

Murphy's story addresses learning to be patient with difficult family members and others. While visiting their grandmother, four cousins find they have a mystery to solve when they visit an old house where their great-great-great-grandfather artistically carved woodwork. At first, Sarah-Jane, Timothy, and Titus think that Patience, their four-year-old third cousin, is quite annoying and a hindrance to their activities. They change their minds, however, when she helps them discover a secret revealed by the words of an old family rhyme and locate some missing jewelry.

33. Newman, Leslea (1996). *Remember That*. Illustrated by Karen Ritz. New York: Clarion. Ages 5–8. Heritage: European American/Jewish.

Bubbe and her granddaughter always celebrate the Jewish sabbath. As the years go by, Bubbe moves from her apartment to her daughter's home and, finally, to a nursing home. Each time Bubbe gives her granddaughter some words of wisdom, she says, "Remember that." Though her surroundings change, Bubbe adapts to her moves each time and is supported by loving family members who are warm and tender.

34. Oppenheim, Shulamith Levey (1995). *The Hundredth Name*. Illustrated by Michael Hays. New York: Caroline House/Boyds Mills. Ages 5–8. Heritage: Middle East.

This is a tale of friendship between Salah and his beloved camel, Qadim. Salah is sad because Qadim always seems so unhappy and solemn. They live in a Muslim village in Egypt, and Salah's father comforts his son and tells him that humans learn to live knowing only 99 names for Allah (the known), when it is the 100th name (the unknown) that is most important. Considering his father's words, Salah unrolls his father's prayer rug and says his first prayer to Allah, asking that Qadim be told the 100th name. The following day, Salah's prayer seems to be answered when he sees that Qadim looks very wise and happy, as if he knows something special and is standing tall—full of pride.

35. Oram, Hiawyn (1994). *The Second Princess*. New York: Artists & Writers. Ages 6–8. Heritage: European/folk literature.

Oram's story is about a second princess who thinks that the first princess gets better treatment at the palace and wants to be rid of her. Her schemes are discovered by her mother, the queen, who finds out how the second princess feels about her sister. In her own peaceful way, the queen helps the two sisters become friends and declares that the first and second princesses will alternate days of being "first" through the royal week (and on Sundays, the entire royal family will be "first" together).

36. Pfeffer, Susan Beth (1979). *Awful Evelina*. Illustrated by Diane Dawson. Chicago: Albert Whitman. Ages 5–8. Heritage: European American.

Meredith is dreading going with her family to visit her aunt, uncle, and cousin, because her cousin, Evelina, always hits her and steps on her toes. She dreads it because none of the grown-ups ever notices. Meredith fantasizes some major disasters that could happen on the way, because she wants to avoid facing the torment dished out by her cousin. When her family arrives, the first thing Meredith asks is, "Are you going to hit me and step on my toes?" Surprisingly, Evelina assures her that only babies do that and suggests they play a game that happens to be Meredith's favorite. The two girls have a wonderful time playing together. When it comes time to go home, Meredith fantasizes a snowstorm that would make it so she would never have to leave—quite a contrast to her feelings when she first arrived.

37. Pinkney, Brian (1995). *JoJo's Flying Side Kick*. Illustrated by the author. New York: Simon & Schuster. Ages 5–7. Heritage: Asian American.

This is a story of intergenerational love, family love, and friendship. JoJo wants to advance from white belt to yellow belt status in her Tae Kwon Do class and, to do this, she must break a board with a flying side kick. Family members offer their support to help her. Her grandfather, a former boxer, suggests that she do fancy footwork similar to what he did before his boxing matches. Her mother suggests visualizing the action, and a friend suggests that JoJo gain power by yelling "KIAH" from deep within herself. When JoJo does all three in her class, she earns the yellow belt she wants.

38. Polacco, Patricia (1988). *The Keeping Quilt*. New York: Simon & Schuster. Ages 6–8. Heritage: European American/Russian.

This is a true story about a quilt and the author's Great-Gramma Anna, who came to America from Russia during the last century. Anna wanted to start life anew in New York and she made a quilt to remember her family members and related events. Each generation used Anna's quilt in different ways as it was handed down—as a Sabbath tablecloth, a wedding canopy, a blanket for new babies, and an imaginary tent in the park.

39. Polacco, Patricia (1994). *My Rotten Red-Headed Older Brother*. New York: Simon & Schuster. Ages 5–8. Heritage: Russian American.

Polacco's story is about a brother who always outdoes his younger sister, Patricia, and rubs in his achievements with a greeny-toothed grin. Patricia makes a special wish on a star that her brother would really care for her, and the following day, she discovers that her brother does care about her—he rescues her after a bad fall.

40. Ransom, Candice F. (1992). *Shooting Star Summer*. Illustrated by Karen Milone. New York: Caroline House/Boyds Mills Pr. Ages 7–9. Heritage: European American.

In this story of hostilities among members of an extended family, two cousins overcome their differences. Cousin Shannon visits for two weeks, and the unnamed narrator thinks her summer is ruined when the cousin arrives with a book to read. Gradually, the narrator loses her hostility toward her cousin and the two find out they have a lot in common. For instance, Shannon teaches the narrator how to make the longest clover chain in the world, and the narrator shows Shannon how fireflies can make her hands glow at night. When Shannon leaves, her cousin is sorry to see her go.

41. Schotter, Roni (1996). *Dreamland*. Illustrated by Kevin Hawkes. New York: Orchard. Ages 5–8. Heritage: European American.

Set in the 1900s in California, this is the story of a struggling immigrant family whose members are warm and sensitive to one another. Hardworking Uncle Gurney toils in the family's tailor shop and his nephew, Theo, makes sketches of something he calls "dream machines." Admiring the sketches, Uncle Gurney and the other family members pitch in and use the sketches as ideas and eventually create a bright, fanciful amusement park to start a new way of life.

42. Schreier, Joshua (1993). *Hank's Work*. Illustrated by the author. New York: E. P. Dutton. Ages 5–6. Heritage: European American.

In this story, Dad yells at Hank when Hank messes up a worktable. So Hank stomps off to his room and in acid-green crayon draws a monster that comes to life, gives frightening roars, and talks back to Hank's dad, saying, "Shhh, don't yell." Later, Hank's dad apologizes, and Hank shows him the picture he drew of the acid-green monster, which has returned to its origin on the paper.

43. Sharmat, Majoria Weinman (1975). *I'm Not Oscar's Friend Anymore*. Illustrated by Tony DeLuna. New York: E. P. Dutton. Ages 5–6. Heritage: European American.

Oscar's friend says Oscar used to be his friend until Oscar said something very fresh to him and he said something fresh right back, then Oscar said something further in return. After this escalating word duel, the two boys aren't friends anymore. In reflection, Oscar's ex-friend gets some satisfaction from daydreaming about how much Oscar will miss him and, when he finally calls Oscar, he offers to let Oscar be his friend again. He is surprised to discover that Oscar has forgotten all about the fight.

44. Stamm, Claus (1990). *Three Strong Women: A Tall Tale*. Illustrated by Jean and Mou-sien Tseung. New York: Viking. Ages 5–8. Heritage: Asian/folk literature.

In this tale of exaggeration, Forever-Mountain, the best wrestler in Japan from his point of view, meets Maru-me and plays a joke on her. She takes him home to meet her family—her mother and grandmother—and with their help, to teach him what strength really is from their points of view. During his 90-day stay, he learns to stop his boasting and begins to understand humility, as he prepares for the country's wrestling championship.

45. Stanek, Muriel (1989). *I Speak English for My Mom*. Chicago: Albert Whitman. Ages 5–8. Heritage: Mexican American.

Stanek's story centers on helping family members. At home, bilingual Lupe is an essential family member when others need help. Lupe helps her mother, who speaks and reads only Spanish. Mrs. Gomez needs her daughter's help as she completes her tasks and activities in her daily life. Lupe helps her with trips to the dentist and with shopping, even though Lupe acknowledges she would rather play. Even though she would rather be with her friends, Lupe does not pout or become unhappy about the demands on her time, but stays with the job of translating for her mother—and in this way avoids disappointing her mother.

46. Steig, William (1995). *The Toy Brother*. Illustrated by the author. New York: HarperCollins. Ages 6–8. Heritage: European American.

Steig's story is set in medieval times, as the parents in a family leave for a wedding. At home, Yorick, the elder son, who wants to be an alchemist like his father, tries out his magic formula. The results are unexpected, and he diminishes to the size of a sausage. This change of events delights his younger brother, Charles, and the two gain a new affection for one another as Charles takes care of his older brother. Charles makes his brother a miniature house, feeds him with bread crumbs and clabbered cheese, and carries him in his pocket. Yorick is anxious to get back to his normal size, however, and finally remembers what went wrong—an ingredient was missing from the magic potion. It is supplied and all is normal again, but the two brothers do not lose the new appreciation they now have for one another.

47. Torres, Leyla (1995). *Saturday Sancocho*. New York: Farrar, Straus and Giroux. Ages 5–8. Heritage: Latino/Hispanic.

This is the story of Maria Lili and her grandmother, Mama Ana. Every Saturday, Maria goes to visit her grandparents and they make *sancocho*, a chicken stew that Maria thinks is the best she has ever tasted. One Saturday, Maria discovers that the only food in the kitchen is eggs and that they lack all the ingredients to make the favorite stew. Mama Ana and Maria put the eggs in a basket and go to the open-air market, where they barter their eggs from stall to stall to get what they need for the stew.

48. Tusa, Tricia (1995). *Sisters*. Illustrated by the author. New York: Crown. Ages 5–7. Heritage: European American.

Two eccentrically dressed sisters, Eeda and Lucy, go to bed angry when they argue over the best way to cook an artichoke. In an unusual retaliatory approach, they each hide an artichoke to surprise the other. The artichoke is found in a sister's purse, the bathtub, in oatmeal, and other places until, finally, Lucy discovers it in the oven—Eeda has baked it in garlic lemon butter stuffed with crabmeat and bread crumbs—knowing this is Lucy's favorite way to cook an artichoke. Instead of a verbal apology, Lucy, in turn, prepares Eeda's favorite dish. With this, the two sisters end their argument and enjoy a dinner together, until a similar argument gets under way and surprise events begin all over again.

49. Viorst, Judith (1974). *Rosie and Michael*. Illustrated by Lorna Tomer. New York: Atheneum. Ages 5–8. Heritage: European American.

This story describes the meaning of friendship from the vantage points of Rosie and Michael, two best friends. Both point out that friendship endures the vicissitudes of life. Rosie likes Michael when he's dopey, not just when he's smart. And Michael likes Rosie when she's grouchy, not just when she's nice. Even when he sprays Kool Whip in her sneakers, Rosie remains Michael's friend. Rosie and Michael give testimony to the fact that true friendship overcomes all problems. It inspires jokes, laughter, sharing, and helping each other out (or promising to) and it can withstand anger (once in a while). That's what friendships are for, according to Rosie and Michael. The two children clearly can tell a reader much about maintaining peaceful, harmonious relationships.

50. Wallace, Ian (1984). *Chin Chang and the Dragon's Dance*. Illustrated by the author. New York: Atheneum. Ages 5–7. Heritage: Asian American.

All his young life, Chin wanted to dance the dragon's dance on the first day of the new year and he had practiced the dance with his grandfather. Now, it seems, he would get his chance, but instead of being happy and excited about it, Chin is sad and afraid because he fears that he will not dance well enough to make his grandfather proud of him. On the eve of the festivities for the Year of the Dragon, Chin runs away and hides on the roof of the public library. There, he meets Pu Yee, an elderly woman, who talks to him and helps him gain the courage to return to the dance and face his fears.

51. Weiss, Nicki (1985). *Battle Day at Camp Delmont*. Illustrated by the author. New York: Greenwillow. Ages 6–8. Heritage: European American/multiethnic.

Maude is going to Camp Delmont with her best friend, Sally. She reassures her worried mother that she will be fine because Sally will be with her. Everything is fine—until Battle Day, a day full of sports competitions, and Sally and Maude find themselves on opposite sides. Maude has a difficult time coming to terms with trying to beat Sally, her best friend. With the support of her other team members, however, Maude begins to realize that there is nothing wrong with wanting to win and that she can still keep her friendship with Sally.

COMMUNITY, NEIGHBORHOOD, AND SCHOOL FRIENDSHIPS

52. Aliki (1995). *Best Friends Together*. Illustrated by the author. New York: Greenwillow. Ages 5–7. Heritage: European American.

Neighborhood children welcome Peter back with their own version of a friendship reunion when Peter arrives to spend two weeks with his best friend, Robert. The boys are anxious about how the other might have changed and how their friendship might be affected, but their anxiety soon fades as they realize they are as happy as old friends could possibly be. In moments of reflection, they talk about their new friends and recall their good times and shared experiences. A young reader who wants another story about the friendship between the boys can turn to *We Are Best Friends* (Greenwillow, 1982), also by Aliki.

53. Angelou, Maya (1994). *My Painted House, My Friendly Chicken, and Me*. Illustrated by Margaret Courtney-Clarke. New York: Potter. Ages 7–8. Heritage: African.

Angelou depicts the goodness of South African life in a Ndebele village. The story is narrated by eight-year-old Thandi, a young girl who begins her story with the words, "Hello, stranger-friend." Her anecdotes portray her people, their friendships, and their village life.

54. Aylesworth, Jim (1995). *McGraw's Emporium*. New York: Holt, Rinehart. Ages 5–6. Heritage: European American.

Aylesworth's story is about the caring actions of friends. A young fellow who wants to buy a present for a sick friend goes into McGraw's Emporium in search of a gift. Many, many items are there, ranging from a Franklin stove to a cricket bat. The items include a little knife for spreading jam, a sweater with a monogram, and others mentioned in rhyme. Finally, an announcement on the wall catches the boy's eye and leads him to a special gift—a kitten.

55. Battle-Lavert, Gwendolyn (1994). *The Barber's Cutting Edge*. Illustrated by Raymond Holbert. New York: Children's Book Press. Ages 6–9. Heritage: African American.

Battle-Lavert's topic in the story is community friendship. Rashaad, an African American boy, visits a local barber. Mr. Bigalow is known as the best barber in town, and his shop is brightly decorated with posters and pictures on the walls. Customers can play checkers at a table or read books from a bookshelf. Playfully, Rashaad tries to stump the barber by giving him difficult words to define in an amusing and entertaining exchange. The illustrations are an integral part of the story and show that Mr. Bigalow keeps walking into his back room—perhaps to look in a dictionary.

56. Bushey, Jeanne (1994). *A Sled Dog for Moshi*. Illustrated by Germaine Amaktauyok. New York: Hyperion. Ages 6–8. Heritage: Canadian Eskimo.

Bushey's story is about the budding friendship between two girls—Moshi, a Canadian Eskimo who wants a dog of her own, and her new friend from New York City. The two become lost in a snowy whiteout, but are saved by Moshi's skills and her father's lead sled dog.

57. Champion, Joyce (1995). *Emily and Alice Again*. Illustrated by Sucie Stevenson. New York: Gulliver/Harcourt. Ages 6–8. Heritage: European American.

Champion's chaptered story is about the friendship of two young girls. The special bond between Emily and Alice is shown in the way they support one another in whatever they do. For example, the two girls share their fears of a sleepover; they wear the same clothes to school; and they trade their sunglasses for a little "sister."

58. Chinn, Karen (1995). *Sam and the Lucky Money*. Illustrated by Cornelius Van Wright and Ying-Hwa Hu. New York: Lee & Low. Ages 5–7. Heritage: Asian American/Chinese.

This story focuses on the theme "it is better to give than receive." It is set in Chinatown in New York City during a traditional New Year celebration. For the celebration, Sam receives four bright red envelopes decorated with shiny gold emblems. Each contains a lucky dollar. Sam considers ways to spend his money as he goes with his mother through Chinatown, but discovers that things cost more than he thought they would. He encounters a barefoot stranger on the street and concludes that his money would be best spent on helping the man in the street who has no shoes.

59. Chmielarz, Sharon (1994). *Down at Angel's*. Illustrated by Jill Kastner. New York: Ticknor & Fields. Ages 6–8. Heritage: European American.

Chmielarz's story is about a neighborhood friendship. Two sisters develop a friendship with an elderly neighbor, Angel, a widower and woodcutter from Bulgaria. At Christmas time, the girls and their mother prepare a gift of homemade sauces, preserves, and other foods for him. In return, Angel gives them a hand-carved table they had previously admired.

60. Cristaldi, Kathryn (1994). *Samantha the Snob*. Illustrated by Denise Brunkus. New York: Random House. Ages 5–8. Heritage: European American.

A female classmate at school narrates this story about a new girl, Samantha S. Van Dorf. Samantha's family is wealthy and she wears fancy hats and a fur coat and rides in the back of a long back limousine instead of a school bus. Seeing this, the narrator thinks that Samantha's middle initial S probably stands for snob. The narrator, however, changes her mind when she is invited to Samantha's birthday party, gets to know the new girl, and discovers that Samantha is really a nice person who could be a new friend.

61. de Paola, Tomie (1983). *The Legend of the Bluebonnet*. Illustrated by the author. New York: Scholastic. Ages 5–8. Heritage: Native American.

In this legend, a shaman tells the Comanche people that the drought and famine has come upon them because the people are selfish. They are to sacrifice a treasured possession to the great spirits to restore life as it was before the famine. A small girl, She-Who-Is-Alone, is without parents or grandparents and is the only one to sacrifice and burn a valued possession—a warrior doll her mother made for her. When she scatters the doll's ashes on the hillside, bluebonnet flowers appear and the people believe the flowers are a sign of forgiveness from the great spirits. They recognize her contribution to the Comanche people and rename the small girl One-Who-Dearly-Loved-Her-People.

62. de Paola, Tomie (1988). *The Legend of the Indian Paintbrush*. Illustrated by the author. New York: Putnam Group. Ages 5–7. Heritage: Native American.

A small boy, Little Gopher, uses his artistic skills to make a special gift for his people. He paints the deeds of his tribe. As a reward, he is given magical paintbrushes that hold bright colors of red, orange, and yellow. These colors enable him to paint his version of the colorful evening sky. When the brushes are discarded, they take root and bloom across the hillside.

63. Dooley, Norah (1996). *Everybody Bakes Bread*. Illustrated by Peter J. Thornton. New York: Carolrhoda. Ages 7–9. Heritage: Multiethnic.

In a friendly multiethnic neighborhood, Carrie is sent on a tongue-in-cheek errand to find a three-handled rolling pin as a rainy day activity. As she visits her neighbors, she tastes different kinds of bread. The samples include braided bread from Italy, Jewish challah, chapatis bread from India, coconut bread from Barbados, corn bread from South Carolina, pocket bread from Lebanon, and pupusa from El Salvador. When the rain stops, she discovers she has found enough friends to play a game of kickball.

64. Duffey, Betsy (1996). *Hey, New Kid!* Illustrated by Ellen Thompson. New York: Viking. Ages 8–9. Heritage: European American.

Cody, a newly enrolled third-grader at school, dreads facing unknown classmates and decides, in his own humorous way, to impress the kids and to build up his image as a super kid who has a lot going for him. In the role of a super kid, he tells others that his dad is an FBI agent, that he is a world-class roller skater, and that he has an emu for a pet. Of course, this all backfires on Cody. For instance, when Cody (a nonskater) is invited to a friend's skating party, he rolls out of control and into the girl's bathroom, where he becomes entangled in the toilet paper and comes out looking like an Egyptian mummy. Cody, however, meets some kids who give him another chance and he makes some friends in spite of his so-called super image. Cody's mother helps and supports him, and his teacher understands what is going on.

65. Egan, Tim (1995). *Chestnut Cove*. Illustrated by the author. Boston: Houghton Mifflin. Ages 5–7. Heritage: European American.

In this original folktale, King Milford offers his kingdom to the one who grows the largest watermelon. The attitude of the inhabitants of Chestnut Cove changes from friendly to distrustful and jealous as residents strive for the big prize. At summer's end, on the day before judging, the people turn out to rescue Mrs. Lark's pet pig, Eloise, from a confining spot and, in working together, realize how silly they had been to mistrust one another. To make amends and reestablish their friendships, they decide on an all-night melon feast, and King Milford is left to judge only the remains of the melon feast.

66. Ernst, Lisa Campbell (1995). *Miss Penny and Mr. Grubbs*. Illustrated by the author. New York: Aladdin. Ages 5–7. Heritage: European American.

Ernst's story is about two neighbors who become rivals. Miss Penny's prizewinning vegetables from her garden make Mr. Grubbs green with envy. Envy gets the upper hand and mean-spirited Mr. Grubbs sabotages Miss Penny's crop with two hungry rabbits. Kindhearted Miss Penny takes in the rabbits and learns that she has a talent for raising them, too.

67. Gackenbach, Dick (1993). *Claude Has a Picnic*. Illustrated by the author. New York: Clarion. Ages 5–7. Heritage: Multiethnic.

Gackenbach's story begins one morning when Claude, a basset hound, tours his neighborhood and discovers that all of his human neighbors have a problem. No one is feeling friendly, but wise Claude helps out and becomes a goodwill canine ambassador. For instance, Claude learns that Mickey is tired of his old ball and Buddy is bored with his Frisbee. To make the boys happy, Claude carries the ball to Buddy and gives the Frisbee to Mickey. At the story's end, Claude has helped everyone with his acts of love and kindness, and they all celebrate and have a good time at a neighborhood picnic.

68. Garrison, Susan (1995). *How Emily Blair Got Her Fabulous Hair*. Illustrated by Marjorie Priceman. Watertown, MA: Bridgewater Books. Ages 5–7. Heritage: European American.

Emily and her friend, Pamela, like to play beauty parlor. Emily fixes Pamela's hair in lovely golden waves, but her own hair is a problem—it stays straight. To fight her straight hair, Emily tries different approaches—she eats carrots and puts macaroni on her head with glue. Finally, Emily finds a stylish hairdo that is just right for her.

69. Giff, Patricia Reilly (1995). *Say Hola, Sarah.* Illustrated by DyAnne DiSalvo-Ryan. New York: Dell/Yearling. Ages 6–8. Heritage: Multiethnic.

Unhappily, Sarah Cole discovers that Benjamin, a pest in class, has volunteered *her* to help *him* give a report on Columbus. She wants to work with her friend, Anna, who is helping her learn Spanish. Sarah meets Anna's cousin, visiting from the country of Colombia, who helps the two children prepare a bilingual report on Columbus. The experience improves Sarah's mood as she sees working with Benjamin in a different way.

70. Greene, Stephanie (1996). *Owen Foote, Second Grade Strongman.* Illustrated by Dee Derosa. New York: Clarion. Ages 6–8. Heritage: European American.

This is the story of an ongoing, supportive friendship between two second graders—Owen, undersized, and Joseph, oversized. Naturally, the two boys dread seeing the school nurse on height-and-weight day at school and start lifting weights (just as Owen's grandfather did as a professional strongman) to bring about positive changes in each one's size.

71. Grimes, Nikki (1994). *Meet Danitra Brown.* Illustrated by Floyd Cooper. New York: Lothrop, Lee & Shepard. Ages 7–9. Heritage: African American.

This is a collection of poems narrated by Zuei Jackson about her friend, Danitra. The poems tell about moments of friendship the two girls have. The words are related to their thoughts and feelings about pride in their heritage, future plans, their self-assurance, as well as some disappointments and pain.

72. Guthrie, Donna (1985). *The Witch Who Lives Down the Hall.* Illustrated by the author. Boston: Harcourt, Brace. Ages 5–8. Heritage: European American.

This story focuses on overcoming suspicions about neighbors who act in mysterious ways. A young boy observes a neighbor and thinks she acts like a witch. His mother, however, believes she can logically explain his concerns away. She tries, but the boy is difficult to convince until he meets the neighbor face-to-face.

73. Hamanaka, Sheila (1995). *Behop-a-De-Walk!* Illustrated by the author. New York: Simon & Schuster. Ages 6–8. Heritage: Asian American/African American/Multiethnic.

Set in the 1950s on the lower east side of New York, this story is about the friendship of Emi, a young Asian girl, and Martha, her best friend, who is African

American. The two girls go with Emi's father for a walk to Central Park, and the whole community turns out to give them a send-off. The girls greet people as they notice the different sights on the way to the park—Washington Square Park, the Empire State Building, and the Museum of Modern Art. After a day of walking, Emi's father treats them to a bus ride home at the end of their wonderful outing.

74. Havill, Juanita (1993). *Jamaica and Brianna*. Illustrated by Anne Sibley O'Brien. Boston: Houghton Mifflin. Ages 5–8. Heritage: African American/Asian American/Multiethnic.

This is a story of rivalry, envy, and jealousy. Jamaica, a young African American, and Brianna, an Asian American, let envy affect their friendship. One snowy day, Jamaica has to wear her brother's hand-me-down boots, and Brianna makes some unfeeling comments. When she gets some new boots, Brianna again makes remarks that seem mean to Jamaica. Upset and angry, it takes a while for the two to work out their negative feelings in a satisfactory manner.

75. Havill, Juanita (1995). *Jamaica's Blue Marker*. Illustrated by Anne Sibley O'Brien. Boston: Houghton Mifflin. Ages 5–7. Heritage: African American/Multiethnic.

At school, Russell never has the school supplies he needs and Jamaica, a classmate, is unhappy when she has to share her blue marker with him and he draws all over her picture. At home, her father helps her understand her feelings, as well as those felt by Russell—that the boy could be mean because he is unhappy about having to move away. Jamaica, now considerate, gives him the blue marker as a good-bye gift and something to remember her by in his new classroom.

76. Hess, Debra (1994). *Wilson Sat Alone*. Illustrated by Diane Greenseid. New York: Simon & Schuster. Ages 5–8. Heritage: European American.

This story espouses being persistent when trying to make new friends. When a new girl arrives in class, she makes friends but notices that Wilson eats, reads, plays, and walks home alone. She makes an effort to be friendly, but the other children tell her that Wilson *wants* to be left alone. She prevails, however, and, surprisingly, Wilson responds to her friendly actions and is not alone anymore thanks to the new girl's persistence and friendship.

77. Hooks, William H. (1995). *The Girl Who Could Fly*. Illustrated by Kees de Kiefte. New York: Macmillan. Ages 7–8. Heritage: African American.

In Hooks' story, nine-year-old Adam Lee tells about his friendship with a newcomer—an alien girl. His new next-door neighbor, Tomasina Jones, asks if he will be her new best friend, and Adam discovers that Tomasina (called Tom) Jones can suspend balls in the air, read his mind, move with incredible speed, draw magical maps of the world, and even fly. After helping his team win a game against their rivals, Tom unexpectedly tells Adam good-bye and leaves.

78. Hopkinson, Deborah (1993). *Sweet Clara and the Freedom Quilt.* Illustrated by the author. New York: Knopf. Ages 6–8. Heritage: African American.

Hopkinson's story is about a young slave who works as a seamstress and dreams of freedom and peace from the harshness of slavery. Overhearing the talk of others escaping to the north, she gets the directions she needs and makes an escape map from quilt patches. When she escapes to Canada, she leaves the quilt behind to guide others—an act of assistance, support, and friendship.

79. Howard, Arthur (1996). *When I Was Five.* New York: Harcourt, Brace. Ages 5–7. Heritage: European American.

Jeremy, sporting freckles and round eyeglasses, has just had his sixth birthday and describes how he has changed since he was five. It seems that at age five, he was satisfied with little toy cars and plant-eating flying dinosaurs. Now, at six, he favors fast racing cars and the meat-eating tyrannosaurus rex. At five, he thought he wanted to be a cowboy or an astronaut, but now he wants to be a deep-sea diver or a famous baseball player. One thing, however, hasn't changed during the year—his best friend is still the same, a boy named Mark.

80. Howe, James (1995). *Pinky and Rex and the Double-Dad Weekend.* Illustrated by Melissa Sweet. New York: Atheneum. Ages 5–6. Heritage: European American.

This story emphasizes the way family members and friends can enjoy being together despite adversity. Pinky and Rex, two best friends, and their fathers go on a weekend camping trip. Caught in a seemingly never-ending rainstorm, the four have fun in spite of the gray, wet, damp days. They set up camp in their motel room and explore the area by visiting a reptile museum, a train museum, and a puppetmaker's studio.

81. Hutchins, Pat (1993). *My Best Friend.* Illustrated by the author. New York: Greenwillow. Ages 5–6. Heritage: European American.

In Hutchins' story, two girls are best friends yet decidedly different. One is a can-do girl and can button her clothes, climb, jump, and run well, paint without spilling anything, and untie her shoes. The other girl cannot do these things as well. One night during a sleepover, when the wind blows the bedroom curtains and frightens them, the can't-do girl is brave and uses her common sense to calm her friend.

82. Jackson, Isaac (1996). *Somebody's New Pajamas.* Illustrated by David Soman. New York: Dial. Ages 5–8. Heritage: African American.

This is a story of warmth and consideration between friends. Friends Jerome and Robert are from different economic backgrounds and home environments. When Jerome, who lives in a small, cluttered apartment with thin walls and hot water problems, spends the night with Robert, who lives in a brownstone, he is embarrassed to say that he does not have any pajamas. At home, Jerome's father tells him that their family has its own way of doing things, and when Robert spends the night with Jerome, he sleeps in his underwear just like Jerome does. Later, two pairs of birthday gift pajamas make the story's ending warm and friendly.

83. Johnson, Angela (1995). *Shoes Like Miss Alice's*. Illustrated by Ken Page. New York: Orchard. Ages 5–7. Heritage: Multiethnic.
      Young Sara narrates her activities with a new baby-sitter. Young Sara is anxious about her new baby-sitter, but it is not long before Miss Alice and her unique warmth and friendliness win the little girl over. Miss Alice captures Sara's attention and interest when Miss Alice changes into her dancing shoes to dance, then into her walking shoes to walk, her napping shoes to nap, and finally, her bare feet to play.

84. Keats, Ezra Jack (1971). *Apt. 3*. Illustrated by the author. New York: Macmillan. Ages 6–8. Heritage: African American/Multiethnic.
      In his apartment on a rainy day, Sam hears harmonica music and wonders who is playing. Sam and his little brother, Ben, listen at the doors to locate the music and its player. When Sam peeks in an open door at Apt. 3, he sees it is a blind man's apartment, and the man invites the two boys to come in and sit down. The man begins to play his harmonica and he plays magic—purples and gray and rain and smoke and the sounds of night. Sam seems to float with the music as it evokes sights and sounds and colors. When it stops, Sam invites the man to take a walk with him and Ben the next day. The man's music begins again with wild happy sounds, and Sam and Ben think it is so wonderful that they can hardly wait until the next day.

85. Keats, Ezra Jack (1968). *A Letter to Amy*. Illustrated by the author. New York: Harper & Row. Ages 5–8. Heritage: Multiethnic.
      Peter wants to invite his friend Amy to his birthday party, even though he knows his other friends will make fun of her because she is a girl. Amy clearly is one of his favorite people, shown by the fact that he sends her a special invitation, even though he has just asked everyone else. Peter is seen as a sensitive little boy who values his friendship with Amy; he doesn't even react negatively when the other boys say, "A girl—ugh!" when Amy arrives.

86. Lacapa, Michael (1990). *The Flute Player: An Apache Folktale*. Flagstaff, AZ: Northland Pub. Ages 8 up. Heritage: Native American.
      Lacapa retells an Apache tale about a young girl and boy, a flute player, who are attracted to one another during an Apache hoop dance. The girl says that when she hears his flute, she will place a leaf in the river that runs through the canyon. The floating leaf will tell him that she likes his music. When he leaves to join his companions for a long hunt, the girl becomes ill and dies before his return. To

this day, when the people hear nature's echoes through the canyon and see leaves falling into the river, they say the girl still likes the music of the flute player.

87. Larson, Kirby (1996). *Cody and Quinn, Sitting in a Tree*. Illustrated by Nancy Poydar. New York: Holiday. Ages 7–8. Heritage: Multiethnic.
A second grade bully, Royce, picks on Cody and teases him about being friends with a girl named Quill. When Cody fights back against the teasing, he learns that Royce only wants to be accepted by the rest of the children in the class. In an act of turning the other cheek, Cody finds a way to help Royce become accepted.

88. Larson, Kirby (1994). *Second Grade Pig Pals*. Illustrated by Nancy Poydar. New York: Holiday. Ages 7–8. Heritage: Multicultural.
This story centers on making new friends. Quinn Kelley's second grade class is preparing for a pig patch display, for which each child will bring in something special to exhibit. A new student, Manuela, enrolls in class and Quinn tries to be friendly, but some misunderstandings occur between the two. Quinn has nothing to bring to the class display, and when Manuela's pet project of a pig balloon is popped by another student's pet Vietnamese pot belly pig named Jelly Belly, the two girls are both without projects. The two get together on a cooperative project and write their own pig rhymes after reading the book *Pigericks,* by Arnold Lobel.

89. Lasky, Kathryn (1995). *Pond Buddies*. Illustrated by Mike Bostock. New York: Candlewick. Ages 6–8. Heritage: European American.
This is the story of two curious six-year-old girls who play together near the pond in their neighborhood. Their friendship grows as they learn a great deal about life in the pond water and discover not only tadpoles (and how they grow) but also dragonflies and other inhabitants that live in and near water.

90. Leghorn, Lindsay (1995). *Proud of Our Feelings*. Illustrated by the author. New York: Magination. Ages 5–7. Heritage: Multiethnic.
A young girl, Priscilla, introduces Shelly and her other friends to a reader and tells about each one's feelings. The friends' feelings cover a wide range, including not only confidence, happiness, and friendliness, but anger, fear, frustration, loneliness, sadness, and shyness. As an example, Priscilla says that meeting new people makes Shelly feel shy. Each child is shown acting out the feelings, and Priscilla is shown mimicking the actions.

91. Leverich, Kathleen (1995). *Brigid the Bad*. Illustrated by Dan Andreasen. New York: Random House. Ages 7–9. Heritage: Multiethnic.
Bossy Brigid asks her godmother, Maribel, for a spell to make the members of her family and her friends obey her. Maribel does so, and Brigid has her way—she does not have to do chores at home or homework for school and can wear her

best party dress to class if she wants to. Brigid, however, is not totally happy, because she wants something more. She wants everyone to be happy under her control and asks Maribel for another spell. This makes her family and friends obey her in a cheerful but nonhumanlike manner. Brigid still has some problems with this and receives still more help that resolves the problem of what it's like to have others obey you and to make them unhappy.

92. Lonborg, Rosemary (1995). *Helping Bugs*. Illustrated by Diane R. Houghton. New York: Little Friend Pub. Ages 5–6. Heritage: European American.

When Hannah's family moves to a new neighborhood, her parents are busy unpacking and taking care of the baby. So lonely Hannah goes outside and meets Douglas, the boy next door. She thinks he must be someone important because he is dressed in an unusual way—a fireman's hat, cowboy boots, and a backpack, and he sports a sheriff's badge. He asks her to help him make a bug village out of grass, leaves, and sticks, and the two have so much fun that they decide to play together again the next day.

93. Lyon, George Ella (1996). *A Day at Damp Camp*. Illustrated by Peter Catalanotto. New York: Orchard Books. Ages 5–8. Heritage: Multiethnic.

Arriving at camp, both Sarah and Megan are each alone and lonely, but they get acquainted as they participate in daily activities and become friends. Their friendship grows as they attend craft classes, swim and hike together, and enjoy the fellowship of others around evening campfires.

94. MacDonald, Maryann (1994). *The Pink Party*. Illustrated by Abby Carter. New York: Hyperion. Ages 6–7. Heritage: European American.

MacDonald's friendship story is a humorous portrayal of one-upmanship. Two girls, Lisa and Amy, both like the color pink and they try to outdo one another. For instance, when Lisa gets pink shoes, Amy gets a pink lunch box. This one-upmanship eventually turns into envy, rivalry, and jealousy but all ends well at a party when they realize that their friendship, not the color pink, is the thing to value.

95. McLerran, Alice (1991). *Roxaboxen*. Illustrated by Barbara Cooney. New York: Lothrop, Lee & Shepard. Ages 6–8. Heritage: Multiethnic.

McLerran's story is based on her mother's childhood experience. It is about an imagined world of play for friends in a community in Yuma, Ariz. The children transform a rocky hill into an imagined town called Roxaboxen for their playtime. They use broken bits of pottery, sticks, and pebbles to represent the objects they need in their town. They elect a mayor, drive their imagined cars like the wind, and build homes, streets lined with rocks, businesses, and, interestingly, a jail.

96. Markel, Michelle (1995). *Gracias, Rosa*. Illustrated by Diane Paterson. Chicago: Albert Whitman. Ages 5–7. Heritage: Multiethnic.

Markel's warm story is narrated by Kate, a young girl, and concerns her developing friendship with Rosa, a new baby-sitter. Rosa is from Guatemala and doesn't speak much English. Unable to fully communicate, Kate is not sure that she likes Rosa. Rosa, however, gives Kate a gift—a cloth doll—for which Kate thanks her and learns a new word, *gracias*. Over time, the two develop a special bond and become friends.

97. Medearis, Angela Shelf (1995). *The Adventures of Sugar and Junior*. Illustrated by Nancy Poydar. New York: Holiday. Ages 7–8. Heritage: African American/Latino Hispanic American/Multiethnic.

This is a chaptered book about meeting new people and making new friends. It is told through the adventures of an African American girl, Sugar Johnson, and a Hispanic boy, Santiago Ramirez. Sugar calls him Junior. Their story includes how the two children first met, how Sugar got her name, baking cookies together, reassuring one another while seeing a scary movie, and buying their favorite flavor of ice cream together.

98. Merriam, Eve (1992). *Fighting Words*. Illustrated by David Small. New York: William Morrow. Ages 5–9. Heritage: European American.

Dale and Leda are the best of enemies and are envious of what the other has. Ready to do battle, the two rivals meet halfway between their two homes and fight verbally—insulting one another as they chase each other through the city. They verbally duel in the streets, the sports stadium, and at the zoo. When they finally cross the river, they realize they are out in the countryside far from home. At this point, they shake hands and praise one another for their good fight and promise to meet and fight again with the power of their words.

99. Ness, Evaline (1966). *Sam, Bangs and Moonshine*. Illustrated by the author. New York: Holt, Rinehart & Winston. Ages 6–8. Heritage: European American.

In this story, Samantha (Sam) has trouble distinguishing between what is real and what is imaginary, i.e., moonshine. When Sam's imagination jeopardizes the life of her good friend, Thomas, the difference becomes clear to her. Sam tells Thomas she has a baby kangaroo (she's talking moonshine) and sends him off to Blue Rock to find it. A storm blows up and the tide comes in, stranding Thomas and Bangs, Sam's cat, on a rock. Thomas is rescued by Sam's father, but Bangs is swept away. As Sam goes to bed, she knows that her moonshine was responsible for Bangs' death and Thomas' dangerous situation. Later that night, a scratching at the window alerts her to a waterlogged cat outside that is indeed Bangs. At the hospital, Sam visits Thomas in friendship and gives him a gerbil (named Moonshine) because she thinks it looks just like a baby kangaroo.

100. Penn, Malka (1994). *The Miracle of the Potato Latkes*. Illustrated by Gloria Carmi. New York: Holiday. Ages 5–7. Heritage: European/Jewish.

This is a warmhearted Hanukkah story about friendship toward others. Tante Golda and other villages have a poor harvest, and everyone feels the hunger and the unhappiness of their situation. Through Golda's faith and her generosity toward others, she becomes the spirit of change toward happiness and creates the miracle of the potato cakes.

101. Polacco, Patricia (1992). *Chicken Sunday.* Illustrated by the author. New York: Philomel. Ages 6–8. Heritage: African American/Russian American/Multiethnic.

Without a thought as to race or religion, Patricia is a best friend of Winston and Stewart Washington and considers Miss Eula, their African American grandmother, as dear as her own Russian grandmother. On Sundays, she attends Baptist services with them and enjoys a fried chicken dinner at their house. The children know that Miss Eula likes one of the hats in Mr. Kodinski's shop, but the Russian American store owner accuses them of pelting his shop with eggs. To make peace with him, they give him a lovely gift of hand-dyed eggs in the Russian style that Patricia's grandmother had taught her. The shop owner, feeling nostalgic when he sees the eggs of his homeland, lets the children sell the eggs in his shop and rewards them by giving them a hat which Miss Eula proudly wears on Easter Sunday.

102. Raschka, Chris (1993). *Yo! Yes?* Illustrated by the author. New York: Orchard Books. Ages 5–7. Heritage: African American/European American/Multiethnic.

Meeting on the street, two boys talk to one another and start a conversation that leads to a friendship. Their conversation consists of extremely brief exchanges and begins with, "What's up?" "Not much." They agree that nothing is up because they have no friends. "No friends?" With that, they agree to be friends and close the deal by jumping up in the air and yelling, "Yow!"

103. Ring, Elizabeth. *Some Stuff* (1995). Illustrated by Anne Canevari. New York: Millbrook. Ages 5–6. Heritage: European American.

Ring's story is about a new boy on the block who reaches out to meet a friend and comes over to play with a lonely little girl. The girl overwhelms him, however, with toys and playthings she pulls out. When the boy is taken aback with so much stuff and hides under the accumulated clutter, the girl comes up with a friendly resolution and politely asks what *he* would like to do. His idea is that they go outside—away from the clutter—to play.

104. Ryan, Cheryl (1996). *Sally Arnold.* Illustrated by Bill Farnsworth. New York: Cobblehill. Ages 5–8. Heritage: European American.

In a mountain community during a summer visit, an affectionate relationship develops between a young girl, Jenny, and a unique elderly woman, Sally Arnold.

At first, Jenny thinks Sally is a witch and spies on her in her shack at the end of the hollow. Later, when Jenny falls in the creek, Sally rescues her and they get to know and appreciate one another and their abilities.

105. Shipton, Jonathan (1995). *No Biting, Horrible Crocodile!* Illustrated by Claudia Munoz. New York: Artists & Writers. Ages 5–6. Heritage: Multiethnic.

In class, Flora, a bully, pretends to be a mean biting crocodile when she wears a paper mask and snaps at everyone, scaring all the other children. One day, she bites Monkey, the children's favorite toy in the classroom. Flora cries over the incident and decides that she does not want to be a horrible crocodile any longer. She takes off her paper mask and the others accept her and make her feel like part of the class.

106. Tamar, Erika (1996). *The Garden of Happiness.* Illustrated by Barbara Lambase. New York: Harcourt. Ages 5–8. Heritage: Multiethnic.

On New York City's east side, Marisol wakes up one morning to discover that the neighbors are cleaning up a trash-filled lot to plant a garden. They plant the vegetables that remind them of the places of their childhood. Mr. Castro plants tomato seedlings. Mr. Singh has beans from Bangladesh. Mrs. Washington plants seeds for black-eyed peas. A small space remains for Marisol, and she plants one seed—a seed that grows into a beautiful big sunflower. When fall comes, the plants die—including the sunflower—but neighborhood teenagers help it remain in the gardeners' memories by painting a wall mural of giant yellow flowers across the street.

107. Walsh, Jill Paton (1996). *Connie Came to Play.* Illustrated by Stephen Lambert. New York: Viking. Ages 6–8. Heritage: European American.

On a visit to Robert's house, Connie creates her own imaginative world when Robert refuses to share his toys with her. At each refusal, Connie elaborates on each toy in her mind to imagine a wonderful rich world of play and make-believe. Double-page illustrations show the colorful world of Connie's fanciful play, in contrast to the white backgrounds that envelop Robert and his toys. When Robert finally decides to share the toys and play with Connie, she tells him an intriguing story that begins their friendship.

108. Willner-Pardo, Gina (1995). *When Jane-Marie Told My Secret.* Illustrated by Nancy Poydar. New York: Clarion. Ages 6–8. Heritage: European American.

In this chaptered story, Carolyn, a third grader, is angry that her one best friend, Jane-Marie, told her secret about wanting the most popular girl in the class to like *her*. After this betrayal, Carolyn confronts Jane-Marie and decides to make new friends to be with at school. Later, Jane-Marie apologizes and a reconciliation takes place when each girl brings one of their new friends along to the meeting.

109. Yamaka, Sara (1995). *The Gift of Driscoll Lipscomb*. Illustrated by Joung Un Kim. New York: Simon & Schuster. Ages 5–8. Heritage: European American/Asian American/Multiethnic.

Four-year-old Molly receives a gift of red paint from her elderly artist friend, Driscoll Lipscomb, so she paints objects that are red—tomatoes, apples and roses. The next year, she receives orange paint from the artist and on subsequent birthdays, yellow, green, blue, and purple paints. On her 12th birthday, Molly sees all the colors of the rainbow in the world around her and she reflects on the gift she'd been given—to celebrate the ways in which art and the colors of nature's rainbow add richness, variety, and diversity to life.

FRIENDSHIPS AROUND THE WORLD

110. Accorsi, William (1992). *My Name Is Pocahontas*. New York: Holiday House. Ages 5–7. Heritage: Native American.

This is a fictionalized biography told by Princess Pocahontas, beginning with her childhood. The princess tells about her life in two cultures—her friendship with John Smith and then her marriage to John Rolfe. The story ends with her trip to England as Rolfe's wife.

111. Baer, Edith (1995). *This Is the Way We Eat Our Lunch: A Book about Children Around the World*. Illustrated by Steve Bjorkman. New York: Scholastic. Ages 5–7. Heritage: Multicultural.

This book introduces a reader to foods eaten by girls and boys around the world such as curry, pita bread, rice, gumbo, couscous, and Chinese dumplings. Each of the introductions about a food features a particular location, beginning with places in the United States of America and then in Canada, South America, and so on. A map of the world highlights the locations where the food is enjoyed by children and their families. Types of cookery and a list of the dishes from different cultures are included.

112. Bains, Rae (1982). *Harriet Tubman: The Road to Freedom*. Illustrated by Larry Johnson. Mawah, NJ: Troll. Ages 7–8. Heritage: African American.

This is the life story of Harriet Tubman (1821–1913), who is acknowledged in the United States, Africa, and other countries as one who brought peaceful times to her people. After Harriet escaped from field work in the South and went to the North, she performed the ultimate act of friendship—she risked her life to help others escape from slavery. To do this, Harriet went back into slave territory and led more than 300 slaves to freedom. After the Civil War (also known as the War Between the States), she got involved in another supportive venture for her people—organizing schools for freed slaves in North Carolina.

113. D'Aulaire, Ingri and Edgar Parin D'Aulaire (1957). *Abraham Lincoln*. Illustrated by the authors. New York: Doubleday. Ages 6–8. Heritage: Multiethnic.

This story covers Lincoln's childhood, life as a young adult, his friendships with family and others, and his success in becoming president of the United States. The text, published in the 1950s, provides words for discussion by readers, i.e., words that portray the image of Native Americans and African Americans that may not be seen as politically friendly and correct in modern times. Note that the text coverage ends with the last days of the Civil War, and Lincoln's assassination is not mentioned in the book.

114. Gershator, Phillis (1995). *Honi's Circle of Trees*. Illustrated by Mimi Green. New York: Jewish Publication Society. Ages 5–7. Heritage: Jewish/Middle Eastern legend.

This story introduces Honi as an elderly, legendary character who selflessly wanders across the land of ancient Israel planting carob seeds for generations to come. Honi comes to a village, where a friendly man remembers his rain miracle from years before and encourages the old man to take a rest. When Honi awakens from what he thought was a nap, he learns that 70 years have passed and is confused and upset. He soon discovers, however, that he has been granted the extension of the years so he can see his trees bear fruit.

115. Glass, Andrew (1995). *Folks Call Me Appleseed John*. New York: Doubleday, Ages 7–8. Heritage: European American.

This fictional story offers John Chapman's story of the friendship and caring between him and Nathaniel, his younger half-brother, as well as their friendly relationship with Native Americans they met. John tells about some of the exciting experiences they had while traveling in Western Pennsylvania. The basis for the narrative comes from *Johnny Appleseed* (Peter Smith, 1954), by Robert Price. Map and biographical notes are included.

116. Goble, Paul (1984). *Buffalo Woman*. Illustrated by the author. New York: Bradbury. Ages 8–9. Heritage: Native American.

This story emphasizes the way native people depended on the buffalo and the bond between two nations—the Sioux people of the Plains and the Buffalo people. This relationship is shown through the main character's transformation to the Buffalo nation. In his author's notes, Goble explains the meaning of *mitakuye oyasin*, a phrase of value that originated with the Sioux. The phrase emphasizes that people are all related. The author discusses how the lives of the people and the buffalo were closely interwoven.

117. Greene, Carol (1989). *Robert E. Lee: Leader in War and Peace*. Illustrated by the author. Chicago: Childrens Press. Ages 6–8. Heritage: European American.

In simple text, this is the story of Robert E. Lee as it relates to his family, early life, and education in Virginia. Humility, prayer, faith and kindness to others were part of Lee's upbringing and stand out in contrast to his role in the Civil War. This biography also includes some background about slavery, the Civil War years, and his leadership toward peace, and points out that Robert was opposed to slavery, believing it had an evil effect on all people.

118. Hamanaka, Sheila (1994). *All the Colors of the Earth*. Illustrated by the author. New York: William Morrow. Ages 6–9. Heritage: Multiethnic.

The poetic text clearly highlights love for diverse children and describes their hair and skin tones through descriptive colors and flavors. For example, the author mentions that love can come in the flavors/colors of cinnamon, walnut, and wheat. The word *brown* is poetically embellished and becomes the "roaring browns of bears." Further, hair is described as curled like sleeping cats in snoozy cat colors.

119. Hamanaka, Sheila (1995). *The Peace Crane*. Illustrated by the author. New York: William Morrow. Ages 7–8. Heritage: Multiethnic.

The author emphasizes a worldwide view of the needs of people in this fanciful story. An African American girl folds her wishes for peace into a paper crane. Later, the peace crane visits her in a dream and takes her on a flight over farms, hills, and landscapes to show her benevolent people and the ways they care for one another. The flight of the bird takes the girl away from the violence of her world and allows her to see the goodness of others, who want to be part of a caring Earth without weapons and violence.

120. Knutson, Kimberley (1995). *Bed Bouncers*. Illustrated by the author. New York: Macmillan. Ages 5–7. Heritage: Multiethnic.

In this fanciful story, some children are bouncing on the bed and they bounce so high that they fly into space. In the air, they meet other multicultural bed bouncers from around the world and they all start to orbit Earth. All the children (of all colors and sizes) laugh and holler at the fun of it. When an authoritative voice reminds them to stop jumping on the bed, the original bed bouncers return to their bedroom. They get under the covers and pretend they are sleeping.

121. Lee, Betsy (1983). *Mother Teresa: Caring for God's Children*. Minneapolis: Dillon Press. Ages 7–8. Heritage: European.

Mother Teresa recently received the Nobel Prize for her peaceful and selfless work with the sick and dying people of India. At age 12, she left her home and family in Yugoslavia to become a nun and, years later, traveled to India to show her love for others in need. Filled with a desire to help the needy, Mother Teresa first became a teacher and then a friend to the street people living among the desperate and the poor in Calcutta, India.

122. Lobe, Tamara Awad (1995). *Let's Make a Garden*. Waterloo, Ontario: Herald Press. Ages 5–8. Heritage: Multiethnic.

This colorful easy-to-read story about sharing with friends shows how children of different cultures, nationalities, and races can work together in an unusual way—making a garden that represents foods from around the world. In the story, children from 11 nations plant foods such as an orange tree from Swaziland and brown beans from Mexico.

123. Martin, Nora (1995). *The Stone Dancers*. Illustrated by Jill Kastner. New York: Simon & Schuster. Ages 7–9. Heritage: European.

Set in Europe, perhaps southern France, this is a story about welcoming newcomers. A poor family arrives in Anise's village and first encounters suspicion and rejection by the inhabitants. Anise remembers the stories her grandfather told her about the castle near their peasant village. It seems that the original owners of the castle journeyed from a faraway land to seek refuge, just as the newly arrived family had done. All that was left now were the remains of the castle, but in the moonlight, the tall stone ruins looked like people dancing and celebrating their new home to Anise. After meeting the new family, Anise remembers this story and helps persuade others in the village to welcome the newcomers and accept them as friends and neighbors.

124. Meeker, Clare Hodgson, adapter (1994). *A Tale of Two Rice Birds*. Illustrated by Christine Lamb. New York: Sasquatch Books. Ages 6–9. Heritage: Asian, Thailand.

This is a Thai folktale about friendship and enduring love. Three small rice birds perish when a fire burns their tree and the parent birds, in grief, fly into the smoldering ashes to death. The mother bird, who vowed never to speak again, is reborn a princess, and the father bird, a farmer's son. The princess' father declares she will marry the man who persuades her to speak. The farmer's son wins her hand; to get her to talk, he tells her a story that requires an ending that she supplies.

125. Ringgold, Faith (1995). *My Dream of Martin Luther King*. Illustrated by the author. New York: Crown. Ages 7–9. Heritage: African American.

Dr. King received the world-renowned Nobel Peace Prize, and this is a fictionalized account of some of the major events and messages in Dr. King's life that led to the honor. The events of his life story are shown in a dream sequence, and Martin first is portrayed as a young boy who encountered racial prejudice and hatred. Later, he is shown as a celebrated pacifist leader working for civil rights for all Americans. The dream features images of various people in the world (varied ages, gender, race) who eliminate prejudice and hate and accept freedom, hope, friendship, love, and peace. Quotes from Dr. King's "I Have a Dream" speech are included.

126. Rosenberg, Liz (1996). *Grandmother and the Runaway Shadow*. Illustrated by Beth Peck. New York: Harcourt. Ages 6–8. Heritage: Russian/Russian American.

The author describes her grandmother's immigration experience as a young woman journeying from Europe to escape persecution by the Cossacks. During these times, the woman needed company, and her shadow was her only and best friend. Arriving in America, the woman was still alone, but courageously fought loneliness by keeping her shadow as her best friend—they provided companionship for one another in the new land. Author's note about the immigrant experience is included.

127. Schuett, Stacey (1995). *Somewhere in the World Right Now*. Illustrated by the author. New York: Knopf. Ages 6–8. Heritage: Multiethnic.

This story takes children around the world to see what other children (who could be world pen pals and friends) are doing at the very same moment in time. It points out that when children in North America are getting ready to go to bed, children in other parts of the world are getting up and beginning a new day. Other scenes show what it is like for children in the early morning on African plains, in the rain forests, in swamps, as well as in busy cities. Includes time zone maps and names of geographical places shown in the illustrations.

128. Sisulu, Elinor Batezat (1996). *The Day Gogo Went to Vote: South Africa, April, 1994*. Illustrated by Sharon Wilson. Boston: Little, Brown. Ages 6–8. Heritage: South African.

This is the story of a granddaughter's warm and loving relationship with her Gogo—her ailing great-grandmother in Soweto, South Africa. Six-year-old Thembi and the rest of her family are excited when her father announces that a date has been set for the now-historic elections in South Africa and that they'll make the trip to vote. Everyone is upset, however, when they hear that Gogo, in spite of her ill health, wants to travel and vote, too. They are concerned that the hardships of the trip will affect her and that she might not survive. In a caring, supportive way, everyone does everything possible to make Gogo's trip a reality, and she asks Thembi to be the one to stay by her side and accompany her on the journey. Indeed, Thembi has the special responsibility of caring for Gogo's attractive blue cloth bag as they travel.

129. Yashima, Taro, and Mitsu Yashima (1955). *Crow Boy*. Illustrated by Taro Yashima. New York: Viking. Ages 5–9. Heritage: Japanese.

In Japan on the first day of school in the village, a small boy named Chibi is afraid of others and can not learn a thing. The other children avoid him, and he is left alone. Students call him "stupid" and "slowpoke." The years go by, but Chibi doesn't miss a day of school. In sixth grade, the last grade in school, Mr. Isobe, a new teacher, arrives and gets acquainted with Chibi. He is surprised to find out how much Chibi knows and, at the end-of-the-year talent show, announces that Chibi is going to imitate the voices of crows. Chibi imitates newly hatched crows, a father crow, and early morning crow calls that are sometimes happy, sometimes sad. The teacher explains that Chibi has learned the calls by leaving his home for school at dawn and arriving home at sunset every day for six long years, and he is honored for his perfect attendance. Everyone realizes how much they have wronged Chibi all those years and they fondly nickname him Crow Boy.

8

More Multicultural Friendship Stories for Children Ages 9–14

FAMILY FRIENDSHIPS

130. Ackerman, Karen (1988). *The Song and Dance Man*. New York: Knopf. Ages 9–12. Heritage: European American.

Ackerman's focus in this story is on intergenerational respect and friendship. The grandchildren persuade Grandpa to go to the attic, get out his tap dancing shoes, top hat, and cane and perform his old-fashioned vaudeville song and dance routine.

131. Adoff, Arnold (1982). *All the Colors of the Race*. New York: Lothrop, Lee & Shepard. Ages 9 up. Heritage: African American/Multiethnic.

This is a collection of verses that describe a girl's feelings and thoughts related to her parents' biracial marriage—especially what she calls this "color thing." In her poem, "The Way I See Any Hope for Later," she says she hopes that people will stop looking at how brown or tan a person is and, instead, start loving one another.

132. Banks, Jacqueline Turner (1995). *Egg-Drop Blues*. Boston: Houghton Mifflin. Ages 9–11. Heritage: African American.

Judge and Jury, twins, are involved in a science project for the Einstein Rally at the local college, where they try to determine the best way to cushion an egg so it will not break when dropped off a tall building. Judge, who is the most interested in the project, is sensitive, quiet, and dyslexic. He narrates the story. Jury, a tease, shows his love and friendship for his brother through his willingness to help with the project.

133. Bolden, Tonya (1996). *Just Family*. New York: Cobblehill. Ages 12 up. Heritage: African American.

Part of a warm, loving, and religious African American family living in Harlem in the '60s, Beryl Nelson and her older sister, Randy, are not only siblings but good friends. When Beryl discovers that Randy has a different father and was born out of wedlock, Beryl experiences an upheaval of emotions and resentment—she even goes so far to say that she considers Randy a bastard. Her parents and grandmother are honest about their values and gentle with the two girls as they spend additional time with the sisters to help resolve the strained relationship. Later, on a trip to South Carolina for a family reunion, the two girls come to understand that their family's love for and devotion to one another can overcome the actions of the past.

134. Christopher, Matt (1994). *Fighting Tackle*. Illustrated by Karin Lidbeck. Boston: Little, Brown. Ages 9–11. Heritage: European American.
This is the story of Terry's friendship with and love for his younger brother, Nicky, who has Down's syndrome. Showing his friendship for his brother, Terry plays football and helps his brother practice for the Special Olympics. When their father is injured in an accident, however, both Terry and Nicky (not without some tension between them) work together to help him.

135. Conrad, Pam (1989). *My Daniel*. New York: Harper & Row. Ages 9–11. Heritage: European American.
Eighty-year-old Julia Creath Summerwaite flies to New York to visit her son's family and to take her grandchildren to the Natural History Museum. Through flashbacks, she tells of her love for her older brother, Daniel, and about his love for fossils. She describes his search for dinosaur bones and the competitive nature of paleontologists searching for fossils in Nebraska. At the museum, the children learn of the harshness of pioneer life and the life of their great-uncle, who was so loved by his younger sister.

136. Creech, Sharon (1994). *Walk Two Moons*. New York: HarperCollins. Ages 12 up. Heritage: Native American.
Family life, intergenerational relationships, and friendship are the braided themes in this story of thirteen-year-old Salamanca (Sal) Tree Hiddle, a Seneca Indian who journeys west with her grandparents from Ohio to Idaho to visit her mother. Sal is a storyteller and she entertains her grandparents with a story of Phoebe Winterbottom, a character whose mother disappeared mysteriously. Through it all, Sal wonders why her own mother has not yet returned, but feels the love and support of her grandparents.

137. Fine, Anne (1992). *The Book of the Banshee*. New York: Joy Street. Ages 12–14. Heritage: European American.
In a somewhat humorous way, the author shows that life in the Flowers family has been "hell on earth" ever since the relationships in the family deterio-

rated as Will's sister Estelle became a teenager and, suddenly, a shrieking banshee. Will's house is now considered a war zone and he becomes both observer and victim. With all his parents' energies focused on Estelle now, Will feels neglected and, sometimes, doesn't even get any lunch money. Will tries to see things from his parents' point of view. He realizes that he can hardly blame his mother for climbing in the first floor window after work rather than having to confront her yelling daughter. He also understands why his father, under his breath, calls Estelle "miserable" and "bad-tempered." At other times, he can see Estelle's point of view, too, like when she decides she's not going to go to school anymore because it's a "cosmic" waste of time. Will loses his patience with all of them, however, one night when he comes home late and finds that no one has bothered to feed his four-year-old sister because everyone was too busy fighting. Seeing this, Will gets angry and tells everyone what he thinks about the way they have been behaving. His words help bring peace to the family when everyone begins to communicate again, and important concessions are made on all sides.

138. Fox, Paula (1993). *Western Wind.* New York: Orchard Books. Ages 10–14. Heritage: European American.

When her new baby brother arrives and eleven-year-old Elizabeth Benedict is sent away to spend a month with her eccentric artistic grandmother, she is angry at her parents. She matures at her grandmother's, however, and comes to understand her relationships with others in her family.

139. George, Jean Craighead (1972). *Julie of the Wolves.* New York: Harper & Row. Ages 11–13. Heritage: Eskimo/Native American.

In George's book, thirteen-year-old Julie-Miyax, an Eskimo girl, leaves the husband chosen by her father to cross the Tundra toward Point Hope. At Point Hope, she plans to leave for San Francisco to find her California pen pal, Amy. Getting lost on the way, Julie survives because of her knowledge of Eskimo lore (setting her course by migrating birds and the North Star) and her friendship with Amaroq, the leader of a wolf pack. Two cultures come together as Julie lives as the traditional Eskimo did, adapting to a new way of life. Reluctantly, she returns to live with her father, Kapugen, and accepts the fact that he has abandoned his former way of life, married a *gussak* (white woman) from the lower states, and hunts from a plane for sport rather than for food.

140. Gleeson, L. (1990). *Eleanor, Elizabeth.* New York: Holiday House. Ages 9–11. Heritage: European Australian.

Eleanor, an adolescent girl, finds a diary written in 1895 by her grandmother, Elizabeth. The entries tell how Elizabeth, a newcomer in a land unfamiliar to her, came to understand and love the bush country in western Australia, where she settled and met new friends.

141. Gogol, Sara (1992). *Vatsana's Lucky New Year*. New York: Lerner. Ages 11 up. Heritage: Laotian American.

In Gogol's story, twelve-year-old Vatsana, who was born in Portland, Oregon, to Laotian parents, knows what it is like to hear racial epithets and to be called names. Now, she has Tom Connors constantly bullying her with racial slurs and other name-calling. After her aunt and cousin arrive from a refugee camp in Thailand, Vatsana can't understand why her cousin wants to continue learning a Lao dance when she is now in the United States and can do other things. Later, at a traditional New Year's celebration, she realizes that her dual cultural roots will "fit together" (as her cousin's did) and she comes to terms with her heritage as she looks forward to new friendships.

142. Hamilton, Virginia (1985). *Junius Over Far*. New York: Harper & Row. Ages 9–11. Heritage: African American.

Fourteen-year-old Junius goes looking for Jackaro, his grandfather, on an island in the Caribbean. Junius has a strong relationship with his grandfather and, through his actions, shows respect and love for his elderly relative.

143. Hoyt-Goldsmith, Diane (1990). *Totem Pole*. New York: Holiday House. Ages 9–11. Heritage: Native American.

In the Pacific Northwest, a Native American woodcarver and his son carve a traditional 40-foot totem pole to record their memories. It is a tradition to use the symbols on the pole to represent their people. The two make emblems to honor family members, to record important events, and to memorialize events from their people's legends.

144. Johnson, Angela (1993). *Toning the Sweep*. New York: Orchard Books. Ages 11–14. Heritage: African/African American.

When Grandmother leaves her desert home, Emily, an African American teenager, uses a video camera and recorder to memorialize the surroundings. Emily takes pictures of her grandmother's friends and documents her elderly relative's home and makes a visual record of related objects for her grandmother to remember. In doing so, she learns a great deal about her heritage.

145. McColley, Kevin (1993). *The Walls of Pedro Garcia*. New York: Delacorte. Ages 9–12. Heritage: Latino/Hispanic.

In McColley's story, Pedro Garcia works with his grandfather in the fields of Senor de Lupe's estate. A wall is constructed that blocks the workers' view of the river and the cooling river breeze, and this affects their lives. The act makes Pedro angry, and he confronts the groundskeeper and, later, Sr. de Lupe himself. Pedro knows that the workers rely on the river breezes to cool their huts at night. The hardness of the wall seems to represent other emotional, social, and psychological barriers that prevent friendships from developing among the people on the estate.

146. Mahy, Margaret (1994). *Tangled Fortunes*. Illustrated by Marian Young. New York: Delacorte. Ages 9–11. Heritage: European American.

Jackson Fortune and his older sister, Tracey, have always been a team, but this changes somewhat as they grow older. For instance, Tracey starts wearing dresses instead of jeans and shirts, and Jackson meets new friends who take up his time as they all play in a rock-and-roll band. The two siblings reunite as a team, however, to unravel the mystery of a motorcyclist and, later, attend their cousin's wedding.

147. Martin, Bill and John Archambault (1987). *Knots on a Counting Rope*. New York: Holt, Rinehart & Winston. Ages 9–11. Heritage: Native American.

Boy-Strength-of-Blue Horses, a blind boy, has a warm relationship with his grandfather and asks him to tell again and again the story of the storm on the night he was born. Overcoming his disability as he grows older, the boy teaches his horse to run the trails and to race.

148. Myers, Walter Dean (1990). *The Mouse Rap*. New York: Harper & Row. Ages 11–13. Heritage: African American.

Myers' story is set in Harlem, where fourteen-year-old, quick-thinking, fast-talking Frederick Douglas is known as "the Mouse," a kid who loves basketball. During a busy summer, Mouse is involved in a variety of family and peer relationships and must sort out his feelings. For example, Mouse gets reacquainted with his once-estranged father, who tries to get back into the family. Mouse also deals with his feelings for his friend, Styx, as well as his feelings for his girlfriend when she asks him to dance with her in a talent contest.

149. Russell, Ching Yeung (1995). *Water Ghost*. Illustrated by Christopher Zhong-Yuan Zhang. New York: Caroline House/Boyds Mills. Ages 10 up. Heritage: Chinese.

This story takes place in the 1940s in China, where ten-year-old Ying is raised by her loving and nurturing grandmother, Ah Pau. Ying wants to raise some money, but later, is wrongly accused of theft. It is discovered that a disabled classmate is the real thief; sadly, the student commits suicide as a result. Ying feels sadness (and some guilt) over the tragic experience and spends the money she has earned to help the classmate's needy grandmother.

150. Salisbury, Graham (1992). *Blue Skin of the Sea*. New York: Delacorte. Ages 9–11. Heritage: Hawaiian American.

In Hawaii, in the village of Kailua-Kona in the 1950s, Sonny Mendoza and his father are fishermen and face the dangers of the sea. Sonny's father is very supportive as the boy faces various difficulties in his relationship while growing up. One day, when his father's fishing boat fails to return to shore on time, Sonny is afraid he has lost a close friend—his father—to the dangerous sea.

151. San Souci, Robert (1995). *The Faithful Friend*. Illustrated by Brian Pink-ney. New York: Simon & Schuster. Ages 8–10. Heritage: Multicultural/Mar-tinique folktale.

This is the retelling of an 18th century folktale from Martinique that portrays the ultimate sacrifice for a friend. It is the story of two young men, one of African heritage, one of European heritage, who are brought up together from childhood. The two are best friends, as close as brothers, and live in the same house and are always together. When Clement, the boy of color, falls in love with Pauline, the niece of Monsieur Zabocat, a wizard, they are threatened by his evil doings. Hippolyte tries to save his friend and Pauline from the wizard's zombies. But in the rescue that demonstrates his friendship with Clement, Hip-polyte is turned to stone.

152. Scribner, Virginia (1994). *Gopher Draws Conclusions*. Illustrated by Janet Wilson. New York: Viking. Ages 9–11. Heritage: European American.

This story emphasizes that having a friend is better than being upset and not having a friend. Gopher, talented and artistic, gives one of his drawings to his best friend, Kevin. Kevin enters it in a contest under his name, wins, and gets the prize money, which he uses to buy a skateboard. Gopher, angry about what Kevin did and hurt that Kevin did not share the money, decides to get even and steal the skateboard. When he gets the skateboard, Gopher isn't as happy as he thought he would be—he feels sad about what he did and lonely without his friend. He patches things up with Kevin, who makes some compromising amends, too.

153. Waggoner, Karen (1995). *Partners*. Illustrated by Cat Bowman Smith. New York: Simon & Schuster. Ages 9–11. Heritage: European American.

This is a chapter book about a conflict of interest between Jamie and his older brother, Gordon. The two brothers raise mice, and Jamie wants to sell them as pets, but Gordon has a different idea: He wants to sell them as snake food. Dis-agreeing with Gordon on this, Jamie figures out a way to get out of the partner-ship without upsetting his brother.

154. Yep, Laurence (1977). *Child of the Owl*. New York: Harper & Row. Ages 10–14. Heritage: Chinese American.

Casey, a Chinese American girl, is at odds with her uncle's family, with whom she is living. So she is sent to live with her Chinese grandmother in Chinatown, where she eventually adjusts to the community and accepts it as her own. Help-ing Casey, her grandmother tells her about her true Chinese name and her fam-ily's story, which helps the girl develop additional respect for her heritage.

155. Yep, Laurence (1995). *Thief of Hearts*. New York: HarperCollins. Ages 10–14. Heritage: Chinese American/Multiethnic.

This story shows the perspective of a mixed-race child in a changing world.

Stacy lives with Casey, her Chinese mother, Tai-Paw, her grandmother, and her Caucasian father in San Francisco. Stacy, who narrates the story, considers herself American until the time her parents ask her to befriend a Chinese immigrant, Hong Ch'un. Unfortunately, the two girls instantly dislike one another. When some items that are stolen from school are found in Hong's backpack, a schoolmate calls Stacy a half-breed for defending Hong. Hong feels disgraced by the incident and runs away. Stacy, her mother, and grandmother search Chinatown until they find her.

156. Zolotow, Charlotte (1987). *If You Listen*. New York: Harper & Row. Ages 9–11. Heritage: Multiethnic.

When wealthy Lia, a preteen, arrives at her family's country home for the summer, she makes friends with a poor girl named Sue Ellen, with whom she shares confidences and a growing friendship. Lia needs the friendship because she rarely sees her wealthy father, who is busy working all the time, and her mother takes too many pills. Lia feels caged at the country house because no one ever listens to anyone else in the family and she feels more and more estranged as the days go by. Though a friend, Lia never invites Sue Ellen to her house because Lia fears her mother's prejudices. When the situation finally becomes intolerable for her, Lia runs away from home and is discovered at Sue Ellen's house. Her father comes after her and begs for a chance to be a better parent to her. Lia discovers, through forgiveness, a new and different friendship with her parents.

COMMUNITY, NEIGHBORHOOD, AND SCHOOL FRIENDSHIPS

157. Adler, C. S. (1988). *Always and Forever Friends*. Boston: Houghton Mifflin. Ages 9–12. Heritage: European American.

This is a chaptered story about two girls, Wendy and Honor, who vow to never change and to always be friends. Wendy searches for a friend and, in doing so, meets Honor. Wendy shares her views about friendship with Honor and says friendship is sometimes fleeting due to life and other changes that make people decide to go their separate ways.

158. Adler, C. S. (1995). *Courtyard Cat*. New York: Clarion. Ages 9–10. Heritage: European American.

In this story, the message is that neighborhood friendships can play a part in adjusting to life in a new place and in believing in yourself. A stray cat comes into eleven-year-old Lindsay's life when her family moves from the country to Schenectady and the new neighbors help her find a home for the animal. But that is only part of the adjustment that Lindsay must make to life in the city. She blames herself for her three-year-old brother's injury and his need for plastic surgery as a result of an accident, which is why the family moved—to be near the city's hospital. Through it all, Lindsay matures as she meets new friends and acknowledges the error she made related to her younger brother's safety.

159. Applegate, Katherine, et al. (1995). *See You in September*. New York: Avon. Ages 9–12. Heritage: Multicultural.

This is a collection of back-to-school friendship and love stories. For example, it includes "The Bridge," by Anne Ferguson, a humorous view of teens who are students in a life studies class and are required to participate in mock marriages. Also ⸗ ⸗ lonely teens find each other at the mall in "Destination Unknown," by Ka....... Applegate. "Shadow Girl," by Lee Wardlaw is the story of a boy's infatuation with a new girl. And there's a spoof of Dickens' *Christmas Carol* entitled "A Labor Day Carol," by Ellen Conford.

160. Bawden, Nina (1975). *The Robbers*. New York: Lippincott. Ages 12 up. Heritage: Multiethnic.

In Bawden's story, a reader discovers that a friendship can begin when one appreciates people of different environments. Nine-year-old Philip, a wealthy boy, is new at school, and his life becomes difficult when the children tease him about his fine manners. Philip's perspective changes when he makes friends with Darcy, a girl whose crippled father is a canal worker. Darcy makes friends with Philip after he is attacked by other schoolchildren. The two children come from different backgrounds: Darcy is a street child who lacks fine manners, but is independent and competent in an unprotected world. In contrast, Philip is well-to-do, living in his wealthy grandmother's apartment. With Darcy's friendship, Philip matures, appreciates the friendship of others, and realizes that not everyone lives in a protected environment as he does.

161. Bland, Celia (1995). *The Conspiracy of the Secret Nine*. Illustrated by Donald Williams, Jr. New York: Silver Moon Pr. Ages 9–12. Heritage: African American/European American.

The friendship of Troy, a boy of color whose father owns a successful barber shop, and Randy, a white boy whose out-of-work father drinks too much and is a white supremacist, sees them through the riot of 1898 in Wilmington, N.C.—when some people of color were fleeing the city. Though there is some stereotypical material in this historical novel that can be discussed, background material is included for the setting of the late 1800s.

162. Blos, Joan W. (1987). *Old Henry*. New York: William Morrow. Ages 9–10. Heritage: European American.

Henry is a nonconformist who gardens and cooks instead of spending time repairing his dilapidated old house as the other neighbors do. A dispute starts among the neighbors over how untidy his house looks, and Henry leaves town. Away from his home, he discovers that he misses his home—and even his nagging neighbors. So Henry writes a letter to the mayor of the town and asks for advice on how to solve the problem so he and the neighbors can live together as friends.

163. Bouchard, David (1995). *If You're Not from the Prairie . . .* New York: Atheneum/Simon & Schuster. Ages 9–11. Heritage: European American.

This is a portrayal of a young boy of the prairie and his friendships. The boy and his dog play through the months of the year in a country setting of fields, farms, and roads, and their activities are told through rhythmic verse that gives a feeling for the wind, dirt, grit, sunburned skin, and chapped lips suffered by those who live on the land. In the winter season, the boy and his friends have a snowball fight in front of a large country home and ride the bus to school in a winter blizzard. In the dry summer season, the boy sometimes walks in a creek bed in solitude. On a final page, the boy is a grown farmer still living on the prairie.

164. Cooper, Ilene (1996). *Star-Spangled Summer.* New York: Viking. Ages 10–14. Heritage: Multiethnic.

The importance of friendship is paramount when five friends plan for a summer at Camp Wildwood. Jill and the other girls call their friendship club The Holiday Five. However, the club members soon discover some harsh realities of life—realities that could keep some of the girls from going to camp. For instance, Kathy's father and stepmother want to take the family to Europe for a trip; Jill is striving for a spot on the upcoming Olympic ice-skating team and will have to choose between going to camp to see her friends and going to practice at an ice-skating camp; and it seems that Erin's family does not have the money to send her to camp this year, causing her to resent the other girls who can afford to go. Confronting their various situations, the friends make their decisions and accept the consequences of them.

165. Dickenson, Peter (1992). *AK.* New York: Delacorte. Ages 13 up. Heritage: African/Multicultural.

In Dickenson's story, a reader can discover the need to work toward understanding those who don't strive for friendship and peace. Paul Kagomi has never known peace during his life in Africa. Ever since he lost his family in a war when he was quite young, Paul has faced war. Orphaned, Paul is taken with other children and trained as an African warrior under the leadership of a commando, Michael. In an early event, a recent battle has just ended and Paul buries his gun, an AK. Paul and Michael leave the fighting and journey to the city, where Michael becomes politically active and a member of the government. When there is a government coup, Michael is taken prisoner, and Paul retrieves his AK and gathers others who want to rescue their friend.

166. Dolphin, Laurie (1994). *Never Shalon/Wahat Al-Salam: Oasis of Peace.* Photographed by Ben Dolphin. New York: Scholastic. Ages 9–10. Heritage: Multiethnic.

This is a photographic documentary that emphasizes that friendships can make a difference. Through the photos, the presentation highlights the unlikely friendship between two boys, one Arabic and the other Jewish, who live in a progressive Israeli community that has been nominated for the Nobel Peace Prize on four different occasions. The story of their friendship is a true memorial to the power of being friends and the possibility of global understanding of peace.

167. Donahue, John (1994). *An Island Far From Home*. New York: Carolrhoda. Ages 11–14. Heritage: European American.

This is a story set in Civil War days about a twelve-year-old Yankee boy, Joshua Loring, and a young fourteen-year-old confederate soldier who is a prisoner on nearby George's Island. Joshua's uncle, in charge of the prisoners on the island, tells Joshua about a young prisoner who is scared and alone and asks Joshua to write to him. Barely recovered from his grief over the death of his father, a doctor in the Union Army, Joshua at first rejects the idea of writing to a hated confederate soldier. He later decides to write one letter. The prisoner writes back, and stereotypical views of one another soon fade through subsequent letters, replaced by respect and friendship.

168. Erlbach, Arlene (1994). *The Best Friends Book: True Stories about Real Best Friends, Fun Things to Do with Your Best Friends, Solving Best Friend Problems, Long-Distance Friends, Finding New Friends and More!* Illustrated by Stephen J. Carrera. New York: Free Spirit. Ages 9–12. Heritage: Multiethnic.

This is a collection of first-person stories that shows the pluses and minuses of friendship and being best friends with someone. It includes advice for meeting new friends and activities to do together, such as writing letters and friendship messages whether the friend is near or far away.

169. Ernst, Lisa (1983). *Sam Johnson and the Blue Ribbon Quilt*. New York: Lothrop, Lee & Shepard. Ages 9–10. Heritage: European American.

Sam, a 19th-century farmer, discovers that he enjoys sewing when he repairs an awning over a pigpen. When he asks to join the all-women's quilting club, he is ridiculed by the members and so he forms a separate men's sewing club. The two clubs compete until a fateful circumstance inspires them to cooperate in a friendly manner.

170. Ferguson, Alane (1990). *Cricket and the Crackerbox Kid*. New York: Bradbury. Ages 9–11. Heritage: Multicultural.

In Ferguson's story, a reader can discover that reaching out and establishing new friendships may help keep peace at school and in the neighborhood. Lonely Cricket is the only child of yuppie parents who tries to stay on the fringes of a clique, realizing it is social suicide to be friends with kids from a less affluent neighborhood. A new boy in class, a crackerbox kid named Dominic, is assigned to be her partner for a school project, and they become friends. They soon discover that family income is not a measure of friendship and happiness. Their friendship is tested when Cricket rescues a new dog from the animal shelter and later discovers that it is Dominic's lost dog, Coty. Cricket likes the dog and refuses to give it up. The principal settles the argument by trial: The owner of the dog will be decided by a jury of fifth graders from another class.

171. George, Jean Craighead (1990). *On the Far Side of the Mountain*. Illustrated by the author. New York: E. P. Dutton. Ages 9–11. Heritage: European American/Multiethnic.

In George's story, the reader discovers the friendship that can develop among children living in a peaceful wilderness environment. It is told in a first-person narrative, with journal entries—similar to those found in *My Side of the Mountain* (Dutton, 1988)—that reveal Sam's personal observations and growth. As a mountain dweller, Sam constructs devices to make his rugged life easier. He prepares and stores food, tans and sews deerhide, and carves needed objects. Later, Sam and his friend, Bando, search for their friend Alice in the mountains. During the search, the two discover a ring of illegal falcon dealers.

172. Goodman, Joan Elizabeth (1994). *Songs from Home*. Illustrated by the author. New York: Harcourt Brace. Ages 11–14. Heritage: European/Italian.

The concepts of friendship and family relationships are woven together in this story set in 1960s Rome. After her mother's death, eleven-year-old Anna and her father must make a living singing in cafes for tips. Though she worries about their life of poverty in Signora Rossi's rundown boarding house, she loves her father, her best friend, Fiorella, and Maria, Signora Rossi's kindhearted maid. Anna wonders what it is in America that her father is running from as they continue to live in Italy. She also wonders what happened to the extended family they left behind in the Midwest.

173. Granger, Michele (1955). *Fifth Grade Fever*. New York: E. P. Dutton. Ages 9–10. Heritage: Multiethnic.

This story focuses on friendship in an entertaining way when two friends, Marty and Nina, decide wholeheartedly that they want to be the teacher's pets for the school year. Their new teacher is Mr. Truesdale and he is young and handsome. Their competition is Beverly Bridges, who has been teacher's pet every year. Another obstacle is that the two don't like studying or doing their homework.

174. Hamilton, Virginia (1971). *The Planet of Junior Brown*. New York: Macmillan. Ages 10–13. Heritage: African American.

The author states that the humanity of the boys is the central theme in this story about Junior Brown, a 262-pound eighth grader who is a talented pianist and artist. His friend, Buddy Clark, is brilliant in science and math. Buddy leads a group of homeless boys who live on their own "planet" in the basement of an abandoned house. Junior and Buddy spend most of their time with a janitor, Mr. Poole, a former math and astronomy teacher. Mr. Poole and Buddy show Junior a ten-planet solar system, all lit up and revolving, with the tenth planet, labeled "Junior Brown," shaped in the contours of Junior Brown's own face and glazed in beige and black. Neither boy has attended classes at school for two and a half months, and it seems that frustration after frustration affects Junior Brown as he begins to slip away from his family and reality. Concerned about the boys, Mr. Poole compassionately takes Junior, Buddy, and the ten-planet solar system to the "planet" of homeless boys, a place that Buddy renames "the planet of Junior Brown."

175. Herman, Charlotte (1995). *Millie Cooper and Friends*. Illustrated by Helen Cogancherry. New York: Viking. Ages 8–10. Heritage: European American.

The message in this story, set in a 1947 school, is that jealousy is a problem that can be worked through with others. A new girl enters Miss Brennan's fourth grade class and becomes friends with Millie's best friend, Sandy. Sometimes, the two leave Millie out of their play and she seeks advice from her caring mother. The advice helps Millie work to restore the friendship.

176. Kehret, Peg (1995). *Don't Go Near Mrs. Tallie*. Illustrated by the author. New York: Minstrel, Pocket Books. Ages 9–13. Heritage: Multicultural.

Rosie Saunders and her girlfriend, Kayo Benton, are smart, upbeat kids who care about people and help others in the community through their Care Club. They decide to help Mrs. Tallie, an elderly lady they know very little about, find a home for her cat. The girls discover that their first impression of their neighbor was wrong, as they find themselves involved in a mystery that includes attempted murder and mistaken identity.

177. Lawlor, Laurie (1995). *The Real Johnny Appleseed*. Illustrated by Mary Thompson. Chicago: Albert Whitman. Ages 9–13. Heritage: European American.

With the theme of helping others in need, this biography features brief chapters about Appleseed's adventures, details about the time period he lived in, and facts about the people he befriended and the geography of the country he traveled. Of note is the emphasis on Appleseed's character, including his interest in helping others, his friendship with Native Americans, his fondness for children, his love of books, and his business sense.

178. Lisle, Janet Taylor (1994). *Looking for Juliette*. New York: Orchard Books. Ages 9–10. Heritage: Latino/Hispanic/Multiethnic.

To the dismay of two girls, Poco and Georgina, their best friend, Angela, has moved to Mexico for a year. Poco is taking care of Angela's cat, Juliette, and when the Siamese is hit by a car, the cat mysteriously disappears. The two children, along with a new friend, Walter Kew, suspect foul play and consult a Ouija board. They become convinced that Miss Bone, an elderly woman (who lives in the garage apartment at Angela's vacant house), may be involved. When Juliette is finally found, the friends learn a lesson about misjudging others and offer an apology.

179. McDonald, Megan (1991). *The Potato Man*. Illustrated by Ted Lewin. New York: Orchard Books. Ages 9–10. Heritage: European American.

This is a story set in the days of the first Stanley steamer when horse-drawn wagons carried a seller's wares into the neighborhoods. Grandpa tells his grandchildren some stories about a fruit and vegetable peddler in his childhood neighborhood and some unkind actions toward the man that lead to a change of heart and an act of friendship.

180. Maynard, Meredy (1995). *Dreamcatcher*. New York: Polestar Publishing Co. Ages 10–12. Heritage: Multiethnic.

The longing for a friendship when one moves to a new location is the focus of this story about thirteen-year-old Fran, whose family has moved from Toronto to the country. Exploring the woods, Fran finds a baby racoon and also meets Jo, a Native American girl who becomes his good friend. Together, the two raise the racoon and Fran learns about the beliefs and customs of Jo's ancestors.

181. Michelle, Lonnie (1995). *How Kids Make Friends . . . Secrets for Making Friends, No Matter How Shy You Are*. Buffalo Grove, IL: Freedom Publishing Co. Ages 9–10. Heritage: Multiethnic.

The author has created an informational test to teach readers techniques of reaching out to develop friendly relations with other children of diverse heritages. Good point of view.

182. Moore, Floyd C. (1995). *I Gave Thomas Edison My Sandwich*. Illustrated by Donna Kae Nelson. Chicago: Albert Whitman. Ages 9–10. Heritage: European American.

This story is about the nostalgic reflections of Floyd, an eighty-seven-year-old man. He remembers a time in the early 1900s when his fourth-grade class went to the train station in Iron City, Tenn., to see the celebrity train carrying William Taft, Henry Ford, and Thomas Edison. The elderly gentleman remembers that he stood on his lunch pail to see over the grown-ups in the crowd, and that Thomas Edison came toward him and teased him about standing on his "ham sandwich." Floyd told him that the sandwich was made of souse. Edison replied that he had not thought about souse in a long time. When the train started to pull out, Floyd gave his sandwich to the conductor to pass on to Edison—an impulsive gesture of friendship.

183. Myers, Walter Dean (1994). *Darnell Rock Reporting*. New York: Delacorte. Ages 9–12. Heritage: Multiethnic.

This story is about the evolution of a thirteen-year-old city boy from a do-nothing to a do-good kid. Darnell Rock hangs out with his friends called the South Oakdale Corner Crew and does nothing. Faced with poor grades, misbehavior, and the principal, Mr. Baker, who threatens to call Darnell's parents, Darnell decides to join the school newspaper staff. Looking for a story that others will read, Darnell meets and befriends a homeless man, Sweeby Jones, who served in the Vietnam War with Darnell's father. Sweeby inspires Darnell to write an editorial asking that unused basketball courts be turned into community gardens, instead of parking lots as proposed by city planners. The city paper runs the story and interviews Darnel, who speaks before the city council.

184. Nelson, Theresa (1989). *And One for All*. New York: Orchard. Ages 11 up. Heritage: Multiethnic.

In this peace-versus-war story, Wing, Sam, and Geraldine, three friends in high school, suffer tension in their cross-sex friendship when Wing joins the Marines, knowing he will be sent to Vietnam. Sam gets deeply involved in the peace movement, and Geraldine, Wing's sister, falls in love with Sam. When Wing is killed, Geraldine takes her anger to Sam and discovers that Sam's sole reason for fighting the war was to keep Wing from being killed. Geraldine personifies the theme of the story, which is about love and friendship and the effect of misunderstandings between friends.

185. Paterson, Katherine (1977). *Bridge to Terabithia*. Illustrated by Donna Diamond. New York: Harper & Row. Ages 9 up. Heritage: European American.

Jess Aarons is a ten-year-old boy growing up in rural Virginia who is afraid to swing across a high creek on a rope. He has formed a friendship with Leslie Burke, a little girl whose family has left the city for a better way of life. Leslie's life is filled with books and imagination, and, together, the two create Terabithia, their secret kingdom in the woods where magical, beautiful things happen routinely through the forces of their imaginations.

Jess admires Leslie because she not only has led him to this magical world, but she seems to fear nothing. Later, when Leslie is killed crossing the creek to Terabithia, Jess uses all that Leslie has taught him to cope with the unexpected tragedy that befell his friend.

186. Peake, Katy (1972). *The Indian Heart of Carrie Hodges*. Illustrated by Thomas B. Allen. New York: Viking. Ages 10–11. Heritage: Native American/Multiethnic.

Carrie Hodges is a serious and sensitive girl who loves animals and nature. Growing up in the desert environment of southern California, she has come to appreciate the flora and fauna around her. She is befriended by a desert-seasoned old recluse, Foster, who shares her love of nature and begins teaching her about

Native American ways and the magical relations that once existed between the native people and the animals. Carrie's special friendship with Foster is highlighted by their common love of nature, which brings them close. The old man teaches her all he can from his lifetime of solitary observation. When the ranchers in the valley decide to kill all.the coyotes in the area because one coyote killed some sheep, Carrie is filled with torment. She sets out on a mission to save the coyotes and, at the same time, learns about her own determination and courage.

187. Pfeffer, Susan Beth (1983). *Courage, Dana.* New York: Delacorte. Ages 10–11. Heritage: European American.

Dana is a self-effacing twelve-year-old who inadvertently becomes a local heroine when she rushes into traffic to save a little child's life. She becomes an instant celebrity, but doubts that she is really a brave person. Her best friend, Sharon, devises a test for Dana to prove to herself that she is not a coward: spending an evening in a cemetery.

188. Pico, Fernando (1994). *The Red Comb.* Illustrated by Maria Antonia Ordonez. Watertown, MA: Bridgewater Books. Ages 9–10. Heritage: Latino/Hispanic folktale.

This is a Puerto Rican tale that is said to be based on fact. Two neighbors, Rosa and Vitita, discover and befriend a young, frightened black woman—a runaway from a sugarcane plantation. They feed her and keep her hidden from Pedro Calderon, a man who searches for runaways to claim the rewards. Calderon tries various ways to catch the runaway, but Rosa and Vitita outwit him each time to save their new friend.

189. Radley, Gail (1991). *The Golden Days.* New York: Macmillan. Ages 10–13. Heritage: European American/Multiethnic.

In Radley's story, eleven-year-old Cory, a foster home runaway, and elderly Carlotta, a nursing home runaway, are brought together. Both runaways have a need for friendship, love, acceptance, and something they call their "golden days of freedom." Carlotta, a former circus trouper, takes charge until she is hospitalized, and then young Cory must take over responsibility for their lives. Cory decides to call his social worker and, finally, is reunited with his former foster parents, the Keppermans, who say they will share their home with Carlotta, too. With this reunion, Cory realizes the significance of Carlotta's friendship, as well as the support of the foster parents in his life.

190. Rochman, Hazel and Darlene Z. McCampbell (1993). *Who Do You Think You Are? Stories of Friends and Enemies.* Boston: Joy St./Little, Brown. Ages 12 up. Heritage: Multiethnic.

This is a collection of sensitive stories about teenagers from various ethnic groups, written by North American authors such as Maya Angelou, Richard Peck, and John

Updike. Some of the stories deal with the tension and unhappiness that come with learning some painful truths about friendship. Others deal with teens who try to fit in and with adolescents who lose friends when they move away or face death.

191. Ryden, Hope (1994). *Backyard Rescue*. Illustrated by Ted Rand. New York: Tambourine. Ages 9–11. Heritage: European American.

This is a story of two friends, ten-year-old Lindsay and Greta, an animal lover. Greta, with family financial problems, leads Lindsay, whose family is well-off, into a commitment toward animals and animal rescues. Unfortunately, local laws get in the way of their caring for animals. Their friendship becomes stronger as they face civil disobedience together.

192. Savin, Marcia (1992). *The Moon Bridge*. New York: Scholastic. Ages 9–14. Heritage: Japanese American/Multicultural.

Two fifth-grade girls realize their friendship is jeopardized by the hatred and prejudice of World War II society especially when Mitzi Fujimoto, a Japanese American, and her family are sent to an internment camp.

193. Sharmat, Marjorie W. (1976). *The Lancelot Closes at Five*. Illustrated by Lisl Weil. New York: Macmillan. Ages 9–10. Heritage: European American.

Hutch, a health food fanatic, and Abby, his friend, spend the night in the Lancelot, a model home at the new housing development in which they live. When the local newspaper writes about the unusual vandalism at the home, several confess to spending the night there. The two friends realize that a sock with Abby's name on it was left behind and could tie Hutch and Abby to the scene of the crime. Their friendship sees them through the ordeal.

194. Singer, Marilyn (1978). *It Can't Hurt Forever*. Illustrated by Leigh Grant. New York: Harper & Row. Ages 10–11. Heritage: European American.

Eleven-year-old Ellie Simon has a heart defect, and this story describes her experiences during twelve days of hospitalization for heart surgery. Ellie goes through a wide range of emotions about her impending operation—fear, mistrust of the doctors, anger, as well as affection for Susan, a young nurse, and Sonia, a young patient who already had heart surgery and teaches Ellie all about hospital life. After the operation, there is tremendous pain—more pain than Ellie had ever anticipated. During her hospitalization, Ellie struggles with overwhelming fear and helplessness. She overcomes these feelings through her new friendships and grows as a person through the experience. Ellie makes an important decision while being in the hospital: at peace with herself, she decides to become a surgeon like the one who so skillfully repaired her defective heart.

195. Slepian, Jan (1990). *Risk n' Roses*. New York: Philomel. Ages 10–12. Heritage: Multiethnic.

Slepian's story is about a new girl in the new neighborhood, Skip, who wants to be accepted into Jean Persico's gang. The gang members have a secret club and each must meet a challenge stated by Persico, who is considered a pest in the neighborhood. For example, Persico torments old Mr. Kaminsky, who has befriended Skip's retarded sister, Angela, and everyone knows that he has no use for the gang leader. Feeling the rejection, Persico talks Angela into cutting all the blooms off the man's prize roses. With this tormenting act, Skip stops being mesmerized by Jean and decides to go her own way. In the struggle of being the "new girl," there is hope for Skip that will make the reader think about the tactics a strong-willed neighborhood pest can use to draw a newcomer into a so-called friendship and to impel aggressive, unfriendly behavior toward others.

196. Snyder, Zilpha Keatley (1990). *Libby on Wednesday*. New York: Delacorte. Ages 10–12. Heritage: European American.

In Snyder's story, Libby goes to public middle school, where she feels superior to her classmates because she has been educated at home; they, in turn, feel she is socially inferior to them. Libby takes refuge in writing and she tells her story in third-person narrative journal entries. The writing is helpful to Libby, because at the Wednesday meetings of a writer's club, each member learns of the serious problems faced by the others and develops a deeper understanding of them.

197. Snyder, Zilpha Keatley (1995). *Secret Weapons*. New York: Dell. Ages 9–11. Heritage: Multiethnic.

Several suburban, middle-class, multiethnic friends call themselves the Castle Court Kids. In this story, they are bickering among themselves as they try to keep their science projects secret from one another. The project created by Web Wong, a child genius, gets the most attention, until the kids notice two strangers in a black van in their neighborhood (for no apparent reason) on several subsequent days. Some of the kids discover that the strangers are part of a developer's scheme to pollute the neighborhood's drinking water. The Castle Court Kids save the day with their discovery.

198. Uchida, Yoshiko (1993). *The Bracelet*. New York: Philomel. Ages 11–14. Heritage: Japanese American/Multicultural.

During the days of World War II, two girls, Emi and Laurie, are the best of friends. But they begin to realize that their friendshp might end because of the suspicions of people toward Japanese Americans. Before Japanese American Emi and her family are taken to the relocation center, her friend Laurie gives her a bracelet as a symbol of their friendship.

199. Voight, Cynthia (1996). *Bad Girls*. New York: Scholastic. Ages 9–11. Heritage: Multiethnic.

In Mrs. Chemsky's fifth-grade multiethnic classroom, two new girls—Mikey Elsinger and Margalo Epps—meet and later discover they both are considered troublemakers by often hostile classmates. Though they start a friendship, neither one totally trusts the other and they often argue. When Mikey, loud and aggressive, is in trouble for telling rumors, Margalo stands up for her in front of the others. Later, when Margalo's sneaky rumor-telling and prank-playing catches up with her, Mikey refuses to let her friend be punished alone. With this support, the two begin to trust and extend their friendship from the classroom to their outside lives.

200. Yep, Laurence (1975). *Dragonwings*. Illustrated by David Wiesner. New York: Harper & Row. Ages 9–11. Heritage: Chinese/Chinese American.

In the early 1900s in San Francisco, a boy named Moon Shadow learns to change his feelings and thoughts about the white people living there as he helps his father build an airplane called "Dragonwings."

FRIENDSHIPS AROUND THE WORLD

201. Ayer, Eleanor, with Helen Waterford and Alfons Heck (1995). *Parallel Journeys*. New York: Atheneum. Ages 12 up. Heritage: European.

After forty years of traveling parallel journeys in Germany, Alfons and Helen meet in America and discover a common purpose that helps them build a relationship—speaking to youth groups and helping young people understand that compassion, friendship, and peace are possible between individuals (and countries). The accounts of Alfons and Helen are intertwined. Alfons, in a first-person narrative, relates his change from a caring youngster into a young "Nazi devil," a member of the Hitler youth group in Germany. Helen, in her own first-person account, describes her journey, which began after *Kristallnacht* (Night of Shattered Glass). Fleeing Germany, she is caught by the Nazis in Amsterdam and struggles to survive with the help of others. Her plight worsens, while Alfons' power grows in the youth group. Eventually, when Alfons and his corps face the Russians, Alfons realizes his plight—that Hitler has sacrificed his youth group "children."

202. Blue, Rose and Corinne J. Naden (1994). *People of Peace*. New York: Millbrook. Ages 9–14. Heritage: Multiethnic.

People of Peace includes the biographies of eleven figures who worked for friendship and peace. They include Andrew Carnegie, an American businessman who gave much of his money to charity and Desmond Tutu, a Nobel Peace Prize recipient. Other entries are Jane Addams, Woodrow Wilson, Ralph Bunche, Dag Hammarskjold, Jimmy Carter, Oscar Arias Sanchez, Betty Williams, and Mariread Corrigan Maguire.

203. Bryant, Martha F. (1989). *Sacajawea: A Native American Heroine.* Billings, MT: Council for Indian Education. Ages 9–14. Heritage: Native American.

This is the biography of Sacajawea, a Shoshone Indian girl best known for her role as a link between two cultures and guiding the Lewis and Clark expedition. The author has taken what is known about the girl — biography, myth, and legend with validated events — and woven it together into an account of Sacajawea's life from childhood to maturity, when she lived in a society mostly dominated by men. The author's research relied on a collection of letters, diaries, and textbooks, as well as the journals of Lewis and Clark.

204. Clayton, Ed (1968). *Martin Luther King: The Peaceful Warrior.* Illustrations by David Hodges. New York: Archway Books. Ages 10–14. Heritage: African American.

Dr. King received the Nobel Peace Prize and this biography discusses the events in his life that led up to the award and his recognition as a soldier of friendship, peace, and civil rights. Among the nonviolent events related to the civil rights movement are protest marches, sit-ins, and boycotts, including a bus boycott in Montgomery, Ala., in 1955. America's Congress also honored Dr. King by decreeing a national holiday to remember and celebrate the birthday of this peaceful civil rights leader.

205. Dixon, Ann (1994). *The Sleeping Lady.* Illustrations by Elizabeth Johns. Juneau: Alaska Northwest Books. Ages 9–14. Heritage: Native American/south-central Alaska.

The Sleeping Lady explains Alaska's first snowfall and the formation of Mount Susitna, known in south central Alaska as the "Sleeping Lady." In a village long ago, peace-loving prehistoric giants face the dilemma of how to confront a group of attacking warriors who threaten their homes. The consequences of war contrast with peace and love. It seems that the giants enjoyed living in harmony with nature and one another. When the warriors appear, the giants must make a decision and cooperate together to confront the invaders. What they did is the "How" and "Why" part of the tale that explains Alaska's first snowfall and how Mount Susitna was formed.

206. Filipovic, Zlata (1994). *Zlata's Diary: A Child's Life in Sarajevo.* Introduction by Janine DiGiovanni. Translated by Christina Pribichevich-Zoric. New York: Viking. Ages 10 up. Heritage: European.

Filipovic meticulously depicts the daily life of a contemporary young girl growing up during wartime, and her desire for friendship and peace. Zlata's diary entries are from September 1991 to October 1993, as she and her family coped with all that war brings — bombings, killings, and the destruction of the cities.

207. Fletcher, Ralph (1996). *Buried Alive: The Elements of Love*. Illustrated by Andrew Moore. New York: Atheneum. Ages 12 up. Heritage: Multiethnic.

The author narrates his poems in many teenage personas, with each voice telling of his or her experience related to love. For example, a girl in her teens gets love letters written in Spanish and has to have them translated before she can read the contents. The verses, suitable for reading aloud or for choral reading by groups, are arranged to show some of the universal and fundamental aspects of a loving relationship.

208. Friese, Kai (1989). *Tenzin Gyatso, The Dalai Lama*. Boston: Chelsea House. Ages 10 up. Heritage: Asian/Tibetan.

The Dalai Lama received the Nobel Peace Prize—a worldwide recognition. His achievements leading to this award are chronicled in this life story. It tells of his education to prepare to be the spiritual ruler of Tibet, his success in keeping the Tibetan culture alive, and his life in exile when the Chinese communists invaded his country. Also included are a bibliography for further reading, a chronology, and an index.

209. Galichich, Anne (1987). *Samantha Smith: A Journey for Peace*. Minneapolis: Dillon Press. Ages 9 up. Heritage: European American/European.

When ten-year-old Samantha Smith learned that both the United States and the U.S.S.R. had enough nuclear bombs to destroy each other, she wrote to Yuri Andropov, the Soviet leader in 1982. She told him of her concerns, anxieties, and worries. Her letter made the front page of the newspaper *Pravda* and she got a response from Andropov himself—the genesis of a friendly relationship between the girl and other residents of her hometown and between the Soviet Union and its residents who also wanted peace.

210. Giff, Patricia Reilly (1986). *Mother Teresa: Sister to the Poor*. Illustrated by Ted Levin. New York: Viking/Kestrel. Ages 9–11. Heritage: European.

Mother Teresa grew up in a family in which religion was the link that kept them together. They spent hours in church and working for the poor—an act of compassion and friendship. Teresa answered God's call and traveled to Ireland to join the Sisters of Soreto. Years later, she journeyed to India to teach and worked in the slums caring for the poor, the needy, and the dying. She was the founder of a sheltered community for leprosy patients, Shanti Nagar, and in 1979, she received the Nobel Peace Prize.

211. Greene, Bette (1993). *Summer of My German Soldier*. New York: Kar-Ben, Ages 12 up. Heritage: German/European American/Multiethnic.

In a small town in Arkansas, Patty Bergen, the twelve-year-old daughter of a department-store owner, sees herself as awkward. Her parents fight and are mean to Patty. The Bergens' black cook, however, loves Patty and cares for her. Living in a compassionless home, Patty gives what she needs—compassion—to Anton, a good-looking, well-educated German prisoner of war who lives in a prison camp near town and shops at her father's store. A friendship develops. When she later sees him running down the railroad tracks, she offers him the safety of a special hideout room over the garage. After Anton is captured, Patty's part in his escape is discovered. She is arrested, sent to reform school, and thinks ahead of the time when she will be released and can leave her family.

212. Greene, Carol (1986). *Desmond Tutu: Bishop of Peace*. Chicago: Children's Press. Ages 9–10. Heritage: South African.

In 1984, Bishop Desmond Tutu was chosen to receive the Nobel Peace Prize, a result of his lifelong work. The citation with the award honored *all* South African blacks who had worked for peaceful change. Born in South Africa, Desmond quickly learned some disturbing facts about his country: Although 70 percent of the people in South Africa were black, they could not vote in national elections; they could not live or own land wherever they wanted; and the government could make them move whenever it wanted them to move.

When Desmond was twelve, his mother worked as a cook in a missionary school for the blind. Seeing people helping other people made Desmond decide to help other people, too, in the name of friendship. Tutu became a teacher and then, inspired by a white Anglican priest, he also was ordained as a priest. Tutu became the first black dean in the Anglican church. When the government was moving blacks from cities back to tribal lands, Tutu, who was not a bishop, asked the United States and countries in Europe to stop trading with South Africa. Though this made the South African government angry, the peaceful tactic worked.

213. Hamanaka, Sheila, coordinator (1995). *On the Wings of Peace*. New York: Clarion. Ages 10 up. Heritage: Multicultural.

This collection contains the contributed work of more than 50 artists and authors of children's books that relate to some aspect of friendship and peace. It commemorates the anniversary of the bombings of Hiroshima and Nagasaki and also discusses the dangers of nuclear proliferation. Royalties are donated to peace organizations.

214. Heide, Florence Parry and Judith Heide Gilliland (1992). *Sami and the Time of the Troubles*. Illustrated by Ted Lewin. New York: Clarion. Ages 9 up. Heritage: Lebanese/Middle East.

Living in Beirut, Lebanon, ten-year-old Sami and his friend, Amir, hear gunfire every day. When the danger finally lets up and there is a lull in the fighting, the two friends meet outside and play what they know best—war. Other people in the neighborhood go about their business as peacefully as they can, but the boys notice what is going on: The elderly men drink their coffee with friends and smoke their water pipes, and there is even a bride and groom on the way to their wedding. Everyone faces deadly bombings and gunfire in their neighborhood daily. To escape the danger when it comes, Sami's family stays in the basement of an uncle's house and listens to the radio. Sami says the fighting cannot last forever, but at the end of the story, Sami and his family still seek safety at night in the basement and listen to gunfire in the dark.

215. Holler, Anne (1993). *Pocahontas: Powhatan Peacemaker*. Illustrated by the author. New York: Chelsea. Ages 10–14. Heritage: Native American/Multiethnic.

This is a brief biography of the life of Pocahontas and her act of friendship in helping the English survive at Jamestown. Her life story also portrays the life of the Algonkian people who settled on the coastal lowlands in present-day Virginia, and their friendships (or lack thereof) with the English who settled there. In marrying an Englishman, Pocahontas defied her own people, though she was an important mediator between the different cultures. Ironically, she also suffered because of the very people she had helped settle in the "new land." Includes archival maps and reproductions.

216. Hoyt-Goldsmith, Diane (1992). *Arctic Hunter*. Photographs by Lawrence Migdale. New York: Holiday House. Ages 9–11. Heritage: Inupiat Eskimo.

This is the story of ten-year-old Reggie, an Inupiat boy who lives with his family above the Arctic Circle. In the spring, the family journeys across an ice floe to reach their spring camp on Sadie Creek. Reggie goes on a seal hunt and stays in the boat while the men stalk seals on the ice. When a seal comes close to the boat, Reggie seizes the opportunity to capture his first seal. Out of friendship, Reggie gives his seal to an elderly woman so that she can feed her family with its meat during the long cold days of the coming winter.

217. *I Dream of Peace* (1994). Introduction by James P. Grant, executive director, UNICEF. New York/HarperCollins/UNICEF. Ages 9–11. Heritage: Multiethnic.

A preface by Maurice Sendak describes day-to-day existence in a warring world, where only a few of the fighting care for the human rights of others. This is a compilation of sketches and writings by children who have tried to cope with the realities of war. The sketches show planes bombing houses and buildings, soldiers shooting people, and fires burning structures in the towns. Writings accompany the sketches and drawings and further depict the children's experiences.

218. Laird, Elizabeth (1992). *Kiss the Dust*. New York: E. P. Dutton. Ages 11–15. Heritage: Middle East/Multiethnic.

The need for world friendships is underscored in this story, which focuses on the conflict between the Arabs and the Kurds in northern Iraq. The conflict is brought home when the Iraqi secret police arrive in a Kurdish village looking for Tara Hawrami's father. The family flees into the mountains of Kurdistan, then over the border into Iran, where they join other refugees. This story is well-researched and portrays the fears of the people who live in northern Iran.

219. Lattimore, Deborah Nourse (1987). *The Flame of Peace: A Tale of the Aztecs*. New York: Harper & Row. Ages 9–11. Heritage: Aztec myth/folk literature.

To honor his father's death, a young Aztec boy in Tenochtitlan goes in search of a new temple flame of peace to mark an end to fighting and war. On the way to get the flame from the hill of Lord Morning Star, the boy is challenged by nine demons. When he overcomes the demons and successfully reaches the hill, he receives a reward of feathery fire and returns with it to the temple.

220. Little, Jean (1986). *Different Dragons*. New York: Viking. Ages 9–12. Heritage: Multiethnic.

Set in the north in Canada, a boy lives with a secret fear that he must conquer— a dragon of emotions. When he later makes friends with a neighborhood girl, he discovers that everyone has different dragons to overcome.

221. Long, Cathryn J. (1994). *The Middle East in Search of Peace*. New York: Millbrook. Ages 9–14. Heritage: Multiethnic.

This informational book is a fair and evenhanded overview of the disputes among the people in the Middle East. The disputes include the role of water and oil, the beginnings of self-rule in places like Jericho, and the political role of outside governments. The development of the contemporary conflict and the steps that are being taken to achieve friendship and peace are discussed. A full-color photograph of the historic handshake between Yitzhak Rabin and Yasir Arafat is included.

222. McDonald, Ian (1989). *The Hummingbird Tree*. Portsmouth, NH: Heinemann. Ages 12 up. Heritage: Multiethnic.

This story traces the friendship between twelve-year-old Alan Holmes, a wealthy white boy in Trinidad, and his best friends, Kaiser and Jaillin, the house boy and the girl who work for Alan's parents. The friendship grows as the three grow older until, sadly, the pressures of race and class in Trinidad drive them apart. Alan is not wanted in the village where his friends live, and his friends are not accepted by other children who visit his home. Though they wish to be friends, the older the children become, the more susceptible they are to society's expectations for conformity.

223. Mansani, Shakuntala (1950). *Ghandi's Story*. Illustrated by the author. New York: Henry Z. Walck. Ages 9–10. Heritage: Asian/East Indian.

The author was a contemporary of Ghandi's and knew this peace-loving man quite well. He writes this introduction to Ghandi's life with reverence and affection. He tells how Ghandi's life as a pacifist leader was devoted to the idea of creating change in human rights through peaceful means. This is a simple, direct account of India's great leader and one of the greatest peace-loving figures in history. The shy but lively boy, living in a small Indian town, then studying in England, grows up to become a crusader for human rights in South Africa, a revered pacifist leader in India, and, finally, a friend to all who advocated nonviolence.

224. *My Wish for Tomorrow: Words and Pictures from Children around the World in Celebration of the Fiftieth Anniversary of the United Nations* (1995). Illustrated. New York: Tambourine. Ages 9–11. Heritage: Multiethnic.

There is a foreword by Nelson Mandela and an introduction by Boutros Boutros-Ghali. The text features words and pictures depicting wishes that children around the world send out to people about the future.

225. Namioka, Lensey (1992). *The Coming of the Bear*. New York: HarperCollins. Ages 10–14. Heritage: Asian/Japanese.

In Japan in the 1600s, an impending island war between the native Ainu people and Japanese colonists who want to settle on the land is diverted when a mystery is solved. The mystery: A bear keeps attacking the colonists during the winter, when bears usually hibernate. Two young samurai, Senta and Matsuzo, solve the mystery and avert the fighting between the natives and the colonists.

226. Siegel, Danny (1993). *Tell Me a Mitzvah: Little and Big Ways to Repair the World*. Illustrated by Judith Friedman. New York: Kar-Ben. Ages 9–14. Heritage: Jewish/Multiethnic.

This collection profiles twelve people who have contributed to repairing the world, or *Tikkun Olam*. They are common people doing uncommon acts—a woman collects and distributes shoes to those who need them, a man gathers pennies for the homeless, and some farmers give part of their harvest to feed the hungry. Yiddish and Hebrew terms are included in the text.

227. Sierra Judy and Robert Kaminski (1995). *Children's Traditional Games: Games from 137 Countries and Cultures*. Phoenix: Oryx. Ages 10 up. Heritage: Multiethnic.

More than 200 games, such as hopscotch, marbles, and tag, are organized alphabetically by the country of origin and include rules of play, cultural information, and, where appropriate, diagrams. This is a useful resource for older children researching evidence and anecdotes of friendship in particular cultures. The indices indicate the playing environment, as well as the type of game such as ball games, word games, and so on.

228. Strachan, Ian (1990). *The Flawed Glass*. Boston: Little, Brown. Ages 10–11. Heritage: Scottish/North American.

Strachan's story is set on an island off Scotland, where Shona MacLeod rescues Carl, the island owner's son, from a potentially fatal accident. They become friends. Shona is physically handicapped and unable to walk or talk and she calls herself a piece of "flawed glass." Shona is intellectually clear, however, even though she cannot tell others her thoughts. During their new friendship, Carl teaches Shona to use his dad's computer, and Shona shows Carl the birds on the island—in particular, the eagle hatchlings that, like Shona, struggle for their survival. When Shona and her family face dangerous poachers and are involved in a conflict with the new American owners of the island, she finds a way to communicate the truth when the poachers try to incriminate her father for their deeds. Later, when Carl returns to the United States, the two maintain their friendship, and Shona communicates with him through a computer and a modem.

229. Turnbull, Ann (1995). *No Friend of Mine*. Illustrated by the author. New York: Candlewick. Ages 9–11. Heritage: British/European.

This is the story of the parallel lives of two youngsters who live in the mining town of Culverton, England. Lennie, a miner's son, is teased and tormented by the school bully and is in need of a friend. Ralph, the son of the mine owner, is home from boarding school and needs a friend. They meet and begin a friendship, which eventually is tested when Lennie is falsely accused of stealing from the mine owner's home. With this accusation, the distrust between the classes is crystallized and affects the friendship.

Title, Author, and Illustrator Index

Numbers refer to entry numbers in the bibliography, not page numbers.

Abraham Lincoln (D'Aulaire & D'Aulaire) 113
Accorsi, William 110
Ackerman, Karen 130
Adler, C. S. 157, 158
Adoff, Arnold 1, 131
The Adventures of Sugar and Junior (Medearis & Poydar) 97
AK (Dickenson) 165
Aliki 52
All the Colors of the Earth (Hamanaka) 118
All the Colors of the Race (Adoff) 131
Allen, Thomas B. 186
Always and Forever Friends (Adler) 157
Amaktauyok, Germaine 56
And One for All (Nelson) 184
Andreasen, Dan 31, 91
Angelou, Maya 53
Annie and the Old One (Miles & Parnall) 28
Annie's Gifts (Medearis & Rich) 27
Apt. 3 (Keats) 84
Applegate, Katherine 159
Archambault, John 147
Arctic Hunter (Hoyt-Goldsmith & Migdale) 217
August, Louise 12

Aunt Flossie's Hats and Crab Cakes (Howard & Ransome) 14
Awful Evelina (Pfeffer & Dawson) 36
Ayer, Eleanor 201
Aylesworth, Jim 54

Backyard Rescue (Ryden & Rand) 191
Bad Girls (Voight) 199
Baer, Edith 111
Bains, Rae 112
Banks, Jacqueline Turner 132
The Barber's Cutting Edge (Battle-Lavert & Holbert) 55
Battle Day at Camp Delmont (Weiss) 51
Battle-Lavert, Gwendolyn 55
Bawden, Nina 160
Bed Bouncers (Knutson) 120
Behop-a-De-Walk! (Hamanaka) 73
The Best Friends Book (Erlbach) 168
Best Friends Together (Aliki) 52
Bjorkman, Steve 111
Black Is Brown Is Tan (Adoff) 1
Bland, Celia 161
Blue, Rose 202
Blue Skin of the Sea (Salisbury) 150
Blos, Joan W. 162
Blow Away Soon (James & Vojtech) 15
Bogart, Jo Ellen 2

Bolden, Tonya 133
Bond, Craig 7
The Book of the Banshee (Fine) 137
Bostock, Mike 89
Bouchard, David 163
The Boy and the Quilt (Kurtz) 22
The Bracelet (Uchida) 198
Brave Little Pete of Geranium Street (Lagercrantz & Lagercrantz) 23
Bridge to Terabithia (Paterson & Diamond) 185
Brigid the Bad (Leverich & Andreasen) 91
Brunkus, Denise 60
Bryant, Martha F. 204
Buffalo Woman (Goble) 116
Bunting, Eve 3, 4
Buried Alive: The Elements of Love (Fletcher & Moore) 208
Bushey, Jeanne 56
Byars, Betsy 5

The Canada Geese Quilt (Kinsey-Warnock) 20
Canevari, Anne 103
Carmi, Gloria 100
Carrera, Stephen J. 168
Carter, Abby 94
Catalanotto, Peter 6, 93
Cazet, Denys 7
Champion, Joyce 57
Chestnut Cove (Egan) 65
Chicken Sunday (Polacco) 101
Child of the Owl (Yep) 154
Children's Traditional Games: Games from 137 Countries and Cultures (Sierra & Kaminski) 228
Chin Chang and the Dragon's Dance (Wallace) 50
Chinn, Karen 58
Chmielarz, Sharon 59
Christopher, Matt 134
Claude Has a Picnic (Gackenbach) 67
Clayton, Ed 205
Cody and Quinn, Sitting in a Tree (Larson & Poydar) 87
Coerr, Eleanor 8

Cogancherry, Helen 175
The Coming of the Bear (Namioke) 226
Connie Came to Play (Walsh & Lambert) 107
Conrad, Pam 135
The Conspiracy of the Secret Nine (Bland & Williams) 161
Cooney, Barbara 95
Cooper, Floyd 71
Cooper, Ilene 164
Courage, Dana (Pfeffer) 187
Courtney-Clarke, Margaret 53
Courtyard Cat (Adler) 158
Creech, Sharon 136
Cricket and the Crackerbox Kid (Ferguson) 170
Cristaldi, Kathryn 60
Crow Boy (Yashima & Yashima) 129

Dancing (Cazet & Bond) 7
Darnell Rock Reporting (Myers) 183
D'Aulaire, Edgar Parin 113
D'Aulaire, Ingri 113
Dawson, Diane 36
A Day at Damp Camp (Lyon & Catalanotto) 93
The Day Gogo Went to Vote: South Africa, April, 1994 (Sisulu & Wilson) 128
A Day's Work (Bunting & Himler) 3
de Kiefie, Kees 77
DeLuna, Tony 43
dePaola, Tomie 61, 62
Derosa, Dee 70
Desmond Tutu: Bishop of Peace (Greene) 213
Diamond, Donna 185
Dickenson, Peter 165
Different Dragons (Little) 221
DiGiovanni, Janine 207
DiSalvo-Ryan, DyAnne 69
Dixon, Ann 206
Dolphin, Ben 166
Dolphin, Laurie 166
Donahue, John 167
Don't Go Near Mrs. Tallie (Kehret) 176

Dooley, Norah 63
Down at Angel's (Chmielarz & Kastner) 59
Dragonwings (Yep & Wiesner) 200
Dreamcatcher (Maynard) 180
Dreamland (Schotter & Hawkes) 41
Duffey, Betsy 64

Egan, Tim 65
Egg-Drop Blues (Banks) 132
Eleanor, Elizabeth (Gleeson) 140
Emily and Alice Again (Champion & Stevenson) 57
Erlbach, Arlene 168
Ernst, Lisa Campbell 66, 169
Everybody Bakes Bread (Dooley & Thornton) 63

The Faithful Friend (San Souci & Pinkney) 151
Faraway Families (Loredo & Raja) 24, 122
Farnsworth, Bill 104
Ferguson, Alane 170
Fifth Grade Fever (Granger) 173
Fighting Tackle (Christopher & Lidbeck) 134
Fighting Words (Merriam & Small) 98
Filipovic, Zlata 207
Fine, Anne 137
The Flame of Peace (Lattimore) 220
The Flawed Glass (Strachan) 229
Fletcher, Ralph 208
Flournoy, Valerie 9
The Flute Player: An Apache Folktale (Lacapa) 86
Folks Call Me Appleseed John (Glass) 115
Fox, Paula 138
Friedman, Judith 227
Friese, Kai 209

Gackenbach, Dick 67
Galbraith, Kathryn O. 10
Galichich, Anne 210
Gandhi's Story (Mansani) 224

The Garden of Happiness (Tamar & Lambase) 106
Garrison, Susan 68
George, Jean Craighead 139, 171
Gershator, Phillis 114
Giff, Patricia Reilly 69, 211
The Gift of Driscoll Lipscomb (Yamaka & Kim) 109
Gifts (Bogart & Reid) 2
Gilliland, Judith Heide 215
The Girl Who Could Fly (Hooks & de Kiefie) 77
Glass, Andrew 115
Gleeson, L. 140
Goble, Paul 11, 116
Gogol, Sara 141
The Golden Days (Radley) 189
Goldin, Barbara Diamond 12
Goodman, Joan Elizabeth 172
Gopher Draws Conclusions (Scribner & Wilson) 152
Gracias, Rosa (Markel & Paterson) 96
Grandfather's Trolley (McMillan) 25
Grandma's Smile (Moore & Andreasen) 31
Grandmother and the Runaway Shadow (Rosenberg & Peck) 126
Granger, Michele 173
Grant, Leigh 194
Great Aunt Martha (Jones & Jackson) 18
Green, Mimi 114
Greene, Bette 212
Greene, Carol 117, 213
Greene, Stephanie 70
Greenseid, Diane 76
Grimes, Nikki 71
Guback, Georgia 13
Guthrie, Donna 72

Ha, Ying-Hwa 58
Hamanaka, Sheila 29, 73, 118, 119, 214
Hamilton, Virginia 142, 174
Hank's Work (Schreier) 42
Harriet Tubman: The Road to Freedom (Bains & Johnson) 112

Havill, Juanita 74, 75
Hawkes, Kevin 41
Hays, Michael 10, 34
Heck, Alfons 202
Heide, Florence Parry 215
Helping Bugs (Lonborg &
   Houghton) 92
Her Seven Brothers (Goble) 11
Herman, Charlotte 175
Hess, Debra 76
Hey, New Kid! (Duffey &
   Thompson) 64
Hiawatha (Longfellow & Jeffers) 16
Himler, Ronald 3
Hodges, David 205
Holbert, Raymond 55
Holding onto Sunday (Galbraith &
   Hays) 10
Holler, Anne 216
Honi's Circle of Trees (Gershator &
   Green) 114
Hooks, William H. 77
Hopkinson, Deborah 78
Houghton, Diane R. 92
*How Emily Blair Got Her Fabulous
   Hair* (Garrison & Priceman) 68
*How Kids Make Friends . . . Secrets
   for Making Friends, No Matter
   How Shy You Are* (Michelle)
   181
Howard, Arthur 79
Howard, Elizabeth Fitzgerald 14
Howe, James 80
Hoyt-Goldsmith, Diane 143, 217
Hu, Ying-Hwa 58
The Hummingbird Tree (McDonald)
   223
The Hundredth Name (Oppenheim &
   Hays) 34
Hutchins, Pat 81

An Island Far from Home (Donahue)
   167
I'm Not Oscar's Friend Anymore
   (Sharmat & DeLuna) 43
I Dream of Peace (UNICEF) 218
I Gave Thomas Edison My Sandwich
   (Moore & Nelson) 182

I Speak English for My Mom
   (Stanek) 45
If You Listen (Zolotow) 156
If You're Not from the Prairie . . .
   (Bouchard) 163
The Indian Heart of Carrie Hodges
   (Peake & Allen) 186
It Can't Hurt Forever (Singer &
   Grant) 194

Jackson, Isaac 82
Jackson, Shelley 18
Jacques, Laura 21
Jamaica and Brianna (Havill &
   O'Brien) 74
Jamaica's Blue Marker (Havill &
   O'Brien) 75
James, Betsy 15
Jeffers, Susan 16
Johns, Elizabeth 206
Johnson, Angela 83, 144
Johnson, Larry 112
Johnson, Tony 17
JoJo's Flying Side Kick (Pinkney) 37
Jones, Rebecca C. 18
Jossee, Barbara M. 19
The Josefina Story Quilt (Coerr) 8
Julie of the Wolves (George) 139
Junius over Far (Hamilton) 142
Just Family (Bolden) 133

Kaminski, Robert 228
Kastner, Jill 59, 123
Keats, Ezra Jack 84, 85
The Keeping Quilt (Polacco) 38
Kehret, Peg 176
Kim, Joung Un 109
Kinsey-Warnock, Natalie 20
Kiss the Dust (Laird) 219
Knots on a Counting Rope (Martin &
   Archambault) 147
Knutson, Kimberley 120
Kroll, Virginia 21
Kurtz, Shirley 22

Lacapa, Michael 86
Lagercrantz, Rose 23
Lagercrantz, Samuel 23

Laird, Elizabeth 219
Lamb, Christine 124
Lambase, Barbara 106
Lambert, Stephen 107
The Lancelot Closes at Five (Sharmat & Weil) 193
Larson, Kirby 87, 88
Lasky, Kathryn 89
Lattimore, Deborah Nourse 220
Lawlor, Laurie 177
Lee, Betsy 121
The Legend of the Bluebonnet (dePaola) 61
The Legend of the Indian Paintbrush (dePaola) 62
Leghorn, Lindsay 90
Let's Make a Garden (Lobe) 122
A Letter to Amy (Keats) 85
Leverich, Kathleen 91
Levin, Ted 211
Lewin, Ted 179, 214
Libby on Wednesday (Snyder) 196
Lidbeck, Karin 134
Lisle, Janet Taylor 178
Little, Jean 221
Lobe, Tamara Awad 122
Lonborg, Rosemary 92
Long, Cathryn J. 222
Looking for Juliette (Lisle) 178
Loredo, Betsy 24, 122
Lucy's Picture (Moon) 30
Luka's Quilt (Guback) 13
Lyon, George Ella 93

MacDonald, Maryann 94
McCampbell, Darlene Z. 190
McColley, Kevin 145
McDonald, Ian 223
McDonald, Megan 179
McGraw's Emporium (Aylesworth) 54
McLerran, Alice 95
McMillan, Bruce 25
Mahy, Margaret 26, 146
Markel, Michelle 96
Martin, Bill, Jr. 147

Martin Luther King: The Peaceful Warrior (Clayton & Hodges) 205
Martin, Nora 123
Masani, Shakuntala 224
Maynard, Meredy 180
Medearis, Angela Shelf 27, 97
Meeker, Clare Hodgson 124
Meet Danitra Brown (Grimes & Cooper) 71
Merriam, Eve 98
Michelle, Lonnie 181
The Middle East in Search of Peace (Long) 222
Migdale, Lawrence 217
Miles, Miska 28
Millie Cooper and Friends (Herman & Cogancherry) 175
Mills, Claudia 29
Milone, Karen 40
The Miracle of the Potato Latkes (Penn & Carmi) 100
Miss Penny and Mr. Grubbs (Ernst) 66
The Moon Bridge (Savin) 192
Moon, Nicola 30
Moore, Andrew 208
Moore, Elaine 31
Moore, Floyd C. 182
Mother Teresa: Caring for God's Children (Lee) 121
Mother Teresa: Sister to the Poor (Giff & Levin) 211
The Mouse Rap (Myers) 148
Munoz, Claudia 105
Murphy, Elspeth Campbell 32
My Best Friend (Hutchins) 81
My Brother, Ant (Byars & Simont) 5
My Daniel (Conrad) 135
My Dream of Martin Luther King (Ringgold) 125
My Name Is Pocahontas (Accorsi) 110
My Painted House, My Friendly Chicken, and Me (Angelou & Courtney-Clarke) 53
My Rotten Red-Headed Older Brother (Polacco) 39

My Wish for Tomorrow: Words and Pictures from Children around the World in Celebration of the Fiftieth Anniversary of the United Nations (no author cited) 225
Myers, Walter Dean 148, 183
The Mystery of the Dancing Angels (Murphy) 32

Naden, Corinne J. 203
Namioka, Lensey 226
Nelson, Donna Kae 182
Nelson, Theresa 184
Ness, Evaline 99
Never Shalon/Wahat Al-Salam: Oasis of Peace (Dolphin & Dolphin) 166
Newman, Leslea 33
Night Lights (Goldin & August) 12
No Biting, Horrible Crocodile! (Shipton & Munoz) 105
No Friend of Mine (Turnbull) 230

O'Brien, Anne Sibley 74, 75
Old Henry (Blos) 162
On the Far Side of the Mountain (George) 171
On the Wings of Peace (Hamanaka) 214
Oppenheim, Shulamith Levey 34
Oram, Hiawyn 35
Ordonez, Maria Antonia 188
Owen Foote, Second Grade Strongman (Greene & Derosa) 70

Page, Ken 83
The Painter (Catalanotto) 6
Parallel Journeys (Ayer, Waterford & Heck) 202
Parnall, Peter 28
Partners (Waggoner & Smith) 153
The Patchwork Quilt (Flornoy) 9
Paterson, Diane 96
Paterson, Katherine 185
The Peace Crane (Hamanaka) 119
Peake, Katy 186
Peck, Beth 126
Penn, Malka 100
People of Peace (Blue & Naden) 203

Pfeffer, Susan Beth 36, 187
Pico, Fernando 188
The Pink Party (MacDonald & Carter) 94
Pinkney, Brian 37, 151
Pinky and Rex and the Double-Dad Weekend (Howe & Sweet) 80
The Planet of Junior Brown (Hamilton) 174
Plecas, Jennifer 19
Pocahontas: Powhatan Peacemaker (Holler) 216
Polacco, Patricia 38, 39, 101
Pond Buddies (Lasky & Bostock) 89
The Potato Man (McDonald & Lewin) 179
Poydar, Nancy 87, 88, 97, 108
Pribichevich-Zoric, Christina 207
Priceman, Marjorie 68
Proud of Our Feelings (Leghorn) 90

The Quilt Story (Johnson) 17

Radley, Gail 189
Raja, Monisha 24, 122
Rand, Ted 191
Ransom, Candice F. 40
Ransome, James 14
Raschka, Chris 102
The Real Johnny Appleseed (Lawlor & Thompson) 177
The Red Comb (Pico & Ordonez) 188
Reid, Barbara 2
Remember That (Newman & Ritz) 33
Rich, Anna 27
Ring, Elizabeth 103
Ringgold, Faith 125
Risk n' Roses (Slepian) 195
Ritz, Karen 33
The Robbers (Bawden) 160
Robert E. Lee: Leader in War and Peace (Greene) 117
Rochman, Hazel 190
Rosenberg, Liz 126
Rosie and Michael (Viorst & Tomer) 49
Roxaboxen (McLerran & Cooney) 95
Russell, Ching Yeung 149

Ryan, Cheryl 104
Ryden, Hope 191

Sacajawea: A Native American Heroine (Bryant) 204
Salisburg, Graham 150
Sally Arnold (Ryan & Farnsworth) 104
Sam and the Lucky Money (Chinn, Van Wright & Ha) 58
Sam, Bangs, and Moonshine (Ness) 99
Sam Johnson and the Blue Ribbon Quilt (Ernst) 169
Samantha Smith: A Journey for Peace (Galichich) 210
Samantha the Snob (Cristaldi & Brunkus) 60
Sami and the Time of the Troubles (Heide, Gilliland & Lewin) 215
San Souci, Robert 151
Saturday Sancocho (Torres) 47
Savin, Marcia 192
Say Hola, Sarah (Giff & DiSalvo-Ryan) 69
Schotter, Roni 41
Schreier, Joshua 42
Schuett, Stacey 127
Scribner, Virginia 152
Second Grade Pig Pals (Larson & Poydar) 88
The Second Princess (Oram) 35
Secret Weapons (Snyder) 197
See You in September (Applegate, et al.) 159
The Seven Chinese Brothers (Mahy, Tseung & Tseung) 26
Sharmat, Marjorie W. 43, 193
Shipton, Jonathan 105
Shoes Like Miss Alice's (Johnson & Page) 83
Shooting Star Summer (Ransom & Milone) 40
Siegel, Danny 227
Sierra, Judy 228
Simont, Marc 5
Singer, Marilyn 194
Sisters (Tusa) 48

Sisulu, Elinor Batezat 128
A Sled Dog for Moshi (Bushey & Amaktauyok) 56
The Sleeping Lady (Dixon & Johns) 206
Slepian, Jan 195
Small, David 98
Smith, Cat Bowman 153
Snow Day (Jossee & Plecas) 19
Snyder, Zilpha Keatley 196, 197
Soman, David 82
Some Stuff (Ring & Canevari) 103
Somebody's New Pajamas (Jackson & Soman) 82
Somewhere in the World Right Now (Schuett) 127
The Song and Dance Man (Ackerman) 130
Songs from Home (Goodman) 172
Stamm, Claus 44
Stanek, Muriel 45
Star-Spangled Summer (Cooper) 164
Steig, William 46
Stevenson, Sucie 57
The Stone Dancers (Martin & Kastner) 123
Strachan, Ian 229
Summer of My German Soldier (Greene) 212
Sweet Clara and the Freedom Quilt (Hopkinson) 78
Sweet Magnolia (Kroll & Jacques) 21
Sweet, Melissa 80

A Tale of Two Rice Birds (Meeker & Lamb) 124
Tamar, Erika 106
Tangled Fortunes (Mahy & Young) 146
Tell Me a Mitzvah: Little and Big Ways to Repair the World (Siegel & Friedman) 227
Tenzin Gyatso: The Dalai Lama (Friese) 209
Thief of Hearts (Yep) 155
This Is the Way We Eat Our Lunch (Baer & Bjorkman) 111
Thompson, Ellen 64

Thompson, Mary 177
Thornton, Peter J. 63
Three Strong Women: A Tall Tale
    (Stamm, Tseung & Tseung) 44
Tomer, Lorna 49
Toning the Sweep (Johnson) 144
Torres, Leyla 47
Totem Pole (Hoyt-Goldsmith) 143
The Toy Brother (Steig) 46
Tseung, Jean 26, 44
Tseung, Mou-Sien 26, 44
Tusa, Tricia 48
Turnbull, Ann 230

Uchida, Yoshiko 198

Van Wright, Cornelius 58
Vatsana's Lucky New Year (Gogol)
    141
Viorst, Judith 49
A Visit to Amy-Claire (Mills &
    Hamanaka) 29
Voight, Cynthia 199
Vojtech, Anna 15

Waggoner, Karen 153
Walk Two Moons (Creech) 136
Wallace, Ian 50
The Walls of Pedro Garcia (McCol-
    ley) 145
Walsh, Jill Paton 107
Water Ghost (Russell & Zhang) 149
Waterford, Helen 202

The Wednesday Surprise (Bunting) 4
Weil, Lisl 193
Weiss, Nicki 51
Western Wind (Fox) 138
When I Was Five (Howard) 79
When Jane-Marie Told My Secret
    (Willner-Pardo & Poydar) 108
*Who Do You Think You Are? Stories
    of Friends and Enemies* (Rochman
    & McCampbell) 190
Wiesner, David 200
Williams, Donald, Jr. 161
Willner-Pardo, Gina 108
Wilson, Janet 152
Wilson, Sharon 128
Wilson Sat Alone (Hess &
    Greenseid) 76
The Witch Who Lives down the Hall
    (Guthrie) 72

Yamaka, Sara 109
Yashima, Mitsu 129
Yashima, Taro 129
Yep, Laurence 154, 155, 200
Yo! Yes! (Raschka) 102
Young, Marian 146

Zhang, Christopher Zhong-Yuan
    149
*Zlata's Diary: A Child's Life in Sara-
    jevo* (Filiporio, DiGiovanni &
    Pribichevich-Zoric) 207
Zolotow, Charlotte 156

About the Author

After receiving her Ed.D. at the University of the Pacific, Patricia L. Roberts received the Distinguished Alumnus of the Year Award and joined the faculty in the school of Education at California State University, Sacramento, where she received the California State University's Award of Merit for Teaching. She has taught graduate courses in children's literature, language arts, and reading and served as coordinator of an elementary Teacher Education Center. She also has served as the Chair and Associate Chair of the Department of Teacher Education at California State University, Sacramento. Dr. Roberts is the author of *Alphabet: A Handbook of ABC Books and Book Extensions for the Elementary Classroom. Second Edition* (Scarecrow Press, 1994) and numerous other textbooks and resources for librarians, teachers, and parents.